LUCIO GALLETTO grew up in Liguria, fell in love with an Australian girl, and ended up running one of Australia's most acclaimed restaurants—Lucio's in Paddington, Sydney. In 2008, he was honoured with the OAM for services to the hospitality industry and the arts. His books include *The Art of Food at Lucio's* and *Soffritto: A Delicious Ligurian Memoir*.

DAVID DALE writes and broadcasts about fads, foods, media, the power of places and the peculiarities of people. His books include *The Obsessive Traveller, The 100 Things Everyone Needs to Know about Italy* and *The Little Book of Australia: A Snapshot of Who We Are.*

PAUL GREEN specialises in photography of food, art, fashion and fame. His books include *The Art of Food at Lucio's* and *Soffritto: A Delicious Ligurian Memoir.*

Lucio's

Ligurian Kitchen

THE PLEASURES OF THE ITALIAN RIVIERA

LUCIO GALLETTO
and **DAVID DALE**
Photography by Paul Green

ALLEN&UNWIN

Allen & Unwin
83 Alexander Street
Crows Nest NSW 2065
Australia
Phone: (61 2) 8425 0100
Fax: (61 2) 9906 2218
Email: info@allenandunwin.com
Web: www.allenandunwin.com

Cataloguing-in-Publication details are available
from the National Library of Australia
www.librariesaustralia.nla.gov.au

ISBN 978 1 74237 486 4

Internal design by Pfisterer+Freeman
Colour reproduction by Splitting Image, Clayton, Victoria
Set in 10¼ pt Joanna by Pfisterer+Freeman
Printed in China by Everbest Printing Co

10 9 8 7 6 5 4 3 2 1

Contents

WHERE IT ALL BEGAN

It's hard to believe, but there was once a movement to ban pasta from the Italian diet. It was started by a radical art group called the Futurists, and taken up by Mussolini's fascist government in the 1920s when Italy was having trouble finding enough wheat to meet the national demand.

The leader of the Futurists, Filippo Marinetti, called pasta 'Italy's absurd gastronomic religion'. He argued it was a stodgy symptom of an outdated peasant culture, and the Italy of modern times needed streamlined foods associated with speed and urban progress. In 1931, the Futurists of the Liguria region wrote Marinetti a letter which at first sight seemed to be an expression of support. They condemned as 'mouldy' what they called 'the endless regional cuisines, full of provincial pseudo-glory', and continued: 'Death to the pastasciutta. We Ligurian Futurists put our forces next to yours against maccheroni, vermicelli, spaghetti and tortellini.

'But we have the audacity of addressing to you the following plea: We wish to declare our loyalty to the ravioli … We could send you thousands of testaments proving the exquisiteness, digestibility and the optimism that the ravioli create. They also provoke elasticity of the muscles and the brain in every good Ligurian. The recipe is universally recognised, like our dialect.'

The Ligurian Futurists went on to seek one more exemption to Marinetti's condemnation of pasta—*trenette col pesto* (square spaghetti with basil sauce). They said pesto is 'a spring sauce with the strong perfume of Liguria and an emerald colour that reminds us of the audacious actions at sea of our ancient fathers'. Pesto sauce, they said, has the capacity to turn even the heaviest noodles into 'silk ribbons'.

Futurism and fascism died out, while the two most precious elements of the Ligurian diet survived, flourished and spread round the world, along with a message: Ligurians are different, and proud of it.

Throughout Italy, the stereotype of people from Liguria is similar to the stereotype applied to the Scots in English-speaking countries. It's all in the way you say it. If you were cruel, you'd say the typical Ligurian was 'miserly bordering on anal-retentive'. If you were kind, you'd say frugal, conservative, environmentally aware and leaving a small carbon footprint—perfect role models for anyone who wants to keep the planet turning happily for another few centuries. Theirs may not be the food of futurism. But it is the food of the future.

During our travels to research this book, we had dinner with Margherita Bozzano, the *Assessore* (cabinet minister) in charge of tourism for the Liguria region. We asked her to describe Ligurians: 'I would say understated, very careful with money, reliable, not too much talking, essential, ironic, practical. And from that comes the typical Ligurian cuisine, which is the definition of the Mediterranean diet—very healthy, with herbs, vegetables and fish, all fresh and local.'

The Ligurians are notoriously careful about conserving their resources. If they do a roast on Sunday, they finely chop the remnants on Monday and stuff them inside parcels of pasta. They use

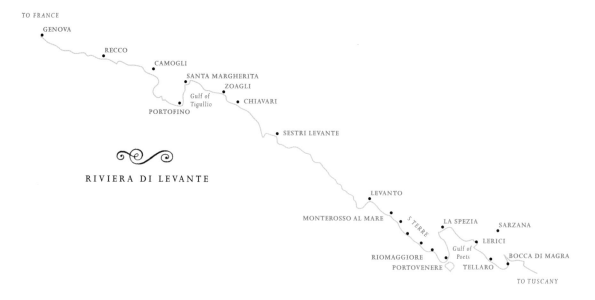

the vegetables they grow in their own gardens and they comb the hills of their neighbourhood for wild herbs to boost flavour. Traditionally, when they fished off their coast, they'd sell the best seafood to outsiders and keep the ugliest and smallest to make soups and stews for themselves. They ended up with a cooking culture that is not just economical and ecological, but also extremely tasty.

The geography explains a lot. Liguria is a thin crescent of land made up of mountains and seashore, with the occasional beach in between. That's wonderful for the climate—so balmy that impoverished Northern Europeans have made it their winter escape for centuries (while the rich shivered in Tuscany)—but not so good for forming associations with the rest of Italy. It has fostered that sense of elegant isolation.

You might picture Liguria as a seagull, with one wingtip touching France and the other touching Tuscany. The seagull's head is Genoa: as it looks to the right, it can see the sun setting in the west; as it looks to the left, it can see the sun rising in the east. The right or west wing is called the Riviera di Ponente. *Lucio's Ligurian Kitchen* focuses on the left or east wing of Liguria, the part known as the Riviera di Levante.

The word 'riviera' means shoreline. 'Ponente' means sinking or setting, as in the sun, and 'Levante' means 'rising'. This is where Lucio Galletto grew up and where he wished to return to rediscover the region.

As a teenager, Lucio worked in his family restaurant: Capannina Ciccio, which is the subject of our last book, *Soffritto: A delicious Ligurian memoir*. Lucio's first experiences of the Levante coast came at the end of every summer, when his cousin Mario would take the restaurant team for a big day out at one of the restaurants further up the coast, as a way of saying thank you for their efforts during the frantic months of July, August and September. Lucio was amazed at how rapidly things changed as he moved up the coast—every village had its own dialect and its own particular approach to the ingredients of Liguria. Even the pesto sauce changed colour, as well as flavour, as he moved further west.

Now, 40 years since he made his first explorations, Lucio embarks on explaining the cooking of his much-loved region to the rest of the world. We begin at the seagull's eastern wingtip.

Bocca di Magra

First there must be dinner at Capannina Ciccio, started in 1950 as a shack on the beach by Lucio's mother and father and aunt and uncle. It will set a standard by which we will judge all else along the coast.

Ciccio's is famous for its seafood, but it wouldn't be Ligurian if it didn't do meat ravioli and we surprise head waiter Giuseppe by ordering that. He says '*Che profumo!*' (What a fragrance) as he sets down a huge bowl of white parcels, steaming with the scent of nutmeg and marjoram. This aroma, invigorating and comforting, will greet us in many a restaurant over the next few weeks.

Cousin Mario Guelfi tells us the fad at the moment along the Riviera is '*catalana*', a salad of poached seafood which grows flashier as the wealth of the neighbourhood increases. By the time we get to Portofino, the scampi will be coated in gold, he predicts. He gives us the secret of Ciccio's version—the dressing of the salad contains a little roe from local lobsters, which sharpens the flavour. 'Nobody else on the coast is doing it that way yet,' he says. 'By the time your book comes out, they'll all have discovered my secret and I'll have moved on to something else.'

Tellaro

Behind Bocca di Magra is a hill called Montemarcello (named for the consul Marcellus, who defeated the Liguri tribe here in 155 BC) and on the other side of the hill, the tall red and orange houses of Tellaro cling to the cliff face and descend 500 steps to the sea. Lapped by the water is a red church, and local legend claims there was once a giant octopus which would reach up from the sea and ring the church bell to annoy the locals—or possibly to warn them of imminent invasion. The villagers now get their revenge, or express their gratitude, by eating octopus at every opportunity.

The octopus tale was first told in English by the sex-obsessed novelist D.H. Lawrence, who holidayed near Tellaro in 1913. In December of that year he wrote to a friend about his cottage, which was 'pink outside, with a red roof ... standing above the vines, against grey olive trees', with an enormous garden full of orange and lemon trees. The kitchen was crammed with red earthenware cooking pots because the local diet consisted mainly of soup. He loved Italian cooking 'when there isn't too much oil' and thought 'one can live quite cheaply'. The people of Tellaro were 'fearfully nice', he wrote, and the place is so ancient you wouldn't be surprised to bump into Jesus Christ in the street. Lawrence acted as a witness at a wedding where the children were 'swarming round like wolves yelling good wishes for the bridal pair: "Evviva gli Sposi—Evviva gli Sposi". The bride's response was to throw them handfuls of sweets.'

These days, the best weddings would be celebrated at Tellaro's Locanda Miranda, which is a seven-room hotel as well as an upmarket restaurant. It is pink outside and yellow inside, with the cooking done by 70-year-old Angelo Cabani, who bears a cheerful resemblance to the video game figure SuperMario. The service is performed with great seriousness by his wife Giovanna and with great friendliness by their son Alessandro, who explains that his dad started cooking there in traditional style (lots of octopus) in 1959 but became lighter and more adventurous in the 1980s.

Of course Angelo does ravioli, but instead of meat and cheese, they are stuffed with *triglie* (sweet-fleshed red mullet). His lasagna is made with the flour of farro, an ancient grain loved by the Romans, and layered with scampi and tomato; his 'carpaccio' is tuna marinated in orange juice, with finely sliced fennel beneath; and his pescatrice (monkfish) is steamed with zucchini and a saffron sauce.

The lightness of Angelo's savoury dishes leaves room for the decadence of his desserts: a bright green mint *semifreddo* in a moat of dark chocolate, and pears poached in red wine with a cinnamon mousse. It's very clever food, and very Ligurian.

TRY TO VISIT: *Locanda Miranda, Via Fiascherino 92, Tellaro, www.locandamiranda.com.*

Lerici

On our walk along Lerici's beachfront towards the cliff-top castle that guards the town, we pass a street called Shelley and a hotel called Byron. This was a favourite holiday spot for the English romantic poets in the early 1820s. Percy Bysshe Shelley, staying there with his wife Mary Wollstonecraft, who had just published her novel *Frankenstein*, wrote that they were inhabiting 'this divine bay, reading dramas and sailing and listening to the most enchanting music' in 'a lonely house close by the soft and sublime scenery of the Bay of Lerici'.

To visit them, Shelley's mate Lord Byron used to swim across the bay from Portovenere, a marathon that took six hours. In July 1822, Shelley drowned when his yacht was wrecked on the way from Tuscany to Lerici. Byron had Shelley's body cremated on the seashore. The story goes that Shelley's heart would not burn, so one of his friends plucked it from the ashes, put it in a bottle and gave it to Mary, who slept with it. This is a coast of strange tales.

As we approach Due Corone restaurant in the shadow of the castle, we see a man struggling with an octopus as big as his head. He has pulled it out of the water with a net and is trying to force it into a plastic bag, but it keeps wrapping its legs around his arm. He has a small knife in his other hand but he can't find a way to stab the octopus without endangering himself. Eating octopus suddenly seems essential.

Under the plastic-roofed marquee that extends Due Corone onto the waterfront, the cooks are happy to oblige, in the form of a pinky-purple terrine. They've chopped the creature into small chunks, boiled it with vegetables and moulded it into a kind of salami shape, sliced it into shimmering discs and served it with a sharp yellow sauce. This is one dish Lucio will want to reproduce in Sydney.

Due Corone gives us our first sight of another local specialty—cuculli, balls of mashed potato and seafood in batter. Its *catalana* is a salad of tomato, carrot, celery and radish on a glass plate elegantly topped with a *scampo* in its shell. Today the waiter is keen to enhance the *catalana* with lobster 'flown in live from Canada'. 'Why would we want to eat Canadian lobster on the Italian Riviera?' we ask. 'Most tourists do,' he replies. Lerici has been a resort town for 200 years. For dessert, Due Corone makes a pine nut *semifreddo* striped with dark chocolate, elaborately described on the menu as '*Piastrellino alla doppia panna e pinoli al cioccolato fondante caldo*' (little tile of double cream and pine nuts with warm chocolate fondant). Another one for the notebook.

Afterwards, as we stroll through the arcades next to the castle, we discover this part of the Riviera has another claim to fame—buildings painted to look as if they have balconies, pediments and tall shuttered windows when their frontages are really blank. The name for this is 'trompe l'oeil', which means 'trick the eye'. It should be called *trompa l'occhio* but just this once the Italians are

IL VICOLETTO

— o —

Spaghetti alle scarpere	€ 7.00
Ravioli al sugo	€ 7.00
Ravioli ai funghi	€ 8.00
Trofie al pesto	€ 8.00
Gnocchi buro e salvie	€ 6.00

— o —

Tortillas spagnole	€ 6.00
Focaccia al formaggio	€ 6.00
Spiedini di carne misti	€ 8.00
Filetto all'aceto balsamico	€ 12.00
" ai funghi	€ 12.00
" alle griglie	€ 10.00

prepared to use a French term. That's not to imply the Italians think the French do it better. It's just that the French were the first (in the seventeenth century) to name this way of decorating façades which was then perfected along the Italian Riviera, where, say the cynics, the canny Ligurians embraced it as a way of saving money.

In Lerici, the *trompe l'oeil* ornamentations on the pink and orange buildings are partly obscured by the washing that hangs between the genuine windows. Later in our journey, we'll come across washing that is actually *trompe l'oeil*.

TRY TO VISIT: *Due Corone, Via Vespucci 14, Lerici, 0187967417.*

Portovenere

The next morning Mario announces he is going out fishing for octopus in the Gulf of Poets. He'll be crossing the stretch of water where Lord Byron used to swim. As we jump aboard the little white launch parked outside Capannina Ciccio, Mario rips off his shirt to catch the sun. We're bumping over the waves while Mario points out the three-storey red house where D.H. Lawrence stayed, next to the Punta Bianca cliffs where the Romans used to mine marble, before they discovered Carrara.

Mario stops in deep water and tosses out a line baited with a reasonably convincing plastic squid with hooks attached. After ten minutes, no octopus has been fooled, so Mario, not the most patient of men, gives up the fishing plan and suggests we go for lunch on the island of Palmaria.

Near the island, we stop to observe two mussel farmers reaching into the water and pulling up ropes festooned with black shells, which they gently detach and deposit in baskets in their boat. Then we approach a wide bungalow with a jetty projecting into the water. From an upper window we're greeted by a man who must be Ernest Hemingway—white-jacketed, with a bushy white beard and ruddy complexion. He yells advice on where to tie up the boat, and Mario whispers that this is the legendary Iseo (real name Giuseppe), who has been running restaurants in the area for decades. His place in Portovenere was a rival of Capannina Ciccio—'When I got a fish tank, Iseo had to go and get a fish tank,' says Mario. 'Let's see what his *catalana* is like.' Iseo comes out and greets Mario like a long-lost brother, and we walk into the restaurant past a framed newspaper clipping headlined '*Il Menu Intrepido*' and photos of Warren Beatty, Lou Reed and assorted Italian singers.

Our table has a view across the mussel farms to the narrow six-storey houses that line the Portovenere waterfront. Most are pink or orange, but a few individualists have gone for light blue or green. From this distance we can't tell which of the green-shuttered windows are real and which are *trompe l'oeil*. The village is enclosed within a thick grey wall which extends up the hill to a Norman castle that Mario says was a meeting place for armies travelling to and from the crusades. This has to be one of the most interesting restaurant panoramas in the world.

Among the antipasti, Lucio is particularly impressed with a yellow puree of capsicum and prawns; a 'tian'—which involves layers of potatoes, anchovies and tomatoes—and with Iseo's version of *catalana*, which contains prawns and scampi. It is decorated with a lobster head and tail and sits on an invigorating salad of tomato, capsicum and basil. Mario and Iseo exchange commiserations about the difficulty of getting good waiters now that Liguria is so wealthy. 'They won't work nights,' complains Iseo, 'the women want their men at home. And this used to be the area where the men would go off for months at a time to work on the cruise ships!'

TRY TO VISIT: *Locanda Lorena on the island of Palmaria (www.locandalorena.com). If you book, they'll pick you up in a boat near Iseo's other restaurant, called Iseo, on the Portovenere waterfront.*

Cinque Terre

As we drive past the dockyards of La Spezia, Lucio is talking about the local specialty—a bean soup called mes-ciua (mess-chew-ah). He's remembering a story from his childhood:

A very rich shipping magnate used to go to a *trattoria* just near here because they made the best mes-ciua. One night he went in with some important clients, but the *trattoria* was very busy so he had to wait a long time to be served. He called the owner over and asked him if he was interested in selling his *trattoria*. The owner said yes and they set a price. The rich man told his assistant to give the owner a cheque for the agreed amount, and asked if the place now officially belonged to him. The host said yes, so the rich man said, 'OK, get rid of all these other people and bring me my mes-ciua.'

What is the name of that restaurant? Lucio can't recall. Are we going to try mes-ciua? Yes, but not in La Spezia, because we're not stopping there. We're on our way to the Cinque Terre, which literally means five earths and which we will henceforth abbreviate to 5T.

The 5T villages and their surrounding vineyards, farms and forests are part of a heritage park protected by an authority set up by Italy's Department of the Environment. Because it has been so well preserved, it has become one of Italy's prime tourist destinations, which puts even more pressure on the preservers. We're staying in the easternmost village, Riomaggiore. As we walk down the steep main street from the tiny car park (the heritage people really really don't want you to bring a car—foot and train are more useful in 5T), we're surrounded on both sides by bars, souvenir stores and takeaway food shops with signs in a mixture of English, German and Italian, including this:

'Le specialite delle 5 Terre
Also spaghetti home made cooking spaghetti carbonara
lasagna al forno roast chcken whit potatoes tipical Ligurian food'.

This is not promising, so we move on. When we look at the menu outside a place called La Lanterna, we're encouraged by this message: 'At the moment, date mussels are a protected species; because of our participation in an initiative for the defence of our sea, the Trattoria La Lanterna apologises to the respectable customers for having suppressed the dishes Zuppa di Datteri and Zuppa Cinque Terre from the menu.' So not every eatery in Riomaggiore has handed its identity to tourism.

These people sound as if they care about their region, so we wander inside. Our impression is supported by the discovery that tonight they are making mes-ciua. Each bowl is like looking into a rockpool: chickpeas, cannellini beans and farro grains at the bottom of clear chicken broth which proves to have an intense and refreshing flavour. We can understand why the rich guy bought the La Spezia specialist.

The park authorities have kindly lent us a three-bedroom 'Writers' Flat', with a view of the ocean and Riomaggiore's tiny port. We're told that the last guest was Italy's prime minister, Romano

Prodi, and his wife, on a secret break from Rome. Prodi apparently liked to travel without luxury, to learn how ordinary Italians experience their holidays. In the Writers' Flat, he would have learned that the drain in the shower is blocked (unless he was the one who left it blocked—he does have a thick head of hair); that the bells in the nearby church toll the time twice every hour, all night long; and that drunken New Zealanders in the bar below have particularly penetrating voices.

When we emerge from the flat around 7 am, we find that the New Zealanders have disappeared and Riomaggiore has been briefly reclaimed by its fishermen, who are sitting over coffees reminiscing about quieter days. At 8 am the Germans burst out of their bed-and-breakfasts, carrying ski poles to help them negotiate the steep streets.

We join them on a walk called the Via dell'Amore, round the cliff face to the next town, Manarola. The path is lined with cactus plants, brought from America in the seventeenth century and now a signature element of the Ligurian landscape.

In Manarola, Matteo Perrone, a botanist employed by the park, collects us in his boat and shows us from the water why 5T has been legendary around Europe for 800 years—every cliff face is draped with hundreds of tiny vineyards in terraces descending to within metres of the waterline. Most of them are now in ruins. The golden age of 5T was the fourteenth century, when selling wines as far away as England enabled every village to build a magnificent church.

The statistics tell a story of decline: a census in 1900 showed 5T had a population of 9000 people servicing 1800 hectares of vineyards; in 1970, 7000 residents were working on 1200 hectares. Then the tourists discovered the rugged beauty of 5T and the winemakers discovered an easier way to make a living: they abandoned their properties and opened cafés and souvenir shops in the villages. Now 5T has a population of 4400 and only 140 hectares of working vineyards.

The park authority wants to entice people back onto the land. It is rebuilding the dry stone walls around the most accessible terraces and employing botanists to grow herbs and vegetables. One of the people attempting to revive the 5T farms is Matteo himself. He uses an English phrase to describe the land he is reclaiming—'my little plot of happiness'—but laments that this year, half his grape crop was destroyed by wild boars wandering down from the forests on top of the hills.

Matteo takes us to a hilltop 'factory' which uses locally grown herbs and fruits to make cosmetics, jams, sauces and liqueurs. To reach it, we have to ride a monorail that is not designed to carry humans. We clamber into metal baskets normally filled with grapes, grip the sides, brace our feet and rattle slowly up a sheer cliff face, trying to keep our gaze outwards to the horizon rather than down to the rocks. As our cages bump and rock, we are inclined to envy the peasants who used stone steps to make their way up and down this cliff every day.

We lunch at a hilltop restaurant called Santuario, which seven centuries ago was a resting point for pilgrims on their way from Paris to Rome. They probably ate the same kind of anchovies that were served to us (caught off Monterosso, one of the 5T), but they wouldn't have consumed these ravioli, which are white on one side and black on the other (half the pasta is dyed with squid ink).

In the afternoon we visit a disused olive mill, and Matteo explains that in pressing the olives, the farmers would boil water in the fireplace and pour it into the olive basket to force more oil out of the fruit. The concept of 'cold-pressed extra virgin' is more a twentieth-century affectation than an ancient tradition.

At dinner that night in Gli Ulivi, we discover another Ligurian classic—the pie. Coming from Australia, where the pie is a national institution, it's a pleasure to learn that the Ligurians were

baking stuffed pastry centuries before Australia existed. In this case, the pies are like little boxes—deep and rectangular and filled with '*soufflé di scampi*', a light seafood mash. Clearly pies will need their own chapter in our book.

Our most spectacular 5T meal happens the next night in the region's smallest restaurant. Cappun Magru, in the village of Groppo, has only twelve tables, and the menu offers only two choices for each course. This enables chef Maurizio Bordoni to focus his full attention on every dish, while his wife Christiane Utsch concentrates on advising every customer on suitable local wines.

Maurizio is ambitious. To give heartiness to his '*vellutata*' (literally 'velvety', because that's the texture of the soup) he sources ancient grains that have almost vanished from the earth—like farro and *amaranto*. He fills his focaccia bread with homemade sausage. His side vegetable is a pumpkin mousse with a porcini mushroom salad. And every night he turns out individual versions of the most complicated construction in the history of Italian cooking: *cappon magro* (of which the restaurant's name is a dialect version). It was originally made only once a year as a family feast to celebrate the return of the sailors from the sea. I wrote down these layers before I gave up counting and started eating: *vongole* (clams), beans, mushrooms, oysters, mussels, prawns, octopus, green sauce, potatoes, biscuits, tuna, beetroot, garlic, olives, cauliflower, mushrooms and carrots.

Lucio's eyes are gleaming. Australia has an abundance of these ingredients and Australians have big appetites. Oh yes, he says, we'll need to create a recipe for *cappon magro*.

TRY TO VISIT: *La Lanterna, Via San Giacomo 46, Riomaggiore, 0187 920589; Santuario di Montenero, hill above Riomaggiore, 0187 760528; Gli Ulivi, Via N.S. della Salute 114, Volastra, 0187 920158; Cappun Magru, Via Volastra 19, Groppo di Manarola, 0187 920563.*

Levanto

The 5T people graciously refer to Levanto as the sixth of the five lands. The Levanto people prefer to consider themselves unique. Their town was a Roman centre for mining red marble in the first century, and became a retreat of the rich who built their summer palaces there from the sixteenth century. The long grey beach has art nouveau mansions at the east end (no *trompe l'oeil* necessary), one of which is a holiday home for the Agnelli family, who own the Fiat factory in Turin.

We head away from the 1920s pink casino on the beachfront, past shops labelled La Focacceria and Il Laboratorio del Pesto, to a quiet square named after Count Camillo Benso di Cavour, first prime minister of Italy (back when it was a new country in 1860). Trattoria Cavour, which opened here in 1911, is alleged to specialise in a dish called *gattafin*, which we're keen to investigate.

We're lucky to get a table in the front courtyard on this busy Sunday, but when we study the menu, there's no sign of *gattafin*. Lucio falls into conversation with two elderly ladies at the next table, who tell us they live in La Spezia but catch the train to Levanto every Sunday to lunch at their favourite restaurant. Lucio asks them if it still serves *gattafin*. 'Of course,' they reply. 'They don't need to put it on the menu. Just ask the waitress and they make them fresh as soon as you ask.'

The *gattafin* arrive with a little pot of dried herbs for optional sprinkling. They are a kind of fried ravioli, and inside the light crunchy pastry is a mixture of chopped greens and ricotta. The chef, a sturdy woman named Adele, emerges to explain that in spring and summer, women come down from the nearby hills with baskets of wild grasses they have picked, and this '*preboggion*' goes

into the filling. Now that the season is over, Adele substitutes *bietole* (silverbeet) for the '*erbette*' (little herbs) and Lucio realises that's what he'll have to do to make the recipe work in Australia.

TRY TO VISIT: *Trattoria Cavour, piazza cavour 1, www.trattoriacavour.com.*

Sestri Levante

It would be easy to mistake Sestri Levante for a modern tourist town with a serious traffic problem. That would happen if you looked only at the main beach, called La Baie delle Favole (the bay of fairytales), so named because Hans Christian Andersen wrote stories here in 1835. When you sneak round the southern headland to a smaller beach called La Baia del Silenzio (the bay of silence), you find two reasons to think better of Sestri: a wonderful collection of *trompe l'oeil* façades (including a mansion which has real Greek columns on one side and an exact painted replica of them on the other side) and a flat-roofed white restaurant called El Pescador (Spanish for 'the fisherman').

Why it has a Spanish name is a mystery, since the food is fully Ligurian. We enjoy a salad of sliced raw porcini mushrooms which were picked in the forest the day before, a 'riso' (not a risotto, which is heavier) with zucchini flowers, scampi and mussels, and a local pasta called *corzetti*. They're shaped like large coins stamped with an image of stalks of wheat, and are served with a sauce of *vongole* (clams) and prawns. Lucio starts thinking of how such a shape could be made at home, if you didn't have the stamp.

TRY TO VISIT: *El Pescador Via Pilade Queirolo 1, Sestri Levante, 0185 428888.*

Chiavari

By this time in our westward journey, along the ancient Roman way called Via Aurelia, photographer Paul is wearying of the rigorous research schedule that requires lunch and dinner every day. He loves snapping the dishes, but his waistline is showing the effects of eating them. He has christened us 'the three mouthketeers'.

Lunch in the Lord Nelson Pub restores his appetite. Once we get past the peculiar name, we have the most interesting meal of the trip, and that's saying a lot. Claudio Modena's food is both individual and traditional. He serves a classic 'pinzimonio'—a selection of raw vegetables with a dip—and adds a raw prawn. He needs to come out of the kitchen to encourage customers to eat it. 'That prawn was caught out there this morning,' he says, gesturing through the window to the glittering ocean. 'Think of it as sashimi.' With it, he provides a pot of pink salt from the banks of Australia's Murray River. He is currently experimenting with matching local ingredients with salts from different parts of the world.

The mixed antipasto plate contains calamari stuffed with octopus, scallop with peanut paste, carrot mousse and rabbit with olives, pine nuts and mushrooms. His appetisers include a thin slice of *cima* (stuffed veal shoulder), which inspires Lucio to try reinventing a dish that was special-occasion-Sunday lunch in his childhood home. There's a 'lettuce parcels' soup, where the lettuce is stuffed with seafood instead of the usual mixed meats and cheese, and the broth is made with shellfish instead of hen.

Claudio mixes chestnut flour and wheat flour to make the wide pappardelle ribbons which he smothers in a pesto that is thickened and sharpened with a kind of sour cheese called 'prescinsoa'. Lucio wonders if you'd get the same effect with yoghurt.

Chef Claudio says his emphasis on local ingredients (apart from the salts) is 'non per campanilismo' (not because of regionalism), but because they give him the best variety of flavours for the kind of food he likes to cook. But what's with the name—Lord Nelson Pub? Claudio introduces us to the owner, Ruth Molinari, who apologises that her English is a bit rusty, since she's barely used it for 30 years. She's a Londoner who fell in love with a Ligurian waiter on a cruise ship. In 1969, they decided to take advantage of the Italian fascination with English mannerisms by opening a classic English pub serving classic Italian food on the Riviera coast, and decorated the interior to resemble Nelson's ship—brass lamps, figureheads, steering wheels, canvas hanging from the ceiling. She says she's been blessed to find a chef who has taken her to the cutting edge of Italian cooking.

That night we drive inland to go to the other extreme in Ligurian eating—mountain food—in a restaurant called La Brinca in a village called Campo di Ne in an area called Valgraveglia. The place has been urged upon us by the officials of the Slow Food movement in Genoa, who insist that to portray Liguria correctly we must experience more than seafood. And there's not a fish to be seen on La Brinca's menu. The padrone Sergio Circella tells us the big farmhouse was an olive mill run by his family since the 1930s and transformed into a restaurant in 1987. The menu is based on local peasant traditions ('The cuisine of leftovers, the cuisine of everything stuffed,' says Sergio), so it's ideal for winter and a bit heavy in summer.

Here's what we ate: barbecued ravioli stuffed with 'prebugiun di Ne' (mashed potatoes and black cabbage); a 'soup' of meat-stuffed lettuce parcels in veal stock; chestnut gnocchi with pesto, potatoes and pumpkin; roast rabbit stuffed with zucchini flowers; 'ravioli di erbette cu tuccu', meat and herb ravioli with an aromatic meat sauce; cima (stuffed veal shoulder) which is roasted rather than boiled, as would be done on the coastline; taglierini al sugo di lepre, noodles with hare sauce; and chestnut tart. Tomorrow we'll need to walk a lot.

TRY TO VISIT: Lord Nelson Pub, Corso Valparaiso 27 (on the beachfront), Chiavari, 0185 302595. La Brinca, Via Campo di Ne 58, Valgraveglia, www.labrinca.it.

Zoagli

For the westernmost part of our explorations, we're basing ourselves in a small bed and breakfast called Cerisola 2003, halfway up the hill behind Chiavari, with a view of the Portofino headland to our right. We arrive to dump our bags around midday, and ask the enthusiastic owner, Raffaele, if he can recommend a nearby place for lunch. He says the seaside village of Zoagli has a good trattoria called Da Belin. 'What did you say?' asks Lucio. 'Da Belin.' Lucio is smiling as we get back in the car, and explains that in his dialect, the name translates as 'Of the dickhead'.

Da Belin's service is a bit vague, but the food is anything but dickheaded: a spectacular torta di verdure (pie filled with a deep green vegetable mix); stuffed calamari; tagliolini al salsa di noci (noodles with walnut sauce) and trofie al pesto (little twists of pasta with green beans, potatoes, pine nuts and a creamy basil sauce).

Opposite, top: Lord Nelson Pub, Chiavari. Opposite, bottom: La Brinca.

17

We're sitting in Da Belin's courtyard on the town square, looking at a beach through giant arches which support part of the railway line from Genoa to La Spezia. Raffaele has told us to look out for this railway bridge (it would be hard to miss it) because it was the site of the most elaborate piece of *trompe l'oeil* trickery in European history. During the First World War, the people of Zoagli covered the sea-facing side of the railway bridge with panels painted to look like houses, and thus fooled the German ships offshore into thinking there was no railway line and thus no reason for bombardment. It's known now as Ponte Mascherato—the masked bridge. Perhaps the *belins* were the German ship captains.

Just up the hill from the town square are the silk and velvet factories for which Zoagli is famous. In Seterie di Zoagli Cordani, we shop for shawls and handbags that will make wives, children and girlfriends less disgruntled about missing this journey.

TRY TO VISIT: *Bed and Breakfast Cerisola 2003, www.rivieradellevante.it/cerisola2003. Da Belin, Piazza XXVII Dicembre 9, Zoagli, 0185 258122.*

Santa Margherita

The long dock area of Santa Margherita is lined with seafood restaurants designed to catch rich tourists. Being in a narrow lane 300 metres back from the waterfront, Ardiciocca (pronounced ardi-chocka, an old dialect word for artichoke) has to try harder. Most of the experiments of chef Massimo work brilliantly, and even when they don't, they are educational, because the local heritage of every ingredient is fully explained by head waiter Peter.

We try a 'vellutata di fagioli di pigna' (smooth pigna bean soup) with a parmesan cheese waffle; poached dover sole on mashed zucchini; wide *pappardelle* noodles with tuna and pork sausage; sundried tomato ravioli with prawns; risotto of octopus and lemon; and a 'pre-dessert' of three little pots of ricotta cream, with mandarin jelly, chocolate almonds and raspberries.

Next morning we return to Santa Margherita for the food markets, where we see the just-picked porcini mushrooms we've been eating in salads all along the coast, and the long 'sticks' of dried salt cod which get soaked for 24 hours and mashed into a dish called *baccala* that has been a peasant staple for centuries.

TRY TO VISIT: *Ardiciocca, Via Maragliano 17, www.ardiciocca.it.*

Portofino

Now we're at the posh end of the Levante coast. We're having lunch on the terrace of the Hotel Splendido and Laura de Bert, the marketing manager, is telling us how she had to say 'No' to Tom Hanks last week. He'd arrived with some American businessmen in a yacht which moored down in Portofino's little bay, and he'd come up for lunch.

It was a hot day, and Hanks asked if he could use the pool. 'I had to explain that it is only for guests,' said Laura. 'I said all he had to do was check in for the night and our water would be at his disposal, but he was staying on the yacht. He took it very well—he knows we wouldn't deserve our reputation if we let anybody use the pool.'

The Splendido, in a former monastery, has been one of the world's most expensive hotels since 1901, and its visitors' book bears the signatures of Ingrid Bergman, Grace Kelly, Richard Burton, Steve Martin, Warren Beatty, Michael Caine, Ashley Judd, Meg Ryan and Rod Stewart. Largely because of the presence of such guests, Portofino (population 1200) has become the most expensive village on Italy's west coast—a flat with two windows recently sold for four million euros, Laura tells us.

Under these circumstances, you wouldn't be surprised if the Splendido's restaurant served the kind of pretentious 'international cuisine' that appears in grand hotels all over the English-speaking world, but Ligurian pride is stronger than that. The menu is a cavalcade of local classics: handmade *taglierini* noodles with potatoes, beans and pesto (made with a rare local garlic called *aglio di versalico*, which is poached in milk before being mashed with oil and basil); a pasta called '*foglia d'ulivo*' in the shape of olive leaves, with tomatoes and prawns; a '*saltimbocca*' of rabbit, prosciutto and sage, served with grilled porcini; and a cheese called *Trarcantu* which is aged in caves for six months and soaked in the grape 'must' left over from the making of sciacchetrá wine in the Cinque Terre.

TRY TO VISIT: *The terrace restaurant of the Hotel Splendido, www.hotelsplendido.com.*

Camogli

There are various theories on how Camogli got its name, but the most plausible comes from the literal translation, 'house of wives'. This was a town where the women waited at home while their husbands sailed away to find and sell fish. The fishing tradition is celebrated on the second Sunday of May every year when the entire catch is cooked in a giant frying pan on the docks and handed out to the poor and hungry of the district.

As we walk downhill from the car park towards a port crammed with fishing boats, we pass the giant frying pan leaning against a wall in an empty square. It is taller than any of us—four metres in diameter, supposedly—and the sight of it almost distracts us from the spectacular *trompe l'oeil* on the apartment blocks that surround the square. This time, the artists have not only painted fake balconies but fake washing hanging between them, fake cats on the windowsills and fake people peeping out from fake half-open shutters.

Up on the hill at the western end of town, Rosa restaurant overlooks the port and serves stuffed sardines, octopus and olive pie, and the best steamed mussels Lucio has ever eaten. 'The important thing is to serve them as soon as they pop open,' he declares. Just as well we didn't order dessert, because on the way back to the car, the bakeries of Camogli fill our noses with the smell of *pandolce*—fruit cake just out of the oven.

TRY TO VISIT: *The bakeries in Via della Repubblica, just back from the port; Rosa (up the hill at the western end of town); Largo F. Casabona 11, 0185 771088.*

Recco

The town of Recco is at the opposite end of the Levante coast from Tellaro. While Tellaro is ancient, quiet and steep, Recco is modern, busy and flat, mainly because it was heavily bombed during the Second World War and is still in the process of rebuilding itself. And while the Tellarans concentrate their culinary curiosity on one very fine restaurant—Miranda—the Reccans spread their interest over a multitude of eateries.

Our guide is another Lucio (surname Bernini, so he is doubly famous), whose business card describes him as 'Esperto di turismo enogastronomico' (expert in food and wine tourism). Lucio II (as we christen him) used to run restaurants. Now he speaks on behalf of Recco's restaurateurs. 'This is the gastronomic capital of Liguria,' he tells us. 'Recco has 10 000 inhabitants and restaurant seating for 4000. Here if you have less than 200 seats, you are a boutique restaurant.' Lucio I points out that his place in Sydney can seat 80.

Recco is famous for one dish: focaccia stuffed with a sharp creamy cheese called *crescenza*. 'It's our answer to pizza, only better,' says Lucio II. Cheese focaccia was mentioned in the records of the nearby Abbey of San Fruttuoso from the year 1189, as a dish served to crusaders before they departed for the holy land. Their meal included '*pagnotte di farro ed orzo impastate con miele, fichi secchi e zibibbo … e una foccacia di semola e di giuncata appena rappresa*' (loaves of farro wheat and barley, kneaded with honey, fresh figs and *zibibbo* grapes and a focaccia of wheat flour and curds and whey). The Consorzio Recco Gastronomica presented this document as evidence for the antiquity and uniqueness of '*focaccia col formaggio*' when it was seeking its registration as a local trademark.

Cheese focaccia was brought back to prominence by a restaurant called Manuelina as part of Recco's post-war revival in the 1950s, and became so popular that now the town serves three million portions a year. Lucio II takes us to the current champion of crust-stuffing—Vitturin, a wide bungalow under the *autostrada* which describes itself in a brochure as 'elegant, futurist, surrounded by green'.

In a kitchen five times the size of Lucio's in Sydney, Roberto the chef demonstrates rolling out the dough, spreading on the cheese, then rolling out an even thinner top sheet which is allowed to settle gently over the cheese before the big circular pan goes into a very hot oven. Roberto also shows us his other specialty—twisting tiny pinches of dough into a pasta shape called 'trofie'. He refers to *trofie* as 'the Princess Snow White', and explains: 'She goes with the seven dwarves that make pesto—basil, garlic, oil, pine nuts, parmesan, pecorino and salt.' In this analogy, the green beans and potatoes that complete the dish would be the prince and the queen.

We emerge from the kitchen to a dining room full of hundreds of Ligurians doing what they love best—eating, at moderate prices, and drinking, at moderate prices, dishes and wines made with ingredients sourced just up the road.

Now you are ready to join them in celebrating the pleasures of the Italian Riviera. Here's where our journey ends and yours begins.

TRY TO VISIT: *Ristorante Vittturin, Via dei Giustiniani 48, Recco, www.vitturin.it; Manuelina, Via Roma 278, Recco, www.manuelina.it.*

BEFORE YOU START …
LUCIO INTRODUCES THE RECIPES

I am lucky and grateful to have spent half my life in Liguria and half my life in Australia, and to be able to draw on both inspirations in the recipes you are about to read. It strikes me now that Australia and Liguria are very similar. Mellow climate, closeness to the sea, great produce and regular infusions of new ideas from other places are all assets that make for interesting eating. The difference is that Ligurians went out into the world, found their inspirations and brought them home. Australia has been blessed by a constant stream of incoming people and ideas.

It seems to me a local cuisine needs regular refreshment from other cultures. In the long run that will make it stronger—as long as the locals know how to interpret and adapt the new ideas. Ligurians didn't blindly absorb every food and technique that landed on their shores. Over hundreds of years, they learned to be discriminating.

One example is spices. From the thirteenth century onwards, the port city of La Spezia, whose name literally means 'the spice', was one of Europe's commercial distribution centres for the myriad ingredients brought back from the Orient. Yet the only spices used in the area until very recently were pepper and nutmeg. The people of La Spezia prefer to get their flavour boosts from the herbs that grow in the nearby hills.

'*La cucina Ligure*' begins with those herbs, along with olive oil and garlic. You could call it '*cucina povera*', because it is based on ingredients available to the poorest farmers and fishermen, but it's rich in quality and freshness. Let's look in more detail at what you'll be using most often when you cook the Riviera way …

THE KEY INGREDIENTS

OLIVE OIL. It's extra virgin, of course, and the Ligurian style is lighter than the kind they produce in Sicily or even in nearby Tuscany, thus making it equally useful for cooking and for dressing salads and soups. Australia produces excellent olive oils but you should taste-test to ensure the flavour is not too aggressive and thus likely to dominate the ingredients cooked or dressed in it. In the recipes, we've tried to give precise quantities for beginners, but really, we hope you'll just have a big bottle handy, and splash it around to your taste.

HERBS. Always fresh, never dried. The main ones we use are basil, bay leaves, fennel, rosemary, sage, marjoram, mint, oregano, thyme and parsley (which should be the flat-leafed Italian variety, not the frizzy English kind). Again, you should not worry about precise quantities in the recipes. Use more or less leaves of oregano, marjoram, parsley etc., according to your taste.

GARLIC. The important thing is not to burn garlic when cooking, because the bitterness will spoil the flavour. To maintain the natural aroma, put the oil over low heat and add the garlic quickly, then let it sizzle gently for only a minute or two before adding other ingredients.

ONIONS. We mean white onions, unless we specify red (for salads). Onions need more cooking than garlic—sizzling for 5 minutes before you add the other parts of your *soffritto* (base of a sauce).

VINEGAR. The white wine version is best for salad dressings and for marinades. Occasionally we'll suggest red wine vinegar. For a dressing we suggest one part vinegar to four parts oil. Please don't use balsamic in cooking, or even in salad dressing, unless it's specifically recommended, because it will overpower everything.

WHITE FLOUR. There's a myth that you need some special rare type of flour to make pasta or pizza. For our recipes, any plain flour will do. The important point is that you need to eat freshly made pasta within a day. You can't keep it as you would spaghetti.

ANCHOVIES. When you buy preserved anchovies, try to find Ligurian ones, because many others are too strong. In some of our recipes we call for salted anchovies (which should be washed before use) but mostly we mean the unsalted ones. Either way, remove the bones.

MUSSELS. They should be the black shell variety. We suggest heating them only long enough to make them pop open. Any that refuse to open after a few minutes should be discarded. And keep the liquid they put out when heated, because it's delicious.

MUSHROOMS. Many varieties are now available in Australia and we suggest you be adventurous and find the ones with the flavour you like best. Personally, I like shiitake. Some of our recipes call for porcini, which we pick in the forests behind the Riviera and which are sold in Australia dried. I suggest you buy dried porcini that are in large slices rather than broken into small pieces. You'll need to soak them before use, but don't use the water in which you soaked them because it could contain residual soil, and it adds no extra flavour.

CAPERS. The best ones are from the Eolian Islands off southern Italy. If they are preserved in salt, wash them thoroughly and dry them before use.

SALT. You should use sea salt for flavouring dishes, and commercial rock salt for adding to water when you are cooking pasta (and always add it after the water has come to the boil).

BOTTARGA. Traditionally this Sardinian and Ligurian specialty was the dried roe of mullet, but these days it is often dried tuna roe. It's hard to find, and some people consider it too bitter-tasting, but it has a unique flavour that can give character to a dish. It can be served thinly sliced with oil, lemon and pepper accompanied by pickled vegetables, or grated on pasta.

OCTOPUS, CUTTLEFISH, CALAMARI. Try to get them already cleaned from your fish shop, even if you have to pay extra. But if your fishmonger refuses, our recipes will show you how to remove the useless bits inside.

BEANS. Fresh fava beans and borlotti beans are a delight in spring, and are increasingly available in Australian greengrocers. The borlotti lose their beautiful pink marbling when cooked, but of course they are still delicious. Cannellini beans are usually available dried, and you need to soak them overnight and change the water before using them.

BREAD. When we mention bread in the recipes, we mean an Italian-style white, crusty oval loaf. You can slice and toast it for *crostini*, and you can pull out the soft white interior for thickening sauces or making breadcrumbs. A ciabatta loaf is a good example. We never use brown or wholemeal in these recipes.

CHEESES. The main ones we use are parmesan, pecorino (sheep's milk), mozzarella (ideally buffalo milk, but always the soft white version, not the yellow rubbery version), ricotta, and soft creamy stracchino (to melt inside focaccia).

OLIVES. There is no such thing as 'fresh' olives. They need to ferment in a salt solution for at least two months before you can eat them. You should wash them thoroughly before using them in any dish. I find the black (fully ripened) ones are best in cooking, the green better in salads. You won't be surprised to hear that I prefer the small black olives from Liguria, but when the recipe calls for pitted olives, I prefer to use the larger kalamata style, because they retain their flavour and texture when the pits are taken out.

PINE NUTS. In pesto, always use them raw, not toasted. Indian ones are smaller. Needless to say, we prefer Italian. They make a great combination with spinach.

TOMATOES. They only arrived in Europe (from South America) in the seventeenth century, so we think of them as a radical new ingredient to be used with care. In making sauce, you can use Italian peeled tinned tomatoes. For salads, the redder the better.

RICE. The ideal form of rice for risotto is big-grained arborio or carnaroli style, rather than the small Asian-style rice more readily available in Australia. We don't suggest substituting basmati or brown—that's just not Ligurian cooking.

SPAGHETTI AND OTHER PACKET PASTA. Mostly Ligurians make their own pasta, with eggs, but some recipes (for example, when the sauce contains whole pieces of seafood) work better with dried pasta. We suggest you buy an imported Italian variety, which is likely to be best served *al dente* (boiled for a short time so it gives a little resistance to the teeth and the texture becomes part of the experience).

THE EQUIPMENT

Large wooden board for chopping vegetables
Even larger wooden board, or a tabletop, for rolling out dough
Mixing bowls, big and small
Wooden spoons
Knives, big and small, all sharp, for dicing and chopping
Mezzaluna—two-handled knife—for fine slicing
Rolling pin, wooden
Saucepans and pots, including a large one capable of boiling five litres of water
Terracotta casserole dish with lid
Frying pans, some non-stick and some high-sided and heavy-bottomed
Baking dishes and trays, of various sizes
Measuring cups or jug
Electric blender
Mortar (heavy) and pestle for grinding pastes
Springform cake tin
Moulds—various sizes and shapes if you want to be showy,
    or you can use a small bowl or ramekin
Mouli mixer for pureeing cooked vegetables and fish
Pasta cutter (though you can use a sharp knife)
Pastry brush
Pepper grinder
Pizza tray—the larger the better
Potato masher (though a fork will do if you have a strong arm)
Scales
Strainer
Ladles
Sieve
Slotted spoons for lifting ravioli out of boiling water
Small wire spider for removing fried foods from hot oil
Whisk
Cooking thermometer (for use in two of the desserts)

We hope that you will enjoy these recipes and use your creativity to make them your own. In most cases the quantities we have given are meant as an indication, not a requirement, and you can toss in more or less according to taste. My greatest satisfaction will be to know that I have contributed towards a memorable gathering around the table, like the Ligurian feast days of my childhood.

THE WINES OF LIGURIA ... AND THE BEST WINES WITH OUR RECIPES

It was not a very proud beginning for wine production in Liguria. The historian Diodoro Siculo wrote in the first century BC: 'There are no olives or grapes in Liguria, only forests. The land is inaccessible to Bacchus.' Little did he know that the ancient Greeks had taught winemaking to the local Liguri tribes, who weren't about to reveal their skills to the Roman invaders. A century later Strabone, a Greek geographer, wrote: 'The little wine that the Ligurians produce is sour and undrinkable.'

Then things started to change. Pliny the Elder, the creator of the world's first encyclopaedia, wrote in the first century AD: 'The wines from Luni [the very beginning of Liguria] are the best in the whole of Etruria.'

Ligurian wines, particularly those from the Cinque Terre, have been improving ever since. Until recently, the types of grapes grown in Liguria were numerous—estimated a century ago at more than one hundred types per province, mainly because the sailors of Liguria kept bringing grapes from the four corners of the world.

In the Riviera di Levante nowadays there are four wine-producing areas, each with its own 'DOC' (Denomination of Origin Controlled) guarantee of consistency. From east to west they are Colli di Luni, Cinque Terre, Colline di Levanto and Golfo del Tigullio. Here are our recommendations of wines for you to try if you are in the area.

COLLI DI LUNI

Colli di Luni Bianco (white) suits vegetable tarts and stuffed vegetables.

Vermentino (white) suits fish, seafood risotto, and pasta with seafood sauce. It's also hardy enough to match pesto and capon magro.

Vermentino Rosso (red) for meat ravioli, rabbit, grilled meats and local mild pecorino cheese.

CINQUE TERRE

This area lies between La Spezia and Levanto. The vineyards are 'heroically' cultivated (by hand, not machine), in terraces down the cliff face along one of the most beautiful coastlines of Italy.

Two very rare wines are produced here. The Cinque Terre Bianco is a dry white in which you can taste the sea air and the local herbs. It is good with sardines and anchovies, seafood, fish and fish-stuffed pastas. And, of course, the local *mes-ciua* (chickpea soup).

Sciacchetrà is a rare sweet wine, made from Albarola, Vermentino and Bosco grapes, and different from vintage to vintage. Harvesting is labour intensive—the vines are low to the ground so the grape pickers have to kneel down.

It was one of the first *passito* styles in Italy ('*passito*' means the grapes are picked late and left to dry for up to six weeks before being crushed, so they become more intense in flavour).

Sciacchetrà is expensive but unique. It is what we call a meditation wine, left for special occasions. If it is younger than three years, you can drink it with dry fruit cakes such as *pan dolce* or *pan forte*. But after three years, savour it by itself.

Don't confuse it with *sciac-tra*, a rosé style made on the Ponente side of Genoa.

COLLINE DI LEVANTO

Past the Cinque Terre, mainly on the coast, still in La Spezia province, the Levanto hills produce a white called Colline di Levanto Bianco, excellent with the local specialty—the *gattafin* (fried ravioli) and fried vegetables. They also produce a red, called Colline di Levanto Rosso similar to the Colli di Luni red but to be drunk very young, within the year of harvesting.

GOLFO DEL TIGULLIO

The province of Genoa has the two most recently declared DOC areas in Liguria. The Tigullio Gulf goes from near Sestri Levante to Genoa along the coast and inland, particularly in Chiavari.

One of Liguria's favourite sons, the poet/singer songwriter Fabrizio de André in one of his most beautiful songs in dialect, tells us of the pleasure of having some deep-fried '*gianchetti*' (whitebait) with a glass of white wine from Portofino (the centre of the Tigullio Gulf).

In the area they produce three whites: Golfo del Tigullio Bianchetta, Golfo del Tigullio Bianco and Golfo del Tigullio Vermentino.

Each of these three wines comes in a sparkling version. They are very light wines to be drunk within the year, great with seafood salads, octopus and potatoes, fish and the *pansotti* with the walnut sauce.

The two reds of the area, also to be drunk young and within the year, are Golfo del Tigullio Rosso and Golfo del Tigullio Ciliegiolo. Apart from cheeses, salamis and meat dishes such as *cima alla Genovese*, they are good with some seafoods like stuffed mussels, cuttlefish with spinach and stuffed calamari.

IN AUSTRALIA

Wine tastes are personal. My tastes are simple: I'd have Pinot Grigio with everything and horrify the wine experts. But I know how important it is to match wine with food to enhance the experience of each dish. The fundamental principle is that the wine should never overpower the food and the food should never overpower the wine. They should complement each other. So light wines with light dishes (fish, salads), heavy wines with heavy dishes (stews, roasts).

With the finger food in our first chapter, I would serve the Italian sparkling called Prosecco, which is an excellent aperitif and also cleanses the palate; however, with the chicken liver *crostini*, you might like to try a slightly sweet white such as Gewurztraminer or some Reislings.

Crisp young whites such as Soave, Reisling or Pinot Grigio would go with raw or steamed seafood and with salads dressed with oil and lemon.

Light and fruity whites such as Sauvignon Blanc or Gavi could go with vegetable antipasti, asparagus and onion-based sauces.

Rich and fruity whites such as Vernaccia, Chardonnay or Semillon could go with a fish soup, a risotto with seafood or vegetables, or mussels with tomato sauce or any vegetable pasta that would be sprinkled with parmesan. But the meatier and cheesier the pasta sauce, the redder the wine.

Light reds such as Chianti, Barbera, Sangiovese, Merlot or dry Pinot Noir could go with seafood cooked with rich sauces, or vegetable soup such as minestrone or quail or chicken.

Medium-bodied red blends such as Cabernet Merlot, Shiraz Grenache, the Italian Vino Nobile and the new 'Supertuscans' (usually blends with Cabernet Sauvignon) could go with most of our pies and with lamb, veal, pork and rabbit.

And big reds such as Barbaresco, Barolo, Brunello di Montalcino, Primitivo, Cabernet Sauvignon and Shiraz could go with duck, beef and tripe.

Most desserts work with a sweet perfumed light white such as Moscato d'Asti, but a richer dessert deserves wine made with the luscious *zibbibo* grape, or a *passito* style, or an Australian sauterne. With chocolate, Italians drink the rich red called Recioto della Valpolicella. In Australia, try something sweet and red that has a little sparkle.

It is preferable not to drink wine with a dessert that contains any strong liqueur, or with ice cream, which freezes the palate and leaves a layer of fat in the mouth.

Now we're ready to drink.

Stuzzichini

Finger food

Finger food

36 **CROSTINI CON SALSA MARÒ** ~ Crostini with broad bean puree

39 **CROSTINI CON TONNO MARINATO** ~ Marinated tuna crostini

40 **CROSTINI CON PÂTÉ DI OLIVE** ~ Olive paste crostini

40 **CROSTINI CON FICHI E ZUCCHINI** ~ Fig and zucchini crostini

41 **CROSTINI CON FEGATINI** ~ Chicken liver crostini

42 **CROSTINI CON PÂTÉ DI POLPO** ~ Octopus paste crostini

43 **ACCIUGHE MARINATE IN ACETO** ~ Anchovies with bread and butter

45 **BRUSCHETTA AL POMODORO** ~ Bruschetta with tomato

46 **BRUSCHETTA CON TRITO DI OLIVE NERE E VERDI** ~ Bruschetta with black and green olives

46 **BRUSCHETTA DI ACCIUGHE PICCANTI** ~ Spicy anchovy bruschetta

48 **BRUSCHETTA DI ACCIUGHE E PEPERONI** ~ Anchovy and roasted capsicum bruschetta

48 **BRUSCHETTA DI MUSCOLI** ~ Mussel bruschetta

50 **OLIVE AL TIMO** ~ Thyme-scented olives

51 **OLIVE LIGURI IN MARINATA CLASSICA** ~ Marinated Ligurian olives

51 **OLIVE NERE CON FINOCCHIO E BASILICO** ~ Olives with fennel and basil

52 **OLIVE PICCANTI ALL'AGLIO** ~ Spicy garlic olives

52 **OSTRICHE E SALMONE CRUDO** ~ Oysters with salmon tartare

55 **CROSTATINA DI CAPPESANTE** ~ Scallop tartlets

56 **FOCACCIA ALL' OLIO E ROSMARINO** ~ Rosemary focaccia bread

57 **FOCACCIA CON LA CIPOLLA** ~ Onion focaccia

58 **FOCACCIA CON IL FORMAGGIO** ~ Cheese focaccia

60 **CUCULLI DI PATATE** ~ Potato and pine nut fritters

61 **CUCULLI DI CECI** ~ Chickpea fritters

By starting this book with what the French might call *canapés*, **we wouldn't want to give the** impression that Ligurians are the sort of people who stand around at cocktail parties: they are much too hardworking and sensible for that.

But it's a happy coincidence that dishes which developed as snacks to be taken aboard fishing boats or into the fields by shepherds and farmers can now be adapted as treats in a more leisurely age.

These dishes are called *stuzzichini* (pronounced stootzikeeni), which comes from the verb *stuzzicare*—to tease, tantalise or flirt. Modern Ligurians see these dishes as a kind of foreplay before a meal or, for that matter, before a relationship.

Most of these palate teasers are served on grilled bread. If the toast is rubbed with garlic and brushed with extra virgin olive oil, it is called a *bruschetta* (pronounced brusketta, not brooshetta—Australian waiters please note). If the bread is cut into circles and remains garlic free, or is dipped in egg and fried, then the treat is called a *crostino*. And if you're eating an oyster, the raw toast is placed in the mouth before you suck the mollusc out of its shell.

The recipes in this chapter are a mixture of regional classics and new ideas based on traditional ingredients.

Crostini con salsa marò

Crostini with broad bean puree

This dish can be prepared only with fresh raw broad (fava) beans, and their short season makes it really special. I have to confess that the topping originated in 'the other Riviera', west of Genoa, but they could not keep the secret for long—'*salsa marò*' has spread all over Liguria.

Like many Ligurian dialect words, the name *marò* comes from the Arabs, who paid many visits to our coastline over the centuries. Their word *mara* means condiment or sauce, and this one was prepared mainly to give the sailors who made daily journeys up and down the Riviera something to spread over their bread.

1 kg (2 lb) fresh broad (fava)
 beans (smallest possible)
1 garlic clove, peeled
5 small mint leaves
pinch of sea salt

100 g (3½ oz) freshly grated
 pecorino cheese
125 ml (4 fl oz) olive oil
1 loaf Italian bread
 (baguette size)

Double peel the broad beans: first, remove from the pod and then slip the rough outer shell off the bean.

Place the broad beans in a mortar with the garlic, mint and salt. Pound everything until you obtain a smooth paste, then transfer to a bowl. Add the pecorino, mix thoroughly with a wooden spoon and, while mixing, slowly add in as much olive oil as the mixture can absorb—it needs to be thick, not runny.

Cut the bread in slices and toast the discs of bread in the oven or under the grill until golden. Spread the *salsa marò* on top.

Salsa marò is also excellent with veal or grilled fish, or tossed through pasta. **SERVES 6**

Crostini con tonno marinato

Marinated tuna crostini

First, prepare all the ingredients for the topping to have them ready 5 minutes before you want to serve. With this dish you have to act fast—you don't want the tuna to sit around too long in the marinade and lose its lively taste.

400 g (13 oz) sashimi-grade
 tuna
10 Ligurian black olives,
 pitted and chopped
1 tsp thyme leaves, picked
 and finely chopped
1 tsp oregano leaves, picked
 and finely chopped
½ red onion, finely chopped

2 tsp salted capers,
 rinsed and dried
1 tsp pine nuts, toasted
juice of ½ lemon
45 ml (1½ fl oz) olive oil
sea salt and freshly ground
 black pepper
1 loaf Italian bread (baguette
 size), sliced and toasted

With a very sharp knife, dice the tuna into small cubes and place in a bowl with the olives, thyme, oregano, onion, capers and pine nuts. Mix thoroughly to amalgamate the flavours. Now add the lemon juice and olive oil, season with salt and pepper and mix well. Place the marinated tuna on the toasted bread and serve.

This dish can also be served as an antipasto for four people. Divide the tuna mixture into four and place a mound in the centre of each plate (you can mould them with a ramekin or egg ring). Arrange five little toasts around the tuna and serve. **SERVES 4**

Crostini con pâté di olive
Olive paste crostini

345 g (11 oz) black olives
in brine, drained and pitted
100 g (3½ oz) capers in brine,
drained
155 g (5 oz) salted anchovy
fillets, rinsed and dried
1 tsp picked tender rosemary
leaves

1 tsp picked thyme leaves
125 ml (4 fl oz) olive oil
(you won't necessarily
use it all)
juice of 1 lemon
freshly ground black pepper
12 slices toasted Italian
bread

Combine the olives, capers, anchovies and herbs in the mortar, and pound until you achieve the consistency of a coarse paté. It is better to make the olive paste in a mortar, but if using a blender, be careful not to make it too fine.

Transfer the olive mixture to a bowl and, while mixing with a wooden spoon, slowly pour in the olive oil—as much as the paté will hold. Add the lemon juice and some pepper, give a last good mix and it is ready. Spread either on toasted bread or on fresh crusty ciabatta.

If you want to keep it for another occasion, put the paté into a jar, cover completely with olive oil and use some baking paper as a lid. **SERVES 4**

Crostini con fichi e zucchini
Fig and zucchini crostini

4 small zucchini (courgettes),
with the flower still attached
if possible
30 ml (1 fl oz) olive oil
sea salt and freshly ground
black pepper
4 figs

2 anchovy fillets, chopped
1 loaf Italian bread (baguette
size), sliced into eight pieces,
crusts removed and toasted
2 sprigs oregano, roughly
chopped

Wash the zucchini, cut off the tips and cut them in half lengthwise.

Heat a few drops of olive oil in a non-stick frying pan, add the zucchini halves and salt and pepper, and fry for about 2 minutes on each side. Set aside to cool.

Wash the figs and dry them. Cut off the tops and slice into eight discs.

Mix the anchovies with the remaining oil, then lightly brush this mixture on top of each disc of toast. Place a disc of fig on each crostino, sprinkle on the oregano and top with a slice of zucchini. Put another drop of anchovy-flavoured oil on each zucchini slice then serve.

Crostini con fegatini

Chicken liver crostini

FOR THE TOPPING
45 ml (1½ fl oz) olive oil
300 g (10 oz) chicken livers,
 trimmed of sinew and chopped
a few sage leaves
sea salt
1 tbsp finely chopped
 flat-leaf parsley
45 ml (1½ fl oz)
 dry white wine
5 anchovy fillets
1 tbsp salted capers,
 rinsed and dried
5 pitted black olives,
 such as kalamata
10 g (⅓ oz) pine nuts

20 g (¾ oz) butter
2 tsp red wine vinegar
2 sprigs oregano, roughly
 chopped

FOR THE BASE
1 loaf Italian bread,
 baguette size
60 ml (2 fl oz) milk
1 handful plain
 (all purpose) flour
2 eggs, lightly beaten
100 ml (3½ fl oz) olive oil,
 for frying

To make the topping, pour the olive oil into a heavy-based frying pan over a medium heat. When the oil is hot, add the chicken livers and sage. Cook for 5 minutes, mixing regularly with a wooden spoon to prevent sticking. Season with salt, sprinkle in the parsley and add the white wine. Gently fry for a further 5 minutes to let the wine evaporate. When ready tip the chicken livers onto a chopping board, add the anchovies, capers, olives and pine nuts, and chop very finely. Use a mezzaluna if you have one. Place this mixture back into the pan. Add the butter and melt over a medium heat. Stir in the vinegar, add the oregano, mix again, and finish cooking for a further 3 minutes. Remove from the heat and pour the ready-to-be-used mixture into a bowl.

Now for the base, cut the loaf of bread into slices about 1 cm (½ inch) thick and remove the crusts. Place the milk, flour and eggs in separate shallow dishes. Put 1 cm (½ inch) of olive oil in a frying pan over a medium heat. Dip both sides of the bread first in the milk, then in the flour and finally in the eggs. Drop the bread into the hot oil and fry until golden and crispy, about 2 minutes each side. Drain on paper towel, spread with the chicken liver mixture and serve hot.

If you can't be bothered frying the bread, you could spread the chicken liver mixture on toasted rounds, as with the other crostini. **SERVES 4**

Crostini con pâté di polpo

Octopus paste crostini

Once upon a time there were small sailboats travelling from the Gulf of La Spezia to the major ports of Genoa and Livorno. These boats wanted heavy weights that would help stabilise them but be disposable when not needed. The cheapest option was to use big rocks found along the seashore.

Sailors and workmen called *zavorristi* (stabilisers) from the villages gathered these rocks and often found octopus living underneath them. In the town of Portovenere, one clever *zavorristo* had the idea of turning the octopus into a paste so that the sailors would have something to spread on their bread during their trips.

1 kg (2 lb) octopus
90 ml (3 fl oz) white wine
 vinegar
45 ml (1½ fl oz) olive oil,
 plus extra
1 garlic clove, finely chopped
1 handful finely chopped
 flat-leaf parsley

1 tbsp salted capers,
 rinsed and dried
freshly ground black pepper
12 small slices toasted
 Italian bread

If the octopus has not been cleaned by your fishmonger, pull the head and legs apart, and cut away the beak and eyes. Simmer the legs and hood gently for about 1 hour and allow to cool down in the water. When cool enough to handle but still warm, lift out the octopus and remove the skin.

Pour the vinegar into a pot full of cold water and immerse the octopus for about 20 minutes. Drain and pat dry with paper towel.

Now cut the octopus into pieces, place in a blender and process to form a paste.

Heat the oil in a frying pan and fry the garlic and parsley for about 1 minute, being careful not to let it burn. Add the capers, octopus paste and some pepper, and sauté for 5 minutes, stirring constantly.

Transfer the mixture to a bowl, mix in a splash of olive oil and it is ready to be spread over the toast. **SERVES 4**

Acciughe marinate in aceto

Anchovies with bread and butter

Anchovies are central to Ligurian cooking because they swim near the shore, and even in the smallest boats, fishermen can net them. Oregano, a herb that grows on the hillsides that descend to the sea, goes so well with the flavour of anchovies that it is known as 'l'erba delle acciughe'— the anchovy's herb.

This recipe suggests you eat anchovies with heavily buttered bread, which complements their saltiness. This is one of the very few occasions we mention butter in this book.

250 g (8 oz) salted anchovies
90 ml (3 fl oz) white
  wine vinegar
olive oil

oregano leaves
100 g (3½ oz) butter
12 slices fresh
  Italian bread

Wash the anchovies under running water to remove all the salt residue. Delicately fillet them by removing the central bone. Dry the fillets with paper towel and place in a deep-sided dish without overlapping. Cover with the vinegar and let them rest for about 1 hour. Then with a fork hold the anchovies in place and tilt the dish to allow the vinegar to drain off. Now cover the anchovies with the olive oil, rest for 30 minutes, sprinkle with a little oregano and they are ready to eat.

Spread butter on the bread and top with the anchovies. **SERVES 4**

Bruschetta al pomodoro

Bruschetta with tomato

3 large ripe tomatoes
6 large slices Italian bread
2 garlic cloves, peeled
1 tbsp olive oil

2 tbsp finely chopped
  baby basil leaves
sea salt and freshly ground
  black pepper

Cut a cross in the base of each tomato and plunge into boiling water for about 1 minute. Immediately remove and immerse in iced water until the skin starts to wrinkle. Drain and when cool, peel. Cut the tomatoes in half and remove the seeds with a spoon. Then dice them and let them drain to remove excess liquid.

Toast the bread and rub garlic over it.

Mix the tomato with the basil, olive oil, salt and pepper and spoon onto the toasts, and serve.

SERVES 6

Bruschetta con trito di olive nere e verdi

Bruschetta with black and green olives

1 small ripe tomato
100 g (3½ oz) Sicilian green
  olives
100 g (3½ oz) Ligurian black
  olives

extra virgin olive oil
pinch of sea salt
6 slices Italian bread
2 garlic cloves, peeled
2 sprigs thyme, leaves picked

Cut a cross in the base of the tomato and plunge into boiling water for 1 minute or so. Immediately transfer to iced water and leave until the skin starts to wrinkle. Remove from the water, and peel, deseed then dice them, and let the tomato drain to remove excess liquid.

Remove the stones from the olives, and roughly chop.

Combine the tomatoes and olives in a bowl and dress with extra virgin olive oil and salt.

Toast the bread. Cut the garlic in half and rub it on the toast.

Spread the tomato and olive mixture on top of each slice of toast and sprinkle with the thyme leaves. **SERVES 4–6**

Bruschetta di acciughe piccanti

Spicy anchovy bruschetta

This is a 'do it yourself' bruschetta, with the elements presented separately at the table.

500 g (1 lb) salted anchovies
1 tomato, peeled, seeded
  and diced
2 small red chillies,
  finely chopped

125 ml (4 fl oz) olive oil
2 garlic cloves, finely chopped
1 loaf crusty Italian bread,
  sliced and toasted

Wash the anchovies under running water, getting rid of all the salt residue. Delicately fillet the anchovies by removing the central bone, being careful not to break the fillets. Dry them gently with paper towel and place them in a deep-sided dish without overlapping.

Combine the tomato, chillies and olive oil in a bowl and mix energetically with a whisk until the sauce is well emulsified. Pour over the anchovies and sprinkle with the garlic. Allow to marinate for 24 hours before serving with a plate of toasted bread. **SERVES 4**

Bruschetta di acciughe e peperoni

Anchovy and roasted capsicum bruschetta

8 anchovy fillets marinated
  in oil, drained
juice of ½ lemon
2 red capsicums (bell peppers)
30 ml (1 fl oz) olive oil

sea salt and freshly ground
  black pepper
1 small garlic clove, chopped
8 slices Italian bread
½ tbsp chopped oregano leaves

Place the anchovies on a plate, pour the lemon juice on top and set aside to marinate for at least 20 minutes.

Now barbecue the capsicums. You could cut them in half and roast them, skin-side up, in the top part of a 250°C (500° F/gas 9) oven until the skin turns black. Or you could put the halves, skin-side up, under a grill. But to achieve the best flavour and consistency, you should burn them over an open flame (such as a large gas ring). To do this, use tongs to hold the capsicums over the flame until they are blackened on all sides. Allow them to cool and peel off the blackened skin. Cut off the tops, cut them in half (if they aren't already), scrape out the seeds and cut the flesh into 2-cm (¾-inch) strips. Place in a bowl and dress with a little olive oil, salt and pepper and garlic.

Toast the bread and arrange on a serving dish, sprinkle with a little olive oil and distribute the sliced capsicums over the toast. Place an anchovy on top of each one, sprinkle with oregano and serve. **SERVES 4**

Bruschetta di muscoli

Mussel bruschetta

500 g (1 lb) mussels, scrubbed
  and de-bearded
80 ml (2½ fl oz) extra virgin
  olive oil
1 garlic clove, crushed
  with the blade of a knife

1 small red chilli,
  finely chopped
½ bunch flat-leaf parsley,
  leaves picked and chopped
sea salt
8 slices Italian bread, toasted

Heat a large frying pan over medium heat, add the mussels and cook until they open, about 2–3 minutes. Remove the mussel meat from the shells and chop finely. Reserve 1 tablespoon of the liquid that has been extracted from the shells.

Heat another frying pan, add the olive oil and garlic. Remove the garlic when it starts to turn golden brown. Add the chilli, chopped mussels and the reserved liquid, and cook until the liquid evaporates. Add the parsley or a sprig of thyme, season with salt and spread on the hot toasted bread. **SERVES 4**

Olive al timo

Thyme-scented olives

This is not really a recipe, just a way to dress olives before leaving them on the table for guests to spoon a few onto their plates. So you can make as many as you like and dress them with as much thyme and olive oil as you like.

black olives in brine
olive oil
a few sprigs thyme

Take the olives (preferably Taggiasca which are Liguria's finest), drain them and using a knife, cut them lengthwise on one side. Dry the olives in the sun for two days (bring them in at night and cover them with a tea towel).

Dress the olives with a good Ligurian olive oil and some thyme leaves. Mix and let them rest for at least 1 hour before serving. If you want to make more to keep, put them in a sterilised glass container with some extra sprigs of thyme and some peeled whole garlic cloves. Cover with extra virgin olive oil.

Olive Liguri in marinata classica

Marinated Ligurian olives

300 g Taggiasca black olives
1 tsp fennel seeds
thinly sliced zest of ½ small
  orange

juice of ½ lemon
5 garlic cloves, peeled
extra virgin olive oil

Rinse the olives under running water and pat dry with paper towel.

Place all ingredients in a large bowl, mix well and cover. Place in the refrigerator for at least 12 hours.

To serve, remove the garlic and orange zest, and drain off liquid.

These olives will keep for up to 1 week if kept covered and refrigerated. **SERVES 4**

Olive nere con finocchio e basilico

Olives with fennel and basil

300 g (10 oz) kalamata olives,
  pitted
1 fennel bulb
3 garlic cloves, peeled and
  crushed slightly using the blade
  of a knife
5 basil leaves, chopped
extra virgin olive oil

Rinse the olives under running water and dry in a salad spinner to remove all traces of water. Cut off the base of the fennel and the leafy top, discard the outer layer and cut the fennel into pieces twice the size of the olives.

Place the olives, fennel, garlic and basil in a large bowl, drizzle with olive oil and mix until all ingredients are well combined. Remove the garlic before serving. **SERVES 4**

Olive piccanti all' aglio
Spicy garlic olives

1 large red chilli
3 garlic cloves
300 g (10 oz) Taggiasca black
  olives in brine
45 ml (1½ fl oz) extra virgin
  olive oil, plus extra

2 celery hearts, chopped into
  1-cm (½-inch) lengths
5 sprigs thyme
1 tbsp oregano leaves

Chop the chilli and garlic together very finely. Drain the olives and pat dry with paper towel. Place the olives in a bowl, pour on the olive oil and mix well. Add the chilli-garlic mixture, celery and herbs. Add a bit more olive oil if it looks a bit dry, mix thoroughly and rest for 20 minutes.

Once the olives have been eaten, the remaining oil is excellent for dipping bread.

This mixture must be eaten within a couple of hours otherwise the celery and herbs will darken. **SERVES 4**

Ostriche e salmone crudo
Oysters with salmon tartare

This dish has nothing to do with Africa's answer to the emu. *Ostriche* (pronounced ostrik-eh) are oysters. They are rare on the Riviera, so we bring them from Sardinia and make a ritual of them.

This is how Ligurians eat oysters: put a small piece of bread in your mouth, suck the oyster from the shell and chew the mixture together. After each oyster take a sip of white wine.

Our recipe adds a favourite form of sashimi, but only for dressing. We've got our priorities right.

250 g (8 oz) sashimi-grade
  salmon fillet
½ bunch chives, finely chopped
4 tsp fish roe
juice of 1 lemon

30 ml (1 fl oz) mild extra virgin
  olive oil (preferably Ligurian)
24 oysters, freshly shucked
lemon wedges, to serve

Finely dice the salmon and combine with the chives, fish roe, lemon juice and olive oil. Arrange the oysters on a platter, top with the salmon tartare and serve with lemon wedges. **SERVES 4**

Crostatina di cappesante

Scallop tartlets

Ligurians often eat tarts, but rarely eat scallops (which are more of a French delicacy). In Australia, it's vice versa. Because this book celebrates Australian produce as much as it celebrates Ligurian traditions, I thought we should create an elegant modern *stuzzichino* using one of this country's favourite shellfish.

1 sheet savoury pastry
  (bought is fine)
2 leeks
30 ml (1 fl oz) olive oil,
  plus extra

sea salt and freshly ground
  black pepper
12 scallops
1 tbsp small basil leaves,
  finely chopped

We're assuming you will buy the pastry already made in sheets from the supermarket. Cut out 12 discs and press them into 12 tartlet moulds about 3 cm (1¼ inches) in diameter. Rest in the fridge for 15 minutes. Take them out, prick the pastry with a fork and bake them in a preheated 180°C (350°F/gas 4) oven for 6–8 minutes.

Trim the leeks by removing the top part, the roots, and the outer leaves, and slice into discs about 3 mm (⅛ inch) thick. Heat the oil in a frying pan over a low heat, add the leeks, season with salt and pepper and sauté gently until soft, about 10 minutes, stirring with a wooden spoon. Drain off the oil and set the leeks aside.

Brush a very hot non-stick frying pan with a little extra olive oil and sear the scallops for 1–2 minutes on each side. Sprinkle with salt.

To assemble, fill each tartlet with the leek mixture, top with a scallop and a sprinkle of basil and serve warm. **SERVES 4**

VARIATION

This *stuzzichino* works just as well served on toasted or pan-fried rounds of crustless Italian bread. Then you'd call it scallop *crostini*.

Focaccia all' olio e rosmarino

Rosemary focaccia bread

Focaccia is Liguria's answer to pizza. We're addicted to it, stuffing it and topping it with all manner of savoury treats, buying slabs of it from food shops mid-morning and mid-afternoon, and making it at home to start meals and to mop up sauces. Here and on the following pages are three variations. Any amount not eaten on the day can be fried in oil and turned into croutons or breadcrumbs.

5 g (⅛ oz) active dry yeast
1 tsp sea salt, plus extra for
  sprinkling
1 tsp sugar
680 ml (22½ fl oz) warm water
1 kg (2 lb) strong white flour,
  preferably Italian
125 ml (4 fl oz) olive oil
1 tbsp chopped rosemary leaves

In a large bowl, whisk the yeast, salt and sugar with the water, and when the yeast has dissolved, stir in half the flour. This will make a sloppy dough. Let it rest, covered, for 2 hours in a warm place so the yeast becomes active and bubbly. It should rise by one-third.

Place the remaining flour in a mound on a bench or large board and make a well in the top. Pour the wet mixture into the well and add 45 ml (1½ fl oz) of the olive oil. Knead the dough until it forms a firm but sticky ball which is springy to the touch—about 10 minutes. Divide into two balls. Brush each with a little of the oil, and leave, covered, in a warm place for another hour.

Turn the balls of dough onto a floured surface, and roll out to a thickness of 2 cm (¾ inch). Transfer the dough to two oiled baking dishes, about 30 x 40 cm (12 x 16 inches) if rectangular, about 30 cm (12 inches) in diameter if round. Flatten the dough to cover the whole dish and press the top with the tips of your fingers, making imprints all over. Let the dough rest, covered, for another 30 minutes. Sprinkle with extra sea salt and rosemary leaves and pour over the remaining olive oil.

Bake at 200°C (400°F/gas 6) for 30 minutes, or until golden. Eat soon. **SERVES 4**

Focaccia con la cipolla

Onion focaccia

Who would have thought that the onion focaccia found in most bars of the Riviera, particularly in the morning, is the result of an act of love—or more precisely, an act of jealousy? Legend has it that this dish was invented by the wives of the sailors. They hoped the onion on the focaccia would make their husbands' breath unpleasant and therefore keep the girls in other ports at a distance. In fact, the girls were probably eating and enjoying the same focaccia, so the plot is unlikely to have worked.

5 g (⅛ oz) active dry yeast
1 tsp sea salt, plus extra for
  sprinkling
1 tsp sugar
680 ml (22½ fl oz) warm water
1 kg (2 lb) strong white flour,
  preferably Italian
125 ml (4 fl oz) olive oil
1 red onion, thinly sliced

Proceed exactly as in the recipe for Rosemary focaccia opposite, but instead of rosemary, layer the surface with the onion rings, which you press into the surface of the dough before baking.

This focaccia can also be made with olives. Pit the olives and mix them into the dough at the second kneading. **SERVES 4**

Focaccia con il formaggio

Cheese focaccia

When the Saracens raided the Ligurian coastline a millennium ago, the villagers were forced to abandon their houses and escape inland. In the mountains there were herds of sheep wandering around the flour-making mills. The Ligurian villagers rapidly came up with the idea of combining the cheese made from the sheep's milk with the focaccia from the mills. After centuries of 'hibernation', the cheese-stuffed focaccia was revived in the 1950s by a restaurateur called Manuelina in the town of Recco. It has become Recco's specialty. Don't even think of comparing it with the cheese-stuffed crust now offered by some pizza chains.

250 g (8 oz) plain (all
  purpose) flour
125 ml (4 fl oz) olive oil
350 g (11 oz) stracchino
  cheese
sea salt

Place the flour and half of the olive oil in a bowl and mix well, adding a few drops of water from a wet hand. Place the dough on a clean flat work surface and knead with your hands, adding some water if necessary, until you obtain a smooth and soft dough. Shape into a ball, cover with a clean tea towel and rest for 1 hour in a warm place. When rested, knead the dough for 3 minutes. Shape into a ball again and rest for another 5 minutes. At this point divide the dough into two equal portions and flatten each with a rolling pin until very, very thin (almost translucent).

Oil the base of a large round baking dish or tray (a pizza tray would be ideal) and place one sheet of the dough on it. Break the cheese into small pieces and dot them all over this base. Cover with the second sheet of dough, cut off the excess and press the sides so that the two sheets stick together.

Pour some of the oil on top of the focaccia and spread it around with the palm of your hand, exerting a small amount of pressure to squash the cheese down a little. Sprinkle with salt and make some holes in the surface by pinching and pulling up a little of the dough.

Bake in a 220°C (425°F/gas 7) oven for 20 minutes or until starting to become crispy.

SERVES 4

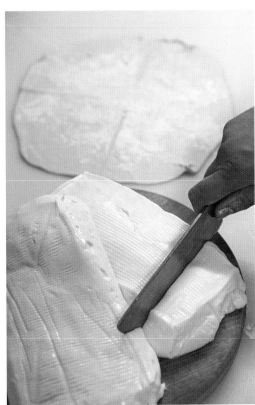

Cuculli di patate

Potato and pine nut fritters

Cuculli are a kind of fried dumpling made either with chickpea flour (besan) or with potatoes and herbs. The name comes from the dialect word *coccoli*, which means lively children (we'd call them hyperactive these days), and they are the biggest audience for this dish.

While the mothers were frying the fritters they would distract the impatient kids with this nursery rhyme: 'It is the dance of Cuculli/ Mother broke the plates/ She broke her best ones/ She'd paid 5 coins for them!' It doesn't make any more sense in the original dialect—which is probably why it slowed down the kids.

1 kg (2 lb) desiree potatoes
100 g (3½ oz) butter, chopped
4 sprigs marjoram leaves,
  picked and chopped
45 g (1½ oz) freshly grated
  parmesan cheese

45 g (1½ oz) pine nuts,
  roughly crushed
sea salt
3 eggs, separated
45 g (1½ oz) breadcrumbs
olive oil

Scrub the potatoes, place in a large saucepan and cover with water. Simmer on a medium heat until tender. Allow to cool enough to peel, then put them in a bowl and mash with a potato masher—or even with your hands. Add the butter and mix with a wooden spoon. Continuing to work the mixture, add the marjoram, parmesan, pine nuts and a few pinches of salt. Add the egg yolks, one at a time, mixing vigorously to amalgamate well and obtain a soft and creamy mixture. Using two spoons, form bullet-shaped balls the size of a walnut.

Pour the breadcrumbs onto a large plate.

Lightly beat the egg whites.

Pour the olive oil into a deep-sided frying pan to a depth of about 5 cm (2 inches) and place on a high heat. Let the oil get very hot—190–200°C (375–400°F) if you have a thermometer, or otherwise drop a piece of bread into the oil and if it sizzles right away it is ready.

Roll the *cuculli* first in the egg white and then in the breadcrumbs. Fry a few at a time in the hot oil until they are golden brown on all sides, about 3 minutes. They will fluff up a little and become soft. Serve hot sprinkled with salt.

Instead of frying, you can bake the *cuculli* on a greased oven tray for 5 minutes in a 200°C (400°F/gas 6) oven. Either way they must be served very hot. **SERVES 4**

Cuculli di ceci
Chickpea fritters

500 g (1 lb) chickpea
  flour (besan)
sea salt
1 litre (32 fl oz) cold
  water (approximately)

5 g (⅛ oz) active dry yeast
60 ml (2 fl oz) warm water
3 sprigs marjoram,
  leaves picked
olive oil

Place the flour in a large bowl with a pinch of salt. Add just enough of the cold water, a little at a time, to make a runny batter, whisking carefully so as not to allow any lumps to form. Dissolve the yeast in the warm water. Add this, with the marjoram, to the flour mixture and continue whisking to obtain a smooth batter. Allow to rest for at least 2 hours.

Pour the olive oil into a frying pan to a depth of about 3 cm (1¼ inches) and place on a high heat. Let the oil get very hot—it is ready when a piece of bread starts sizzling as soon as you drop it in.

Carefully place a few spoonfuls of the batter at a time into the pan and fry the *cuculli* until golden brown and puffed up, about 3 minutes. Drain on paper towel, sprinkle with salt and serve hot. **SERVES 4**

Antipasti

Appetizers

Appetizers

68   **CARPACCIO DI PESCE AGLI AGRUMI** ~ *Fish carpaccio*

68   **FILETTI DI TRIGLIA IN MARINATA** ~ *Marinated red mullet*

71   **PROSCIUTTO IN INSALATA** ~ *Prosciutto with apple, fig and mozzarella salad*

72   **PINZIMONIO** ~ *Raw vegetables with garlic sauce*

74   **CONDIGGION** ~ *Riviera salad*

75   **CARPACCIO ALLA CAPPONADA** ~ *Carpaccio with anchovy salad*

75   **MUSCOLI IN SCABECIO** ~ *Marinated mussels*

76   **MUSCOLI GRATINATI** ~ *Mussels au gratin*

79   **MUSCOLI RIPIENI** ~ *Stuffed mussels*

80   **INSALATA DI MARE** ~ *Seafood salad*

81   **BAGNUN DI ACCIUGHE** ~ *Anchovies in a tomato bath*

82   **ARAGOSTA CON PURÉ DI PEPERONI** ~ *Lobster in a capsicum puree*

83   **TIAN** ~ *Anchovy-potato bake*

84   **VERDURE RIPIENE** ~ *Stuffed vegetables*

87   **GATTAFIN** ~ *Fried ravioli*

88   **FIORI DI ZUCCHINI RIPIENI** ~ *Stuffed zucchini flowers*

90   **GAMBERI E FAGIOLI** ~ *Poached prawns with cannellini beans and caviar*

90   **GAMBERI E CARCIOFI** ~ *Prawns with artichokes*

91   **LINGUA DI BUE CON SALSA DI POMODORI VERDI** ~ *Ox tongue with green tomato salsa*

92   **SFORMATINO DI FAVE** ~ *Broad bean custard*

95   **TERRINA DI POLPO** ~ *Octopus terrine*

You've finished your finger food and now you're ready to move to the table and begin the meal. Italians use the word *antipasto* for the first course—which simply means 'before the repast' (and has nothing to do with pasta, despite what some menu spellings might suggest). In the full scale Italian feast, this would be followed by *primo* (pasta or soup or pie) and then *secondo* (main course of fish or meat, with *contorni* of vegetables or salad).

Every region has a different approach to antipasto. Our rich northern neighbours in Emilia-Romagna like to use a lot of preserved meats. Our southern neighbours in Tuscany like to use a lot of beans. In Liguria, we don't mind borrowing from them, but our antipasto mainly involves the produce most readily available to us—the herbs and vegetables we can pick on the hillsides, and the small molluscs, crustaceans, cephalopods, bivalves and fish that can be pulled off the rocks or netted from the water just off the shoreline. So you won't be surprised to find mussels and anchovies featuring prominently in this chapter. They're central to the daily diet of the Riviera. But because we're adapting Ligurian traditions to the bounty of Australia and the approaches of the twenty-first century, you'll also find ingredients and techniques that would have surprised my mother. We like to think they would also have delighted her.

Carpaccio di pesce agli agrumi
Fish carpaccio

300 g (10 oz) very fresh
  kingfish, (or use sashimi-
  grade tuna or salmon)
1 small orange, peeled and
  cut into 12 segments
1 ruby grapefruit, peeled
  and cut into small pieces
2 limes, peeled and cut into
  small pieces

1 bunch dill
2 radishes, washed, cut into
  discs and then sliced into
  thin strips
45 ml (1½ fl oz) olive oil
15 ml (½ fl oz) lemon juice
pinch of sea salt

Thinly slice the fish and arrange on four plates. Garnish each plate with the orange, grapefruit and lime, a few strands of dill, and some strips of radish.

Mix the oil, lemon juice and a pinch of salt in a bowl, and pour over the fish. Serve immediately.

SERVES 4

Filetti di Triglia in marinata
Marinated red mullet

12 small red mullets
sea salt
juice of 1 blood orange
juice of 1 lemon
juice of 1 grapefruit
juice of 2 mandarins

1 butter lettuce, only the inner
  leaves, washed and dried
45 ml (1½ fl oz) olive oil,
  for dressing
freshly ground black pepper

Wash, clean and fillet the red mullets (if you can't persuade the fishmonger to do it). Place in a wide bowl, sprinkle on a little salt and pour the orange, lemon, grapefruit and mandarin juices over the fish. Marinate for 45 minutes, then drain the juices and gently pat the fillets dry with paper towel.

Dress the lettuce leaves with a little olive oil and arrange on four plates. Top with the red mullet fillets, skin-side up for colour contrast. Drizzle with some more olive oil, sprinkle on some pepper and serve. **SERVES 4**

Prosciutto in insalata

Prosciutto with apple, fig and mozzarella salad

2 red witlof (Belgian endive), trimmed, leaves left whole
1 tbsp olive oil
1 tsp red wine vinegar
pinch of sea salt
3 buffalo mozzarella balls, thickly sliced

12 ripe figs, peeled and left whole
12 very thin slices prosciutto
2 green apples, very thinly sliced

Wash the witlof leaves and dry them well in a salad spinner. Place in a bowl and toss with a tablespoon of oil, vinegar and salt.

Place four plates on a work bench and have all your ingredients ready for assembly.

Drizzle the mozzarella with the remaining oil. At the last minute slice the figs into discs.

Start building the dish by arranging the figs, mozzarella and a slice of prosciutto on each plate. Top with some witlof and apple, then add another slice of prosciutto, more witlof and apple and finish with a third slice of prosciutto on top. **SERVES 4**

Pinziminio
Raw vegetables with garlic sauce

This is a fresh and lively way to energise the tastebuds and the brain before moving on to a heavier pasta or main course. The ingredients and quantities here are determined by what's seasonally available, how much you like each of the fresh vegetables, and how full you want your diners to be before the next part of the meal. Change the quantities any way you like.

2 carrots, peeled
2 red capsicums (bell peppers)
2 fennel bulbs
4 spring onions (scallions)
2 small globe artichokes
1 bunch celery
8 small radishes
2 small cucumbers

FOR THE SAUCE
6 garlic cloves, peeled
1 tbsp of white wine vinegar
20 g (¾ oz) soft inside from
 1 loaf Italian bread
60 ml (2 fl oz) olive oil
pinch of sea salt
freshly ground black pepper

If the carrots are large, slice them into quarters. If they are small, leave them whole.

Wash the capsicums, cut off the tops, remove the stems and cut them in half lengthwise. Remove the core and seeds, and cut into 2-cm (¾-inch) wide strips.

Cut off the end of the fennel, and the leafy top, leaving only the white. Peel off and discard the outer layer. Cut the bulb lengthwise into eighths, wash and pat dry with paper towel.

Cut off the roots and top leaves of the spring onions, peel off the outer layer and wash well.

If artichokes are in season, use only young fresh ones. Remove all the hard outer leaves, so you are left with the yellow interior. Trim the caps and cut the stems so they are not more than 2 cm (¾ inch) long. Cut them in half lengthwise, remove the hairy choke, then cut in half again.

Use only the white heart of the celery (keep the green outer sticks for other recipes). Slice, wash and pat dry with paper towel.

Wash the radishes and cut off most of the leaves. Slice off the bottom and make a cross-like incision in the base, so the sauce can penetrate.

Wash the cucumbers and slice them into pieces about 4 cm (1.5 inches) long.

Arrange the vegetables in bundles on a platter. Place in the centre of the table, and put a small bowl of sauce in front of each person. The diners can take any vegetables they like from the platter and dip them in the sauce.

To make the sauce, place the garlic in a mortar and mash. Pour some vinegar on the bread and add to the garlic. Keep pounding until you have a smooth mixture. Transfer the mixture to a bowl. Add the remaining vinegar, the olive oil and the salt and pepper. Whisk energetically and serve in individual bowls for each diner (so they don't double dip). **SERVES 4**

Condiggion
Riviera salad

Traditionally on the Riviera, this rich salad was served on *gallette*—dry ships' biscuits—but they are now almost impossible to find, even in Italy. So we replace them with toasted bread. It was also served with *mosciame* (dried dolphin fillets), which are now thankfully illegal and can be replaced with thin slices of *bottargá* (compressed and dried tuna or mullet roe) or with anchovies, as we've done in this recipe.

4 large slices Italian bread

4 tomatoes, peeled, seeded and sliced

1 cucumber, peeled, seeded and sliced

1 small red capsicum (bell pepper), peeled, seeded and sliced

1 small yellow capsicum (bell pepper), peeled, seeded and sliced

2 spring onions, (scallions), sliced

20 Ligurian black olives, pitted

8 anchovy fillets, roughly chopped

2 sprigs oregano leaves, picked

1 garlic clove, finely chopped

sea salt

red wine vinegar

olive oil

4 iceberg lettuce leaves

1 small bunch basil, leaves picked and torn

Toast the bread and set aside to cool and harden.

Combine the tomatoes, cucumber, capsicums, spring onions, olives, anchovies, oregano and garlic in a bowl. Sprinkle with salt and a little vinegar. Stir gently to mix thoroughly, add some olive oil and mix again carefully.

Place a slice of bread on each serving plate and sprinkle on a little oil and vinegar. Brush the lettuce leaves lightly with the oil and vinegar and place a leaf on top of each slice of bread.

Place the vegetable mixture in the lettuce leaves, scatter some basil leaves on top and serve.

SERVES 4

Carpaccio alla capponada

Carpaccio with anchovy salad

300 g (10 oz) sashimi-grade
  salmon, swordfish or tuna fillet
18 green olives, pitted
6 anchovy fillets, chopped
1 tsp salted capers, rinsed and
  dried
1 tsp oregano, finely chopped

2 tbsp olive oil
1 tsp red wine vinegar
2 slices Italian bread
1 garlic clove, finely chopped
juice of 1 lemon
sea salt and freshly ground black
  pepper

Thinly slice the fish and arrange on four plates. Roughly chop the olives and place in a bowl. Add the anchovies, capers and oregano. Mix in a tablespoon of olive oil and the vinegar.

Cut the bread into small cubes and place in a small bowl, add the garlic and a splash of oil and mix well. Place on a baking dish and bake in a 180°C (250°F/gas 4) oven until crisp.

Squeeze the lemon on the fish and drizzle over a little olive oil. Arrange the olive mixture on top, sprinkle the bread on top, season with salt and pepper, and serve. **SERVES 4**

Muscoli in scabecio

Marinated mussels

2 kg (4 lb) mussels,
  scrubbed and de-bearded
½ cup plain (all purpose) flour
olive oil
1 garlic clove, finely chopped

1 sprig rosemary
60 ml (2 fl oz) white
  wine vinegar
sea salt and freshly
  ground black pepper

Place the mussels in a heavy-based, deep-sided frying pan over a medium to high heat, taking them out as soon as they open (even one by one!) so they won't dry out. Remove the mussels from their shells and place in a bowl.

Lightly flour the mussels. Pour the oil into a saucepan so it comes 2 cm (¾ inch) up the sides, and put the pan on a high heat. When the oil is hot enough to make a small piece of bread sizzle, fry the mussels for 1–2 minutes, turning them once. Remove and drain on paper towel. Place the mussels in a bowl.

Heat 100 ml (3½ fl oz) of olive oil in a frying pan over a high heat. Add the garlic and rosemary, and when the garlic changes to a gold colour, about 2 minutes, add the vinegar. Season with salt and pepper, and cook for 3 minutes. Allow to cool, remove the rosemary, and pour over the mussels. Serve after the mussels have marinated for at least 2 hours. They are excellent with chopped pickled vegetables. **SERVES 4**

Muscoli gratinati
Mussels au gratin

I am very fond of mussels, not only because of their captivating flavour of the sea, but also for the cultural importance that they have in my region. Being cheap, they are one of the few types of seafood that the farmers and mountain people can eat when they come to the seaside.

I remember when I was a child, in the family restaurant on Sundays, how our little seaside village was inundated by 'strangers' wearing hats and clothing so different from the local fishermen. They would come in to drink white wine (rather than the red they made at home) and work their way through huge bowls of mussels with toasted bread for dipping. It was as if they were on holiday. And I enjoyed watching them have a great time with their satisfied smiles and calls for more mussels and more wine. The following recipe is one of our family favourites.

2 kg (4 lb) mussels, scrubbed and de-bearded
100 g (3½ oz) breadcrumbs
100 ml (3½ fl oz) olive oil, plus extra
1 handful flat-leaf parsley leaves, finely chopped

2 garlic cloves, finely chopped
1 celery stalk, washed and trimmed
freshly ground black pepper
1 small handful oregano leaves, roughly chopped

Place the mussels in a heavy-based, deep-sided frying pan over a medium to high heat, taking them out as soon as they open (even one by one!).

Detach the top shells, and place the half shells with the mussels on oven trays.

Combine the breadcrumbs, olive oil, parsley and garlic in a bowl, grate the celery stalk on top, sprinkle with ground pepper and stir with a wooden spoon until well mixed. Place a teaspoonful on each mussel and sprinkle with oregano. Splash a bit more olive oil on the mussels. Place the tray under a hot grill for 10 minutes or until a crust forms on top. Serve hot. **SERVES 4**

Muscoli ripieni
Stuffed mussels

The traditional way to prepare this dish had mortadella and sometimes salami in the filling. We've adapted the stuffing to include prawns, because in Australia, we can.

500 g (1 lb) green prawns
  (shrimp)
2 kg (4 lb) mussels, scrubbed
  and de-bearded
2 tbsp freshly grated
  parmesan cheese
1 garlic clove, finely chopped
1 handful flat-leaf parsley leaves,
  finely chopped
2 eggs
sea salt and freshly ground
  black pepper

60 ml (2 fl oz) olive oil
1 small white onion,
  finely chopped
125 ml (4 fl oz) dry white wine
5 ripe tomatoes, peeled
  and sliced
2 sprigs oregano,
  roughly chopped
2 sprigs thyme, plus
  more for serving

Peel and devein the prawns, reserving the heads, and finely chop.

With a small knife, force open the mussels slightly, leaving the top shells attached. Reserve any juice from the mussels. Put aside about two-thirds, and remove the mussels from the shells of the remaining third. Finely chop, combine with the prawn meat and place in a bowl. Add the parmesan, garlic, parsley and eggs, one by one. Mix thoroughly and season with salt and pepper. Spoon a little of this mixture into each of the mussel shells, then push the shells closed.

Heat the oil in a heavy-based frying pan over a low heat, and add the prawn heads. Squash the heads with a wooden spoon to release the flavours. When the prawn heads change colour, take them out of the pan and discard. Add the onion and fry for 5 minutes or until translucent. Pour in the white wine and let it bubble for 3 minutes or until the alcohol evaporates. Add the tomatoes, and 4 tablespoons of the juice from the mussels. Sprinkle with oregano, mix well and cook for 5 minutes.

Remove the pan from the heat, add the stuffed mussels and thyme, cover, and place on a medium heat. Cook for 20 minutes, delicately shaking the pan from time to time.

Divide the stuffed mussels between four plates and decorate with a few more sprigs of thyme.

SERVES 4

Insalata di mare

Seafood salad

Making this in our family restaurant at the southern tip of the Riviera di Levante was one of my mother's specialties. By poaching most of the ingredients in the *court-bouillon* (vegetable stock), she made a 'cocktail' in which the individual seafood flavours and textures blended to create a complex new flavour. Then she ensured the little mound of seafood was beautifully composed on the plate—in accordance with the principle that, to give maximum eating pleasure, '*l'occhio vuole la sua parte*' (the eye needs its share). Her cocktail approach is not fashionable today, but for me, there's only one way—Bruna's way.

FOR THE STOCK
3 litres (96 fl oz) water
2 carrots, peeled and cut in half
1 onion, peeled and cut in half
2 celery stalks, cut in half
2 tomatoes, cut in half
1 tsp white peppercorns
6 stalks flat-leaf parsley
60 ml (2 fl oz) white wine
   vinegar
salt

FOR THE SEAFOOD SALAD
200 g (6½ oz) green small to
   medium prawns (shrimp)

300 g (10 oz) small calamari,
   cleaned and rinsed
300 g (10 oz) cuttlefish,
   cleaned and rinsed
1 kg (2 lb) mussels,
   scrubbed and de-bearded
1 garlic clove, peeled
juice of 1 lemon
60 ml (2 fl oz) olive oil
sea salt
1 lemon, cut in wedges,
   to serve
1 handful flat-leaf parsley
   leaves, to serve

To make the stock, fill a large saucepan with the water, add the carrots, onion, celery, tomatoes, peppercorns, parsley and vinegar, and bring to the boil. Continue to boil for 20 minutes.

To make the seafood salad, simmer the prawns in the stock for 3 minutes, remove with a slotted spoon and set aside. Simmer the calamari and cuttlefish in the stock for 15 minutes or until their colour becomes a flat white. Fish them out and set aside.

Meanwhile, place the mussels in a heavy-based saucepan, cover, and cook over high heat until they open. Remove the mussels from the shells, and discard the shells. Place the mussels in the water they put out during cooking, and set aside. Shell and devein the prawns and cut them into 2-cm (¾-inch) pieces. Cut the cuttlefish and calamari into 2-cm (¾-inch) pieces. Cut the mussels in half, and discard their water.

Rub a serving bowl with the garlic, add the seafood, lemon juice and a big splash of oil. Mix well and adjust seasoning with salt, if necessary. Serve garnished with lemon wedges and parsley.
SERVES 4

VARIATION You can serve this seafood salad with potatoes, green beans and a form of pesto sauce made without cheese (see the pesto recipe on page 170, but delete the cheese).

Bagnun di acciughe
Anchovies in a tomato bath

This dish can also be made with sardines. Check with your fish shop about seasonality.

800 g (1 lb 10 oz) fresh
  anchovies
4 ripe tomatoes
60 ml (2 fl oz) olive oil
2 garlic cloves, finely chopped
½ white onion, finely chopped
60 ml (2 fl oz) white wine
sea salt and freshly ground
  black pepper

2 tbsp flat-leaf parsley,
  finely chopped
4 slices (or 8 if small)
  Italian bread, toasted
1 garlic clove, peeled,
  for rubbing on toasts
1 tbsp oregano leaves

Clean and rinse the anchovies, remove the heads, open them like a book and fillet them. Set them aside.

Peel the tomatoes (see Bruschetta with tomato on page 45). Cut the tomatoes in half, remove the seeds with a teaspoon, then cut into strips.

Pour the oil into a saucepan (preferably terracotta) and place over a low heat. When the oil is hot, add the garlic and onion, and sauté for 3 minutes, mixing with a wooden spoon. Add half of the white wine and cook until evaporated, about 5 minutes. Add the tomatoes, mix well, season with salt and pepper and cook for 10 minutes, stirring occasionally. Then put the anchovies in the pan. Sprinkle in the parsley, pour in the remaining wine and cook for about 10 minutes on medium heat, shaking the pot gently every now and then. Don't mix with a spoon or the anchovies will break.

Rub the toasted bread with garlic, and place in four individual dishes. Arrange the anchovies on the toast and cover with the sauce.

Before serving, sprinkle each dish with the oregano leaves. **SERVES 4**

Aragosta con puré di peperoni

Lobster in a capsicum puree

We saw and enjoyed this dish in a little place called Locanda Lorena on the island of Palmaria. From its dining room you can look across the mussel beds of the Gulf of Poets to the mediaeval walled town of Portovenere. One of the most famous restaurateurs of the neighbourhood, who goes by the biblical nickname Iseo, roasts his capsicums and poaches his scampi and combines them in a thick orange-coloured 'soup'.

We decided to adapt it to meet the Australian predilection for lobster. You might find it rather extravagant for an antipasto dish, and feel more inclined to serve it as a main course.

4 x 250–300 g (8–10 oz) lobsters, each	2 yellow capsicums (bell peppers)
1 carrot, cut in half	1 red capsicum (bell pepper)
1 celery stalk	100 ml (3½ fl oz) olive oil
1 onion, cut in half	sea salt and freshly ground
1 handful basil leaves	black pepper
1 tsp black peppercorns	

Tips for buying a fresh lobster: it should be active, flapping its tail when picked up; it should feel heavy, and have a sweet smell, not an ammonia odour. If buying a precooked lobster, it's a sign of freshness and good handling if the lobsters are tightly curled and flip back a bit after being straightened out. You can still make stock with a precooked lobster; you use the heads.

To a large saucepan of boiling salted water add the carrot, celery, half the onion, the basil and peppercorns. Boil for 1 minute, then add the lobsters. Simmer for 15 minutes and remove from the pan, reserving the stock. When cooled a little, detach the heads with a sharp knife and return the heads to the pan. Boil for 15 minutes over a medium heat. Strain the stock into a bowl and discard the heads.

Shell the lobster tails and cut in half.

For the puree, wash the capsicums and cut them in half lengthwise. Remove the core and seeds, and cut in half again. Finely chop the remaining onion. Heat the olive oil in a frying pan over a medium heat, add the onion and fry until translucent. Add the capsicums, season with salt and pepper, and stir in 3 tablespoons of the stock from the lobster heads. Cook for 10 minutes, then pour into a blender and puree.

Return the puree to the stove for 3–4 minutes to reheat, then pour into four shallow bowls. Place the two half lobsters on top of the puree in each plate and serve. **SERVES 4**

Tian

Anchovy-potato bake

4 medium potatoes
1 garlic clove, peeled
  and cut in half
olive oil
3 tomatoes, peeled,
  seeded and diced
sea salt

2 sprigs rosemary leaves, picked
600 g (1 lb 3½ oz) fresh
  anchovies (or sardines),
  cleaned and gutted
1 tbsp chopped flat-leaf
  parsley leaves
1 tbsp oregano leaves

Preheat the oven to 180°C (350°F/gas 4).

Peel the potatoes, wash them well (to remove the starch from the surface so they don't stick to the pan) and slice them.

Rub the garlic over the surface of a large high-sided baking dish. Pour in some oil and tilt the dish to spread it evenly. Place the tomatoes in a bowl with a pinch of salt and a little of the rosemary and splash with some oil. Mix well and spread half the tomatoes in the baking dish. Cover the tomatoes with the thinly sliced potatoes, overlapping if necessary. Brush the top with some oil and bake in the oven for 30 minutes.

In the meantime take the heads off the anchovies, open them out like a book, remove the bones but leave the two halves of the fish attached to each other, with the tail on. Wash under running water and pat dry with paper towel.

When the vegetables are ready, remove the baking dish from the oven and arrange the anchovies on top. Sprinkle with parsley and oregano, and a little more salt. Spread the remaining tomatoes over the anchovies, drizzle with more oil and sprinkle with the remaining rosemary. Increase the oven temperature to 200°C (400°F/gas 6) and return the dish to the oven for 15 minutes.

Serve with a crisp green salad. **SERVES 4**

Verdure ripiene
Stuffed vegetables

4 zucchini (courgettes)
2 capsicums (bell peppers)
4 medium white onions, peeled
8 small eggplants (aubergines)
60 g (2 oz) dried porcini
  mushrooms
2 slices Italian bread,
  crusts removed
75 ml (2½ fl oz) milk
2 eggs
125 ml (4 fl oz) olive oil,
  plus extra

2 garlic cloves, finely chopped
2 tbsp oregano leaves,
  finely chopped
1 tbsp marjoram leaves,
  finely chopped
100 g (3½ oz) freshly
  grated parmesan cheese
pinch of freshly grated nutmeg
sea salt and freshly ground
  black pepper
60 g (2 oz) breadcrumbs

Prepare the vegetables. Wash the zucchini, slice off both ends and cut them in half lengthwise. Wash the capsicums, cut off the tops and cut them in half lengthwise. Remove and discard the core and seeds. Cut the onions in half. Wash the eggplants, cut off the top and cut them in half lengthwise.

Bring a large saucepan of salted water to the boil, add the vegetables and cook for 5 minutes or until softened. Drain well.

With a spoon, scoop out the pulps of the zucchini, onions and eggplants and place in a mixing bowl. You should have a 1-cm (½-inch) thick shell left on the zucchini and eggplants and at least three layers on the onions.

Soak the porcini in warm water for 5 minutes, drain and dry with paper towel. Chop and add to the vegetable pulp.

Soak the bread in the milk for a few minutes and mix into the vegetable pulp. Add the eggs, most of the olive oil, garlic, half the oregano, the marjoram, parmesan and nutmeg. Season with salt and pepper and mix thoroughly.

Preheat the oven to 180°C (350°F/gas 4). Lightly oil an oven tray (or two). Place the vegetable shells on the prepared tray and sprinkle a little salt on top. Fill each vegetable shell with the vegetable pulp mixture, not too compressed. Sprinkle the breadcrumbs on top, drizzle with the remaining olive oil and bake in the oven for 25 minutes.

Serve hot on a platter and sprinkle with the remaining oregano. **SERVES 4**

Gattafin

FRIED RAVIOLI

Traditionally the filling of this classic fried ravioli was made with herbs that grew wild and were gathered by the women of the Ligurian hills, who kept their favourite spots secret. The mixture of wild herbs is called *preboggion* in the province of Genoa and *erbi* in the province of La Spezia, where I come from.

The story goes that this dish was invented in the nineteenth century by the wives of the workers in the sandstone quarry at Gatta, near Levanto, using herbs picked by their husbands around the quarry. When the quarry owner tried the dish, he described it as 'la finezza di Gatta' (the finest of the area), which was condensed into its modern name.

It is impossible to find these wild greens in Australia (and hard enough to find them in the markets of Liguria these days). Instead we are trying to come close to the flavour by using silverbeet, parsley, radicchio and marjoram.

FOR THE DOUGH
300 g (10 oz) plain
  (all purpose) flour
pinch of sea salt
1 tbsp olive oil
60 ml (2 fl oz) water

FOR THE FILLING
1 kg (2 lb) silverbeet, washed
  and white stalks trimmed
½ radicchio, washed and outer
  leaves discarded

1 bunch flat-leaf parsley
  leaves picked, washed
2 eggs
60 g (2 oz) freshly grated
  parmesan cheese
45 g (1½ oz) ricotta cheese
pinch of freshly grated nutmeg
sea salt and freshly ground
  black pepper
1 tbsp olive oil
1 bunch marjoram leaves
olive oil, for frying

We begin with the wrapping for the parcel, which ideally should be made at least an hour before you want to eat. Place the flour in a mound on a flat work surface. Form a well in the centre, sprinkle in the salt, olive oil and water. Start kneading and work the dough with your hands until you obtain a smooth and firm ball. Let it rest for 1 hour. When ready, use a rolling pin to roll out a very thin sheet of dough.

To make the filling, place the silverbeet, radicchio and parsley, with the water from washing still clinging to the leaves, in a saucepan over a medium heat. Steam until soft, 3–5 minutes, and drain in a colander. Squeeze dry in a tea towel, chop finely and place in a bowl. Break in the eggs and add the parmesan, ricotta and nutmeg. Sprinkle in a little salt and pepper, add a spoonful of olive oil and all the marjoram leaves. Mix well with a wooden spoon.

Now cut the sheet of dough into squares about 12 cm (4½ inches) wide. Put a spoonful of the mixture on each square, slightly toward one side, fold the dough over the filling, press with your fingers all around to tightly close the parcel.

Pour the olive oil into a saucepan to a depth of 2 cm (1 inch) and place on a high heat. Fry the Gattafin parcels until golden brown, about 3 minutes on each side. **SERVES 4**

Fiori di zucchini ripieni
Stuffed zucchini flowers

2 bunches English spinach, washed
500 g (1 lb) ricotta cheese
100 g (3½ oz) freshly grated parmesan cheese
2 egg yolks
20 zucchini (courgette) flowers

125 ml (4 fl oz) olive oil
2 bunches asparagus
75 g (2½ oz) parmesan cheese, shaved, plus extra
sea salt and freshly ground black pepper
extra virgin olive oil

Blanch the spinach in a large saucepan of boiling water, drain and squeeze out as much moisture as possible. Chop finely and mix with the ricotta, grated parmesan and egg yolks. Open the zucchini flowers and cut out and discard the stigma. Fill the flowers with the ricotta mixture.

Preheat the oven to 180°C (350°F/gas 4).

Place the zucchini flowers on an oiled baking tray. Drizzle with 60 ml (2 fl oz) of the olive oil and place in the oven to bake for 15 minutes.

Boil the asparagus in salted water for 3 minutes, leaving them a little firm to the touch.

Combine the shaved parmesan, the remaining olive oil and the asparagus in a bowl. Toss gently and season with salt and pepper.

Arrange the asparagus on four plates (tips facing out) and place the zucchini flowers in the centre. Top with some more parmesan shavings, drizzle with a little extra virgin olive oil and serve.

SERVES 4

Gamberi e fagioli

Poached prawns with cannellini beans and caviar

300 g (10 oz) dried
  cannellini beans
1 carrot, cut in half
1 celery stalk, cut in half
½ onion, peeled
1 sprig rosemary
2 sprigs thyme
1 litre (32 fl oz) water
12 green king prawns (shrimp), peeled
  and deveined with tails intact

½ red onion, peeled
  and thinly sliced
juice of ½ lemon
125 ml (4 fl oz) extra
  virgin olive oil, plus extra
sea salt and freshly
  ground black pepper
1 small jar black caviar
  or red salmon roe

Soak the cannellini beans in cold water for 10–12 hours. Drain and place in a saucepan with half a litre of cold salted water, to cover. Add the carrot, celery, peeled onion, rosemary and 1 sprig of thyme, and simmer for 45 minutes. Drain and place the cannellini beans in a bowl, discard everything else.

Bring half a litre of water to the boil, add the remaining thyme and the prawns, reduce the heat to low, and gently poach the prawns for 3 minutes. Drain and keep warm.

Whisk the lemon juice, olive oil, salt and pepper together lightly. Pour over the beans. Add a little caviar or roe and a splash more olive oil, mix well and divide between each serving plate. Place the prawns on top of the beans and add a dollop of caviar to each prawn. **SERVES 4**

Gamberi e carciofi

Prawns with artichokes

1 litre (32 fl oz) water
12 green king prawns (shrimp),
  peeled and deveined with
  tails intact
1 sprig thyme
4 globe artichokes

juice of 1 lemon
extra virgin olive oil
45 g (1½ oz) Parmigiano-
  Reggiano cheese, shaved
sea salt and freshly ground
  black pepper

Bring the water to the boil, add the prawns and thyme, reduce the heat to low and gently poach for 3 minutes. Drain and keep warm to one side.

Peel and discard the tough outer leaves of the artichokes and remove the stems. Cut the artichokes in half and remove any hairy bits. Slice the artichoke hearts very, very thinly, then quickly mix with lemon juice, olive oil and cheese. Season with salt and pepper.

Divide the artichoke mixture between four serving plates. Top with the prawns and a drizzle of olive oil. **SERVES 4**

Lingua di bue con salsa di pomodori verdi

Ox tongue with green tomato salsa

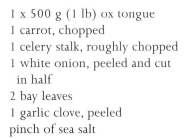

1 x 500 g (1 lb) ox tongue
1 carrot, chopped
1 celery stalk, roughly chopped
1 white onion, peeled and cut
  in half
2 bay leaves
1 garlic clove, peeled
pinch of sea salt

FOR THE GREEN TOMATO SALSA
30 ml (1 fl oz) olive oil,
  plus extra

½ white onion, diced
1 garlic clove, finely chopped
4 green tomatoes, chopped
1 tbsp sultanas, revived in warm
  water, drained, dried and
  chopped, plus extra
sea salt and freshly ground
  black pepper
15 ml (½ fl oz) white
  wine vinegar

Place the ox tongue, carrot, celery, onion, bay leaves and garlic in a large saucepan. Add enough cold water to cover and season with salt. Bring to the boil and simmer on a low heat for 1½ hours or until the tongue is tender. Remove the tongue from the water and discard everything else. Peel the tongue and cut into 5-mm (¼-inch) thick slices (or thinner if you prefer).

To make the green tomato salsa, heat the oil in a heavy-based saucepan on a low heat, add the onion and sauté for 5 minutes, add the garlic, stir with a wooden spoon and cook for 1 minute. Add the tomatoes and sultanas, season with salt and pepper. Mix thoroughly and cook for 5 minutes over a medium high heat, stirring frequently. Transfer to a bowl, allow to cool and add the vinegar.

To serve, arrange the slices of tongue on a plate, brush with a little extra olive oil, and sprinkle with some extra sultanas if you like. Dollop on some green tomato salsa. **SERVES 4**

Sformatino di fave

Broad bean custard

2 kg (4 lb) fresh broad
  (fava) beans
½ bunch flat-leaf parsley, leaves
  picked (or basil for a stronger
  flavour)
2 eggs

4 egg yolks
400 ml (13½ fl oz) single cream
10 g (⅓ oz) freshly grated
  pecorino cheese, not too mild
30 g (1 oz) goat's cheese

Shell the broad beans and blanch them in boiling water for 1 minute, then plunge them into iced water to cool. Drain and remove skin.

Blanch the parsley in boiling water for 1 minute and refresh in iced water.

Combine the eggs, egg yolks, cream, beans and parsley in a blender (or a food processor, which will take a little longer) and blend until smooth.

Mix the pecorino and goat's cheese and the puree in a heatproof bowl. Place the bowl over a saucepan of boiling water, making sure the bowl does not come into contact with the water in the saucepan. Stir continuously for 15 minutes or until thickened. You must not leave it unattended during this time.

Preheat the oven to 120°C (230°F/gas ½). Line the base of a baking dish with a tea towel, place four ramekins on top, and pour in enough water to come halfway up the side of the ramekins. Pour the custard into each ramekin until about two-thirds full. Cover with foil and bake in the oven for 35–45 minutes or until they are no longer liquid and have set (like a custard). Allow to cool.

To serve, turn out the custards and place in the centre of each of four plates.

Serve with salad of choice and crusty bread.

This can also be served in the ramekins as a spreadable dip, with toast for dipping. **SERVES 4**

Terrina di polpo
Octopus terrine

This is one of the most fashionable dishes of modern Liguria, producing shimmering pinky-violet slices that taste as good as they look. Making it is a long process (three days including time for it to set) but rewarding.

In my area they cut the tops off plastic mineral water bottles and shove the boiled octopus into them to set in the fridge. When the 'sausage' is ready to serve, they cut off the plastic and the result is a perfect cylinder. We've suggested you use a terrine mould here, but if you don't have one, you've found a good way to reuse those discardable bottles.

3 kg (6 lb) large octopus or
  8 kg (16 lb) baby octopus
60 ml (2 fl oz) vegetable oil
1 lemon, cut in half
1 long red chilli, cut in half
  lengthwise
1 bay leaf
½ bunch thyme
½ fennel bulb, chopped
60 ml (2 fl oz) dry white wine

1 cork*
1 handful flat-leaf parsley
  leaves, chopped
45 ml (½ fl oz) olive oil
juice of ½ lemon

*The tradition in the Levante
  is to cook the octopus with
  a cork to make it tender.

Wash the octopus thoroughly. Pull the legs and the body apart, and cut off the eyes, the beak and any unpleasant inside bits, so you are left with soft flesh. Wash again and pat dry with paper towel.

Heat the oil in a large heavy-based saucepan over high heat. Carefully add the octopus (it will spit) and cook for 10 minutes, stirring regularly, until the octopus turns pinky red. Add the lemon halves, chilli, bay leaf, thyme, fennel, white wine and the cork. Pour in enough water to cover, put the lid on, and turn the heat to low. Cook for at least 2 hours. Set aside to to cool for 1 hour.

Strain the stock into another saucepan, remove and discard the cork. Reduce the stock for 40 minutes on low simmer until half its original quantity. Put the octopus pieces in a bowl and add the parsley. Pour the reduced stock over the octopus.

Now you are ready to put the octopus into a deep terrine mould 25 x 8 cm (10 x 3¼ inches ideally, but feel free to improvise with what you've got). Spray the mould with oil, and line it with plastic wrap, allowing the wrap to overhang the sides of the mould. Tip in the octopus, ensuring the legs and long parts are running parallel with the longer sides of the mould. Fold the plastic wrap over the top, and poke in a few holes to let out excess juice.

Cut out a rectangular piece of heavy cardboard just big enough to fit into the mould. Wrap in foil and rest on top of the mould. Put a weight on it (two bricks end to end would be good). Leave for at least 48 hours in the fridge.

Lift the top layers of plastic wrap away from the octopus and use them to pull the terrine out. Place the terrine on a platter and slice it as thickly as you like at the table. Do not season the octopus with salt—it is already salty enough. Serve with a lemon dressing made by whisking together the olive oil and lemon juice. **SERVES 4**

Zuppe

Soups

Soups

Here we move from the coastline and go deep into the countryside to visit the homes of inland Liguria, fragrant with the smells from pots that simmer on the stove all morning until the farmers come in from the fields and the children come home from school.

Soup is an ancient way of cooking that flourishes when you have almost no kitchen and space for only one pot in the fireplace; when you must feed a lot of hungry mouths attached to fingers eagerly holding bread to dip; and when you have no time to watch what you are cooking and want something you can leave bubbling on top of the ashes. It's also a handy way to create two courses from one cooking pot—boiled chicken providing the broth as an entrée and then the chicken as the main course.

Ligurian soups come from peasant origins but some, like *burrida*, were born on board the sailing ships which plied their trade up and down the coast.

They range from one-ingredient dishes to the intense multicoloured and multiflavoured minestrone. And in the twenty-first century they are being reinvented as sophisticated creations in the restaurants along the shoreline. We've got a sampling of all types.

Lattughe ripiene di pesce in brodo di pesce

Lettuce parcels in fish broth

Ligurians will create parcels out of anything—even lettuce, which can be folded to look like ravioli. Traditionally this soup, with its stuffing that included lambs' brains and a broth made from boiled old hens, was an Easter dish made in the mountains of Liguria. We decided to adapt the idea for the seashore and came up with something that the Chinese might call *sang choi bau*.

FOR THE FISH BROTH
500 g (1 lb) whole bream,
  cleaned and gutted
500 g (1 lb) whole snapper,
  cleaned and gutted
500 g (1 lb) whole large
  red mullet
45 ml (1½ fl oz) olive oil
20 g (¾ oz) butter
1 white onion, finely chopped
1½ celery stalks, finely chopped
1 carrot, finely chopped
3 sprigs thyme
3 litres (96 fl oz) water
sea salt

FOR THE LETTUCE PARCELS
flesh from fish used to
  make broth
2 eggs
1 tsp chopped marjoram leaves
45 g (1½ oz) ricotta cheese
pinch of freshly grated nutmeg
freshly ground black pepper
1 iceberg lettuce
4 large cherry tomatoes,
  thinly sliced

First prepare the fish broth. Wash the fish well under running water. Heat the oil and butter in a large saucepan. Make a *soffritto* by adding the onion, celery, carrot and thyme. Mix well with a wooden spoon and turn up the heat to medium for 5 minutes, stirring frequently. Add the fish and sear on both sides for 3 minutes altogether. Add the water, season with salt, mix gently, reduce the heat to low and simmer for 30 minutes. Using a slotted spoon, remove the fish from the broth, place on a board and separate the flesh from the bones. Put the flesh into a bowl, return the heads and bones to the stock and simmer for 30 minutes. When the broth is ready, strain through a fine sieve into a clean saucepan.

To prepare the lettuce parcel fillings, check the fish flesh to make sure that there are no bones, and squish it with a fork. Place in a bowl with the eggs, marjoram, ricotta, nutmeg and some ground pepper. Mix well with a wooden spoon and set aside.

Separate the iceberg leaves, allowing 3 per person, and blanch in boiling salted water for 30 seconds. Drain and dry on paper towel and place on a flat work surface. Divide the fish mixture between the lettuce leaves and fold them in a way—rolling and tucking in the ends—so that they will not open during cooking. The parcels should be the size of a matchbox (remember them?).

Bring the fish broth to the boil and cook the lettuce parcels for 2–3 minutes. Remove with a slotted spoon and place in individual bowls. Arrange the sliced tomatoes around the parcels, pour in the fish broth and serve immediately. **SERVES 4**

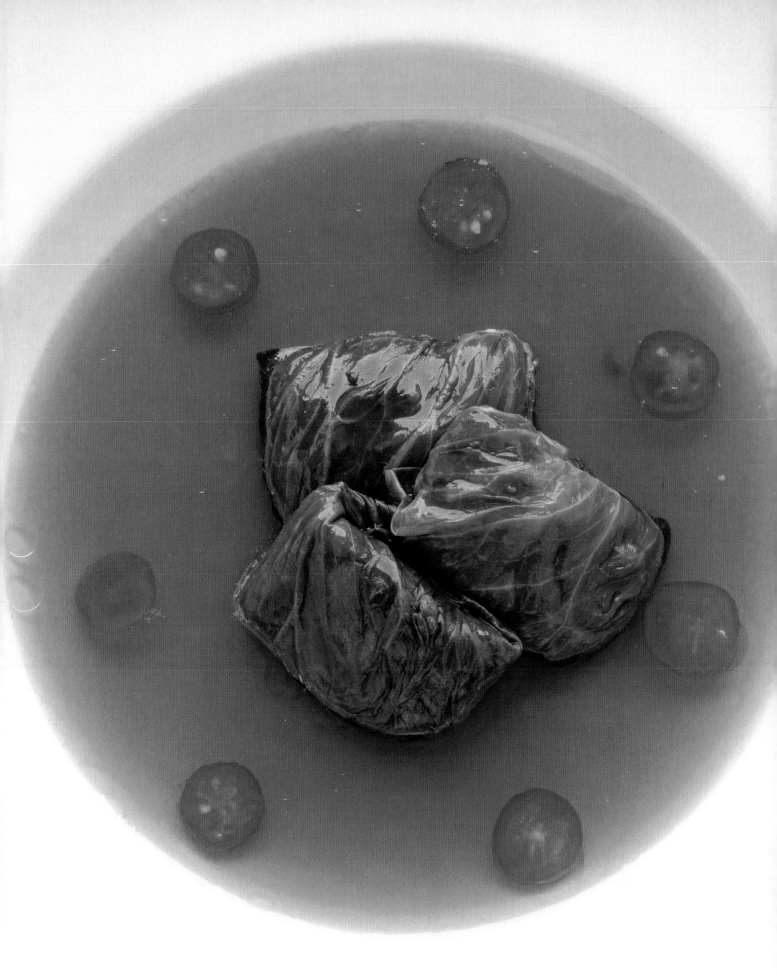

Minestrone alla Genovese

Traditional vegetable soup

An old proverb says: 'If you try the minestrone, you'll never want to leave Genoa.' It was a dish the sailors looked forward to while they were at sea, because it contains only products of the land. It has become popular all over the world, as the sailors carried the idea to their various destinations.

Two centuries ago the port of Genoa was filled with curious floating osterias called *catrai*. They served *burrida* (fish soup) and *troffie* (pasta twists), but they were mainly known for the minestrone that quickly made the sailors forget the months of dried biscuits and salted fish. The *catrai* were so popular that big vessels competed to dock next to the boat of their favourite soup seller.

150 g (5 oz) fresh borlotti
  beans, shelled (or dried if
  you can't find fresh)
3 litres (96 fl oz) water
2 bunches silverbeet, stalks
  removed, chopped
2 zucchini (courgettes),
  washed and sliced
1 eggplant (aubergine),
  diced
2 medium potatoes,
  peeled and diced
150 g (5 oz) green beans,
  cut into small pieces
3 tomatoes, peeled, seeded
  and diced
sea salt and freshly ground
  black pepper

400 g (13 oz) vermicelli
  (or thin spaghetti or macaroni),
  broken into bite-sized pieces
  about 3 cm (1¼ inches) long

FOR THE PESTO
1 anchovy fillet
basil leaves
sea salt
30 g (1 oz) pine nuts
2 garlic cloves
45 ml (1½ fl oz) olive oil
20 g (¾ oz) freshly grated
  parmesan cheese
20 g (¾ oz) freshly grated
  mild pecorino cheese

45 g (1½ oz) freshly grated
  parmesan cheese, to serve

If you have dried borlotti beans, you'll need to soak them in cold water for at least 12 hours, changing the water three times. Fresh beans don't need soaking.

Place the water in a large saucepan over a medium to high heat and bring to the boil. Add the silverbeet, zucchini, eggplant, potatoes, green beans, borlotti beans and the tomatoes. Season with salt and pepper, mix thoroughly with a wooden spoon and cook for 10 minutes, stirring frequently. Cover the pan, reduce the heat to low and cook for 2 hours, stirring occasionally.

In the meantime prepare the pesto. Start by pounding the anchovy in a mortar with the basil leaves and a little of the sea salt (the anchovies are already salty). Add the pine nuts and the garlic, and continue pounding until you obtain a fine mixture. (If you don't have a mortar place all the ingredients in a blender.) Transfer the mixture to a bowl, add the olive oil and cheeses. Mix with a wooden spoon and set aside.

About 20 minutes before you are ready to serve the soup, add the vermicelli, and stir a few times to let the pasta cook. After 10 minutes, turn the heat off, rest for 5 minutes, then serve in individual bowls topped with a spoonful of pesto and some grated parmesan cheese. This soup is also excellent warm, cold or reheated the day after. **SERVES 4**

Zuppa di muscoli
Mussel soup

2 kg (4 lb) mussels, scrubbed
  and de-bearded
60 ml (2 fl oz) dry white wine
200 ml (7 fl oz) olive oil
½ white onion, finely sliced
1 garlic clove, chopped

3 tomatoes, peeled,
  seeded and diced
freshly ground black pepper
1 tbsp chopped oregano leaves
8 slices Italian bread
1 garlic clove, peeled
2 tbsp small basil leaves

Discard any mussels that have already opened. Place the mussels in a large heavy-based saucepan over a medium to high heat and pour in the wine. As soon as the mussels open, transfer to a bowl (discard any that don't open) and retain the liquid in the pan. Take the mussels out of their shells (apart from 4 for the garnish), chop roughly and set aside.

Heat 125 ml (4 fl oz) of oil in a saucepan, add the onion and sauté over a medium heat until translucent, about 5 minutes. Add the chopped garlic and fry for 2 minutes, stirring with a wooden spoon. Add the tomatoes and mix thoroughly, stir in the reserved liquid from the mussels and cook for 15 minutes over a medium heat, stirring regularly. Add the chopped mussels, sprinkle in the pepper and oregano and stir for 3 minutes.

Toast the bread, rub the slices with garlic, place the slices on four plates. Pour the soup over the toast, add a mussel in its shell, sprinkle with basil and serve. **SERVES 4**

Zuppa di primavera
Spring soup

2 kg (4 lb) fresh broad (fava)
  beans
2 kg (4 lb) fresh unshelled peas
60 ml (2 fl oz) olive oil
100 g (3½ oz) pancetta (or
  bacon), finely chopped
500g (1 lb) spring onions
  (scallions), thinly sliced

500 g (1 lb) new potatoes, diced
1 garlic clove, finely chopped
flat-leaf parsley, finely chopped
sea salt
500 ml (16 fl oz) water
1 handful basil leaves, chopped

Shell the broad beans and the peas, set them aside. Heat the oil in a large saucepan over a medium heat, add the pancetta, let it brown a little, then add the spring onions and garlic. Cook for 2 minutes, add the broad beans, the artichokes, potatoes and peas. Sprinkle the parsley on top, mix delicately with a wooden spoon, season with salt and add the water. Stir, reduce the heat to low, cover the pan and cook for 1 hour. Check and gently mix from time to time, adding a couple of spoonfuls of water if it is drying out. Serve this soup hot with a sprinkle of basil. **SERVES 4**

Minestrone di fagioli e tagliatelle

Bean soup with noodles

FOR THE PASTA
150 g (5 oz) plain
  (all purpose) flour
1 egg
30 ml (1 fl oz) water

FOR THE SOUP
450 g (14 oz) cannellini beans
1 white onion, cut in half
2 celery stalks, chopped
1 carrot, chopped
3 litres (96 fl oz) cold water

sea salt and freshly ground
  black pepper
20 g (¾ oz) dried porcini
  mushrooms
45 ml (1½ fl oz) olive oil
3 garlic cloves, finely chopped
1 small red chilli, finely chopped
30 g (1 oz) rosemary leaves,
  finely chopped
8 slices Italian bread
freshly grated parmesan cheese

To make the pasta, follow the instructions in the Basic dough recipe on page 146. Make one round thin sheet. Roll the sheet up into a cylinder and slice into ribbons about 5 mm (¼ inch) wide. Leave them to dry while you make the soup.

The night before you want to eat this soup, soak the cannellini beans in plenty of cold water for at least 12–14 hours. Drain the beans and place them in a saucepan with the onion, celery and carrot. Cover with the water, add some salt, stir, place the lid on top and cook on a low heat for 3 hours, gently stirring from time to time. Keep a saucepan of boiling water on the stove to add to the soup if it seems to be drying out and turning to a paste.

In the meantime, soak the porcini mushrooms for 15 minutes, drain, squeeze dry and finely chop.

After the soup has been simmering for 2½ hours, heat the oil in a saucepan over a low heat and make a *soffritto* by frying the garlic, chilli, mushrooms and rosemary for 3 minutes, stirring constantly with a wooden spoon. When the garlic is just starting to change colour, gently stir the *soffritto* into the soup.

Cook the pasta in boiling salted water for 2 minutes (very *al dente*). Drain and add to the bean soup about 5 minutes before you want to serve it.

Turn the heat off and allow the soup to rest for a few minutes while you toast the bread.

Serve the soup hot with a drop of olive oil on top, plenty of parmesan cheese and the toasted bread. **SERVES 4**

La sbira

Tripe soup

Yes, we use every part of the animal in Liguria, especially an animal we've had to import from a neighbouring region where the land is flat enough for cattle to graze. Some people find tripe alarming, but as with many things, it's all in the way you cook it.

This soup's title comes from the nickname for policemen—*sbirri*—because this substantial and warming dish was a favourite of theirs. It used to be served in the *osterias* until the early hours of the morning.

1.2 kg (2½ lb) veal
  honeycomb tripe
100 g (3½ oz) bone marrow
60 ml (2 fl oz) olive oil
1 white onion, finely chopped
1 small celery stalk, thinly sliced
1 tsp chopped rosemary leaves
1 carrot, diced

4 tomatoes, peeled, seeded
  and diced
sea salt and freshly ground
  black pepper
1 litre (32 fl oz) beef stock

Rinse the tripe under running water a few times, then boil it in unsalted water for 3 hours. When ready, drain and cut into strips about 8 cm (3¼ inches) long.

Heat the oil and the bone marrow in a saucepan over a medium heat and make the *soffritto* by frying the onion, celery and rosemary for 3 minutes, stirring with a wooden spoon. Add the carrot, stir, and cook for a further 3 minutes.

At this point, add the tomatoes, season with salt and pepper, stir well, and cook for 3–5 minutes to let the sauce reduce a little.

Now place the tripe in the sauce and add the stock a little at a time. Turn the heat down and cook for 30 minutes, stirring often. The *sbira* is ready to be eaten with some crusty bread or toast rubbed with garlic. **SERVES 4**

Mes-ciua

Chickpea and farro soup

This traditional soup of La Spezia is a classic example of poor food. It was created by the imaginative wives of the dock workers, who noticed that cereals and beans fell from the sacks during unloading, and asked to be allowed to sweep them up and keep them. It includes the ancient form of wheat called farro, which was a favourite of the Romans and is alleged to keep the men of the Lunigiana mountains fertile until they are in their nineties.

The three main ingredients are cooked separately to preserve their individual flavours and allow for their different cooking times. We give this recipe extra punch by adding a sharp *soffritto*.

300 g (10 oz) dried chickpeas
300 g (10 oz) dried cannellini
  beans
100 g (3½ oz) farro
3 tsp baking soda
2 litres (64 fl oz) cold water
sea salt
olive oil, to serve
freshly ground black pepper

FOR THE SOFFRITTO
45 ml (1½ fl oz) olive oil
1 small onion, finely chopped
1 garlic clove, finely chopped
2 small red chillies, finely
  chopped
30 g (1 oz) flat-leaf parsley
  leaves, finely chopped
10 basil leaves, finely chopped

Put the chickpeas, cannellini and farro into three large individual bowls. Cover with abundant warm water, place 1 teaspoon of baking soda in each bowl and set aside to soak for at least 14 hours.

Four hours before you intend to eat this dish, drain the farro and chickpeas and place in a saucepan. Pour in 1 litre (32 fl oz) of cold water, add a pinch of salt and bring to the boil over a medium heat. Reduce heat to low and simmer for 3½ hours.

Half an hour after the farro and chickpeas start cooking, drain the cannellini beans and place them in another saucepan with the remaining water. Add a pinch of salt and bring to the boil over a medium to high heat. Reduce the heat to low and cook for 3 hours. Pour the beans and their broth into the farro and chickpea saucepan and mix thoroughly. Adjust with salt and cook for 15 minutes, gently stirring every 5 minutes.

Pour the soup into a serving dish or individual bowls and serve hot. Each diner flavours their *mes-ciua* with a drop of olive oil and some pepper. Cheese is not recommended for this soup.
SERVES 4

VARIATION
I hope I will not be excommunicated for suggesting that the *mes-ciua* can be enhanced by adding a spicy *soffritto* just before serving.

To make the soffritto, heat the oil in a saucepan over a low heat, add the onion and garlic and sauté for 2 minutes. Add the chilli, parsley and basil, mix thoroughly with a wooden spoon, and cook for another 2 minutes. Remove from the heat and pour the *soffritto* into the soup just before serving, mixing delicately a few times.

Vellutata di porri

Creamy leek and potato soup

The term *vellutata* comes from the Italian word for velvet, and refers to the texture of the soup, which should slide sensuously over the tongue.

3 medium leeks, trimmed
30 g (1 oz) butter
45 ml (1½ fl oz) olive oil,
  plus extra
2 medium desiree potatoes,
  peeled and diced
sea salt and freshly ground
  black pepper

2 tsp thyme leaves
1 litre (32 fl oz) vegetable
  stock or water
pinch of saffron
8 slices Italian bread,
  crusts removed

Peel off and discard the green outer leaves of the leeks. Slice into thin discs.

Place the butter and half the oil in a large saucepan over a low heat. When the butter is melted and the oil hot, add the leeks and fry for 5 minutes, stirring with a wooden spoon. Add the potatoes, season with salt and pepper, sprinkle with the thyme, and stir. Pour in the stock and cook for 1 hour, stirring regularly. At the last minute, stir in the saffron.

Take the soup off the heat and puree with a hand-held blender. If you don't have a hand-held blender, allow the soup to cool down and process in a blender until it becomes a creamy puree.

Cut the bread into dice, heat the remaining oil in a non-stick pan over a medium heat and fry bread until golden brown. Set aside. Reheat the *vellutata* and when hot serve in individual bowls topped with a little extra olive oil and the croutons. **SERVES 4**

Burrida

Seafood soup

Burrida is one of the many dialect words derived from Arabic. In the beginning *burrida* referred only to the way the *stoccafisso* (dried cod) was cooked in a tomato and herb sauce; today it refers to any preparation of fish and seafood prepared in this way.

Once it could be found in many *osterias* around the big Riviera ports and was eaten by the workers, passers-by and guards as an alternative to heavy portions of tripe.

It was also prepared on board sailing ships to feed the crew by throwing leftover bits of seafood into huge frying pans and adding olive oil, tomato and garlic. The fish was slowly reduced in quantity but increased in quality and this became one of the most popular 'soups' (really a stew) on the Riviera. Today, sadly, it is rare to find it in restaurants or *trattorias*.

Ideally select at least three types of rock fish weighing 200–400 g (6½–13 oz) each, or cut larger ones into 2–3 cm (¾–1¼-inch) cutlets.

1.2 kg (2½ lb) small fish such as mullet, bream and rock cod
200 g (6½ oz) baby octopus
200 g (6½ oz) calamari
200 g (6½ oz) cuttlefish
100 ml (3½ fl oz) extra virgin olive oil
1 kg (2 lb) mussels, scrubbed and de-bearded
500 g (1 lb) *vongole* (clams), rinsed
1.2 kg (2½ lb) ripe tomatoes, peeled and diced

2 garlic cloves, finely chopped
1 medium red chilli, finely chopped
1 small blue swimmer crab
90 ml (3 fl oz) dry white wine
2 tbsp flat-leaf parsley, finely chopped
12 slices toasted Italian bread, rubbed with garlic
1 tbsp chopped oregano (optional)

Clean the fish, then rinse and pat dry with paper towel.

Clean, rinse and pat dry the octopus, calamari and cuttlefish and slice into bite-sized pieces. If they are very small they can be left whole.

Heat 20 ml (½ fl oz) of the olive oil in a large frying pan, add the mussels and *vongole*, and cook until they open. Remove from the pan and place to one side. Strain the juices and reserve.

Drain excess liquid from the tomatoes.

In the same pan, heat 90 ml (3 fl oz) of the oil, add the garlic and chilli and gently fry until lightly coloured. Add the crab and gently squash it to release the juices that will flavour the base of the soup. Increase the heat, add the octopus, calamari and cuttlefish, and cook, stirring often, until coloured, about 5 minutes. Add the white wine, and cook gently until it evaporates. Add the tomatoes and four tablespoons of the mussel and *vongole* juice, and cook for 3 minutes. Add the fish, the big ones first, and cook on low heat for 10 minutes, gently shaking the pan often so the fish don't stick. Add the mussels and *vongole*, and continue cooking for about 3 minutes. You can tell when it is ready, because the oil starts separating from the sauce.

Sprinkle with parsley and serve this beautiful *zuppa di pesce* in individual warmed bowls with toasted bread.

If you like a stronger taste of herbs, you can sprinkle on some oregano as well as the parsley.

SERVES 6

Ciuppin
Smooth fish soup

100 ml (3½ fl oz) olive oil
½ onion, finely chopped
2 garlic cloves, crushed in
  a mortar
1 tbsp chopped flat-leaf
  parsley leaves
1 small carrot, chopped
1 celery stalk, chopped
90 ml (3 fl oz) dry white wine
4 ripe tomatoes, peeled, seeded
  and chopped
1 tsp oregano leaves, chopped
sea salt and freshly ground
  black pepper

1.5 kg (3 lb) assorted small fish
  (rock cod, red mullet, bream),
  filleted, with heads and bones
  reserved for the fish stock
8 slices Italian bread
1 garlic clove, peeled

FOR THE FISH STOCK
1 litre (32 fl oz) water
heads and bones of the fish
½ onion, cut in half
1 carrot, cut in half
1 celery stalk, cut in half
sea salt

First prepare the stock. Combine all the ingredients in a large saucepan and bring to the boil. Reduce heat to low and simmer for at least 30 minutes. Strain, keeping the broth and discarding the solids.

In the meantime, heat the oil in a saucepan over a low heat. Add the onion, crushed garlic, parsley, carrot and celery and sauté for 3 minutes, stirring frequently. Add half of the white wine, let it evaporate, add the tomatoes, season with salt and pepper, stir, add the rest of the wine and the fish stock. Bring to the boil, add the fish fillets, mix gently, and cook for 20 minutes or until the fish are almost melting.

Pass everything, fish and sauce, first through a mouli then through a sieve. Toast the bread, rub with the peeled garlic and place in the base of four serving bowls. Reheat the *ciuppin* for 3 minutes, and then with a ladle divide it between the bowls. **SERVES 4**

Torte salate

Pies

Pies

It's an ancient argument: which came first, the pie or the *raviolo*? Is a *raviolo* a small pie, or is a pie a big *raviolo* that is baked instead of boiled? Either one is a testament to the Ligurian habit of stuffing stuff inside other stuff, to be sure nothing is wasted.

When asked to describe Ligurian cooking, one Riviera restaurateur we visited used a very short sentence: '*la cucina dei ripieni*'—the cuisine of fillings. The pie is the pinnacle of this approach.

Liguria is famous for its savoury pies utilising every conceivable vegetable, but it is unique in its use of aromatic herbs, either picked wild or grown in the sunny terraced vegetable gardens dotting the landscape. Marjoram features prominently, followed by parsley, sage, rosemary and thyme. And apart from traditional vegetable pies, we also make seafood pies using octopus, mussels, anchovies, etc.

Some pies are completely enclosed by pastry; others, called *cielo aperto* (open sky) have a pastry base only. Still others are latticed on top, similar to a jam tart. The varying appearances are not crucial to the cooking. Eating so many pies so often, Ligurians just need regular changes of scenery. You should play around with shapes and garnishes.

Torta pasqualina
Easter pie

This gastronomic masterpiece prepared for the Christian Easter celebration is, like many other dishes, a victim of our modern world where everything is simplified and done in a hurry.

The greatness of this egg and vegetable tart is the way the pastry is worked. The *torta pasqualina* originally had very thin pastry in 33 layers (Christ's age at his death), then over the years it became 20 layers, ten, eight or even less. A century ago the women of the village would make the tart and carry it to the communal oven, making sure to scratch their initials on the top layer of pastry, in order to identify it when it was baked. Only their own recipe could possibly be good enough.

In our recipe we use six layers of pastry, three on the bottom and three on top. It is still quite a task in our modern way of life and in our modern kitchens. But if you make it properly it will be very rewarding. It is like going to a museum—but instead of looking at history you can taste it.

FOR THE PASTRY
450 g (14 oz) plain
  (all purpose) flour
sea salt
45 ml (1½ fl oz) extra
  virgin olive oil
90 ml (3 fl oz) warm water

FOR THE FILLING
1.2 kg (2½ lb) silverbeet
olive oil
1 white onion, finely chopped

2 garlic cloves, crushed with
  the blade of a knife
sea salt and freshly ground
  black pepper
1 handful flat-leaf parsley
  leaves, finely chopped
7 eggs
120 g (4 oz) freshly grated
  parmesan cheese
3 sprigs marjoram,
  roughly chopped
300 g (10 oz) ricotta cheese

To make the pastry, place the flour in a mound on a clean flat work surface. Form a well in the middle, sprinkle some salt all over and pour in the olive oil. Start kneading and add warm water as required to achieve a smooth and soft dough, about 5 minutes. Divide into six balls, making one larger than the others for the first layer at the base of the pie, which is folded up and over the filling. Flour the bottom of a ceramic container, and place the six balls of dough in it. Cover with a damp tea towel and allow to rest for 1 hour.

While the dough is resting make the filling.

To prepare the silverbeet remove the white stalks, roll the leaves up tightly and cut into thin strips. Heat 60 ml (2 fl oz) olive oil in a heavy-based frying pan over a low heat, add the onions and garlic, and stir with a wooden spoon. Just as the garlic starts to change colour, discard it and continue cooking the onions until soft and translucent, stirring regularly so they do not stick to the pan. At this point add the silverbeet, season with salt and add the parsley. Mix thoroughly and continue to cook over a low heat for 3 minutes.

Strain the silverbeet and place it into a bowl. Break in 2 eggs, beat with a little salt and pepper and pour over the silverbeet. Add all the ricotta and all but 1 tablespoon of the parmesan, and stir in the marjoram.

... **Recipe continued on page 124**

You can start building the pie now, flattening the layers of pastry one by one as you need them. With a brush, oil the base and sides of a 28–30-cm (11¼–12-inch) springform cake tin.

Flour the work surface, take the bigger ball of dough and first, with your fists, then with a rolling pin, flatten it until really thin, almost like silk. Line the base and sides of the prepared cake tin with the dough, letting it overhang the sides.

With a brush, gently oil the surface of this first layer of pastry. Roll out another thin sheet of dough and place on top of the first one without squashing. Again, with a brush, delicately oil the surface. Roll out the third sheet of dough and place on top of the second. This one must not be oiled. Instead place the silverbeet and cheese mixture on top and uniformly flatten the surface. Sprinkle with some more marjoram.

With the back of a tablespoon, make five wells in the ricotta and silverbeet mix. Break 1 egg into each hole, being careful to leave the yolk intact. On each egg pour a few drops of olive oil, season with salt and pepper and scatter the remaining parmesan on top.

Now you are ready to close the pie. Roll out another sheet of very thin dough and place over the filling. Brush the surface with oil and place the remaining two sheets on top in the same manner. Fold the overhanging pastry over the top to seal the pie. Prick some holes on the surface with a fork, being careful not to break the eggs, and brush the top with a little more olive oil.

Bake in an oven preheated to 180°C (350°F/gas 4) for 60 minutes or until the crust is golden brown. **SERVES 4**

Torta di farro
Farro and ricotta cake

200 g (6½ oz) farro grains
3 eggs
500 ml (16 fl oz) milk
150 g (5 oz) freshly grated
  parmesan cheese

pinch of freshly grated nutmeg
sea salt and freshly ground black
  pepper
60 ml (2 fl oz) olive oil

Cook the farro grains in abundant salted water following the instructions on the packet. Drain, place in a mixing bowl and combine with the eggs, milk, parmesan, nutmeg and some salt and pepper. Amalgamate well.

Brush the base of a 35–40 cm (14–16 inch) pie dish with half of the olive oil, pour in the cake mixture, sprinkle the rest of the oil on top and bake in an oven preheated to 180°C (350°F/gas 4) for about 45 minutes or until the top is golden brown.

Can be served hot or warm, accompanied by a green salad. **SERVES 4**

Pisciarada
Potato pie

Originally from the outskirts of Genoa, this pie is better known as *torta di patate* (potato pie). It is one of those pies that we call a *cielo aperto* (open sky) because the pastry is only partly covering the top.

FOR THE PASTRY
200 g (6½ oz) plain
  (all purpose) flour
sea salt
30 ml (1 fl oz) olive oil
warm water

FOR THE FILLING
1 kg (2 lb) desiree potatoes,
  scrubbed
500 ml (16 fl oz) milk at
  room temperature

60 g (2 oz) parmesan cheese,
  freshly grated, plus extra for
  sprinkling
45 g (1½ oz) butter, melted
pinch of freshly ground nutmeg
sea salt and freshly ground
  black pepper
olive oil
2 tbsp breadcrumbs

Prepare the dough as per the Easter pie recipe on page 122, roll into a ball and rest in a warm place, covered with a tea towel for 1 hour.

In the meantime, cook the potatoes in boiling salted water, drain and as soon as they are cool enough to handle, peel and place in a bowl. Mash the potatoes, add the milk, parmesan, butter and nutmeg. Season with salt and pepper and mix thoroughly with a wooden spoon to amalgamate the ingredients and obtain a uniform mixture.

On a lightly floured work surface, use a rolling pin to roll out the dough into a very firm round sheet.

Lightly oil a 30-cm (12-inch) pie dish and line the base and sides with the dough, allowing it to overhang. Sprinkle the breadcrumbs over the dough, pour the potato mixture on top and spread evenly. Brush with a little olive oil and add an extra sprinkle of parmesan. Fold the overhanging pastry back onto the tart to form a border, cutting off any excess. Bake in an oven preheated to 220°C (425°F/gas 7) for 30 minutes or until you have a golden crust. **SERVES 4**

Frittata di pesciolini
Whitebait frittata

5 eggs, lightly beaten
30 g (1 oz) freshly grated
  parmesan cheese
2 slices Italian bread, crusts
  removed, finely chopped
2 sprigs marjoram, leaves picked
  and roughly chopped

sea salt and freshly ground
  black pepper
45 ml (1½ fl oz) olive oil
½ white onion, finely chopped
300 g (10 oz) whitebait
  (the tiniest you can find),
  washed and dried

Combine the eggs, cheese, bread and marjoram in a bowl, and season with salt and pepper. Mix thoroughly.

Preheat the grill to high. Heat the oil in a 30-cm (12-inch) non-stick frying pan with a heatproof handle over a low heat. Cook the onion until soft, about 5 minutes. Add the whitebait and a pinch of salt and cook for 1 minute, gently tossing the pan occasionally. Pour in the egg mixture and stir. Cook until the mixture thickens but the top is still runny. Place the pan under the grill until the top starts to brown and become firm. Slide the frittata onto a plate and serve warm.

SERVES 4

Torta di melanzane

Eggplant tart

FOR THE PASTRY
125 g (4 oz) plain (all purpose)
  flour
30 ml (1 fl oz) olive oil
warm water
sea salt

FOR THE FILLING
sea salt
2 large round eggplants
  (aubergines), thinly sliced

olive oil
1 garlic clove, finely chopped
plain (all purpose) flour, for
  coating the eggplant
1 tbsp marjoram leaves
freshly ground black pepper
2 eggs
30 g (1 oz) parmesan cheese,
  grated
20 g (¾ oz) breadcrumbs

Prepare the dough as per the recipe for the Easter pie on page 122 and roll into a ball. Cover with a tea towel and rest for 1 hour.

To make the filling, salt the slices of eggplant and place in a colander for 10 minutes to sweat out the bitter juices. Pat dry with paper towel.

Pour the oil into a frying pan to a depth of 2 cm (¾ inch) and place on a low to medium heat and sauté the garlic until it startes to change colour, about 2 minutes. Flour the eggplant lightly, add a few slices at a time to the pan and cook them on each side for 2 minutes; sprinkle on half of the marjoram and salt and pepper.

Drain eggplant on paper towel to absorb any excess oil and set aside.

Take the dough and roll out to make an extremely thin, round sheet of pastry, using first your hands then a rolling pin.

Oil the base and sides of a 30-cm (12-inch) pie dish and line with the dough, allowing it to overhang the edge.

In a bowl, beat the eggs, parmesan and the rest of the marjoram, and spread a couple of tablespoons over the dough. Now place the eggplant on top, in an overlapping pattern. Cover the eggplant evenly with the rest of the egg mixture. Dust the top with a thin layer of breadcrumbs. Fold the overhanging pastry towards the centre so you have a border around the tart.

Bake in an oven preheated to 180°C (350°F/gas 4) for 25–30 minutes or until the crust is golden brown. **SERVES 4**

Torta di peperoni

Capsicum pie

FOR THE PASTRY
350 g (11 oz) plain
  (all purpose) flour
45 ml (1½ fl oz) extra virgin
  olive oil
warm water
sea salt

FOR THE FILLING
2 yellow capsicums (bell
  peppers)

2 red capsicums (bell peppers)
75 ml (2½ fl oz) olive oil
1 white onion, finely chopped
6 anchovy fillets, chopped
1 tbsp chopped oregano leaves
sea salt and freshly ground
  black pepper
3 eggs
45 g (1½ oz) freshly grated
  parmesan cheese
100 g (3½ oz) ricotta cheese

Prepare the dough as per the Easter pie recipe on page 122 and divide into two balls, one a little bigger than the other. Cover with a tea towel and rest for 1 hour.

In the meantime, wash the capsicums, chop off the base, cut them in half and remove the seeds. Peel off the skin with a very sharp knife and cut each half into thin strips.

Heat the oil in a saucepan over a low heat. Add the onion and fry until translucent. Add the capsicum, anchovies and half the oregano. Season with salt and pepper, mix well, and cook for 12 minutes. Drain and place in a bowl.

In a separate bowl, gently beat the eggs, parmesan, ricotta, remaining oregano and a pinch of salt. Add this mixture to the capsicum mixture, and stir well to amalgamate everything.

Using a rolling pin, flatten the two balls of dough into extremely thin sheets.

Lightly oil the base and sides of a 30-cm (12-inch) pie dish and line with the larger sheet of dough, allowing it to hang over the edge a little. Place the capsicum mixture on top and spread out evenly. With a pasta cutter or a knife, cut the second sheet of dough into 2-cm (¾-inch) wide ribbons and arrange them on top of the tart in a lattice pattern. Bake in an oven preheated to 180°C (350°F/gas 4) for 30–35 minutes or until the crust is golden brown, and serve warm. **SERVES 4**

Torta di carciofi

Artichoke tart

FOR THE PASTRY
350 g (11 oz) plain
   (all purpose) flour
45 ml (1½ fl oz) extra virgin
   olive oil
warm water
sea salt

FOR THE FILLING
12 globe artichokes
juice of ½ lemon

60 ml (2 fl oz) olive oil,
   plus extra
1 white onion, finely chopped
1 tbsp chopped marjoram leaves
8 eggs
200 g (6½ oz) ricotta cheese
60 g (2 oz) freshly grated
   parmesan cheese
sea salt and freshly ground
   black pepper

Prepare the dough as per the Easter pie recipe on page 122 and divide into three balls, one a bit bigger than the others. Cover with a tea towel and rest for 1 hour.

In the meantime, clean the artichokes. Pull off the tough outer leaves, leaving only the yellow heart. Cut off the stem, leaving about 2 cm (¾ inch) attached. Peel the remaining stem with a knife and shape it nicely. With a sharp knife cut off the top, a third of the way down. Cut them in half and remove the points and the hairy choke.

Cut the artichokes lengthwise into thin segments and immerse in a bowl of acidulated water (water with the juice of ½ lemon added).

Heat the oil in a saucepan over a medium heat. Add the onion and marjoram, stir with a wooden spoon and fry until the onions change colour, about 5 minutes. Add the artichoke slices, stir well, and cook until tender, about 10 minutes.

Tip the artichokes into a bowl and allow to cool down a little. When tepid, add 3 of the eggs, the ricotta and parmesan, and season with salt and pepper. Mix well to amalgamate all the ingredients.

Now, roll out the dough to make three round, extremely thin sheets, one a little larger than the others.

Oil the base and sides of a 30-cm (12-inch) pie dish and line with the largest sheet of dough, allowing it to overhang the edge.

Place the artichoke mixture on top of the dough and spread out evenly. Make five wells in the filling with the back of a tablespoon and break an egg into each, being careful not to break the yolks. Pour a little olive oil onto each egg. Cover the tart with the second sheet of dough, brush with olive oil, and place the third sheet on top.

Flip the overhanging dough towards the centre and press down to form a border around the tart. Brush more oil on the top layer and prick some holes with a fork on the surface. Bake in a preheated 180°C (350°F/gas 4) oven for 30 minutes or until golden brown. Serve warm. **SERVES 4**

Scarpazza
Greens pie

FOR THE PASTRY
250 g (8 oz) plain (all purpose)
  flour
175 ml (6 fl oz) warm water
45 ml (1½ fl oz) extra virgin
  olive oil
sea salt

FOR THE FILLING
500 g (1 lb) silverbeet

2 large leeks, trimmed
75 ml (2½ fl oz) extra virgin
  olive oil
6 eggs
60 g (2 oz) freshly grated
  parmesan cheese
30 g (1 oz) freshly grated
  pecorino cheese
pinch of salt

To make the pastry, combine the flour with a little of the water, the oil and a pinch of salt, and knead until you achieve a uniform elastic dough, adding more water as necessary.

Divide the dough into two balls, one bigger than the other. The larger ball of dough is for the base of the pie, and the smaller is for the top.

On a lightly floured work surface, and using a rolling pin, roll out both balls of dough in a circular shape to a thickness of 2 mm (¹⁄₁₆ inch).

Remove the white stalks of the silverbeet. Wash the leaves and chop them roughly. Drop them in boiling water for a few seconds, strain, squeeze out any excess moisture and set to one side.

Peel off and discard the outer layers of the leeks and cut into thin discs.

Heat the olive oil in a saucepan over a medium heat and cook the leeks for 5 minutes, stirring with a wooden spoon. Remove and set to one side.

In the same pan gently sauté the silverbeet for 5 minutes.

In a bowl, combine the silverbeet, leeks, eggs, both cheeses and salt, and mix well.

Using the larger sheet of dough, line the base and sides of a 35–40-cm (14–16-inch) pie dish. Pour in the leek mixture and shake the dish to make sure it is spread evenly. Cut the smaller sheet of dough into strips and place in a lattice pattern over the top of the filling.

Bake in an oven preheated to 200°C (400°F/gas 6) for 40 minutes or until the crust is golden brown. **SERVES 4**

VARIATION
Instead of silverbeet, you can mix the leeks with mashed potato. You would then not use eggs. With the leek and potato *torta*, the custom is to roll out the pastry so it is wider than the baking dish, then fold the overhanging pastry around the edge to form a rim.

Sardenaira

Ligurian pizza

The people of Naples like to claim they invented the pizza, and point to the presence of fossilised pizza bases in the ashes of Pompeii. However, flatbreads with toppings have been baked all along the Mediterranean coastline for centuries, varying only with the availability of local ingredients.

Around the corner from us, in Nice, they do a *pissaladiére* topped with onions, olives and anchovies. The Ligurian version is known by an assortment of names. In the Ponente it is called *machettara*, from the word *machetto*, which is a way of preserving whole anchovies or sardines in salt. In other places it is called *piscialandrea* (or *pizza all'Andrea*—in honour of the Genoese admiral Andréa Doria). The name *sardenaira* is more familiar on our side of Genoa (because originally it was made with sardines instead of the anchovies used today).

FOR THE PASTRY
500 g (1 lb) plain
  (all purpose) flour
5 g (⅛ oz) dry active yeast
125 ml (4 fl oz) warm water
30 ml (1 fl oz) olive oil
30 ml (1 fl oz) milk
sea salt

FOR THE TOPPING
4 salted anchovies
2 onions, thinly sliced

500 g (1 lb) tomatoes,
  peeled, seeded and diced
1 handful basil leaves, torn
1 handful black olives, such as
  kalamata, pitted and cut in half
5 garlic cloves, whole and
  unpeeled
1 tsp oregano leaves

Place the flour in a mound on a clean flat work surface, make a well in the middle. Dissolve the yeast in the warm water and pour into the well with half the olive oil, the milk and a pinch of salt. Knead until you obtain a smooth and soft dough, at least 15 minutes. Rest in a warm place, covered with a tea towel, for 1 hour.

In the meantime, prepare the topping. Wash the anchovies under running water, fillet them and roughly chop.

Heat the rest of the oil in a frying pan over a medium heat. Add the onions and sauté until beginning to colour. Add the anchovies, tomatoes and basil, and cook for 15 minutes, stirring regularly. Remove from the heat.

With a rolling pin, roll the dough into a round thick sheet. Oil a baking tray. Transfer the dough to the prepared tray. Scatter the olives over the surface, arrange the garlic cloves over the top and pour the sauce over everything. Season with salt and finish with a sprinkle of oregano. Bake in an oven preheated to 180°C (350°F/gas 4) for 30 minutes or until the crust is golden brown.

SERVES 4

Pizza ripiena alla Ligure
Ligurian stuffed pizza

FOR THE PASTRY

500 g (1 lb) plain (all purpose)
  flour
5 g (⅛ oz) dry active yeast
125 ml (4 fl oz) warm water
45 ml (1½ fl oz) olive oil
pinch of sea salt

FOR STUFFING

5 eggs
60 g (2 oz) freshly grated
  parmesan cheese
10 basil leaves, finely chopped
125 g (4 oz) ricotta cheese,
  pushed through a sieve
30 ml (1 fl oz) olive oil
sea salt and freshly ground
  black pepper

Place the flour in a mound on a clean flat work surface and make a well in the middle. Dissolve the yeast in the warm water and pour into the well with the olive oil and salt. Knead until you obtain a smooth and soft dough, at least 15 minutes. Rest in a warm place, covered with a tea towel for 1 hour.

In the meantime, beat the eggs in a bowl, add the parmesan, basil and ricotta. Drizzle with the olive oil, season with salt and pepper and mix with care to amalgamate thoroughly.

Divide the dough in half and, using a rolling pin, roll out 2 thin round sheets roughly the same size. Brush a baking tray with some olive oil. Transfer one of the dough sheets to the prepared tray. Evenly spread the ricotta mixture on top, cover with the other sheet of dough. Seal the 2 sheets together, cutting off the excess dough. Prick some holes with a fork on the surface to let some steam escape during the cooking. Bake in an oven preheated to 200°C (400°F/gas 6) for 25–30 minutes, or until the crust is golden brown. **SERVES 4**

Torta di asparagi

Asparagus pie

FOR THE PASTRY
350 g (11 oz) plain
  (all purpose) flour
45 ml (1½ fl oz) extra
  virgin olive oil
sea salt

FOR THE FILLING
2.5 kg (5 lb) asparagus
75 g (2½ oz) butter
sea salt and freshly ground
  black pepper
6 eggs
200 g (6½ oz) freshly grated
  parmesan cheese
30 ml (1 fl oz) olive oil,
  plus extra

Prepare the dough as per the Easter pie recipe on page 122 and divide it into two balls, one a bit bigger than the other. Cover with a tea towel and rest them for 1 hour.

In the meantime, cook the asparagus in boiling salted water for 1 minute (they will be half cooked). Drain and cut off the woody ends and discard them. Cut off the tips and chop the remaining stem into pieces the same size as the tips.

Melt the butter in a frying pan over a medium heat, add the asparagus and sauté for 3 minutes, seasoning with salt and pepper. Transfer the asparagus to a bowl, add the eggs, parmesan and the olive oil. Mix thoroughly to amalgamate.

Take the larger ball of dough and flatten it with a rolling pin to achieve a very thin sheet. Lightly oil a 30-cm (12-inch) pie dish, and line with the dough. Allow the dough to hang over the edge of the dish. Pour in the asparagus mixture and spread evenly. Roll out the other ball of dough and use this to cover the tart. Fold the overlapping edges together and seal, cutting off any excess dough. Brush the surface with olive oil and prick with a fork. Bake in an oven preheated to 180°C (350°F/gas 4) for 30–35 minutes, or until the top is golden. **SERVES 4**

Torta di polpi e olive nere

Octopus and olive pie

Octopus is not a common ingredient in Australian cooking, though the leggy swimmers are just as plentiful along our shores as they are off the Italian Riviera. Ligurians love to include them in every kind of dish. Here and in the following recipe we're suggesting two ways to wrap them in pastry. The first more traditional recipe was inspired by the huge and delicious pie we found at a restaurant called Rosa, which overlooks the port of Camogli, not far from Genoa. It's a handy way to overcome any prejudices from which your guests might suffer—the octopus is so finely sliced, they will never know what they're enjoying until you tell them. The second is a more modern interpretation, where prejudices are overcome by the sheer beauty of the pink and green ingredients on full display.

FOR THE PASTRY
300 g (10 oz) plain
  (all purpose) flour
sea salt
45 ml (1½ fl oz) olive oil
warm water

FOR THE FILLING
1.5 kg (3 lb) octopus
3 bay leaves
1 onion, cut in half
2 celery stalks, cut in half
10 black peppercorns
1 kg (2 lb) mussels, scrubbed
  and de-bearded
30 ml (1 fl oz) olive oil,
  plus extra

1 garlic clove, peeled
1 tbsp chopped onion
1 tbsp marjoram leaves, chopped
3 sprigs thyme, leaves picked
2 slices Italian bread, crusts
  removed
75 ml (2½ fl oz) milk
100 g (3½ oz) ricotta cheese
1 tbsp flat-leaf parsley leaves,
  finely chopped
2 eggs, lightly beaten
200 g (6½ oz) black olives,
  pitted and chopped
sea salt and freshly ground
  black pepper

To make the pastry, place the flour in a mound on a clean work surface. Form a well in the middle, sprinkle in a little salt and pour in the olive oil. Start kneading, adding a little warm water, as necessary, to achieve a soft and smooth dough. Knead energetically for a few minutes and divide the dough into two balls, one bigger than the other. Place the two balls of dough in a lightly floured bowl, cover with a tea towel, and rest in a warm place for about 1 hour.

Now for the filling. Prepare the octopus as described in the Octopus terrine recipe on page 95. Wash well under running water and place in a large saucepan. Add the bay leaves, onion, celery, peppercorns and, as per local tradition, a cork (to make the octopus tender). Cover with water and simmer gently for about 1 hour, or until the octopus is very tender. Let it cool a little in the water. Remove the octopus, discarding the stock. Place the octopus on a chopping board, and using a mezzaluna, chop finely and set aside.

Place a large saucepan over a medium heat and add the mussels. Remove the mussels from the pan as soon as they open. Extract the mussels from the shells and chop finely.

Heat the oil in a heavy-based saucepan over a low heat. Add the garlic and rub it over the entire surface of the pan with a wooden spoon. After 1 minute, discard the garlic and add the onions. Sauté for 3 minutes, stirring often. Add the mussels and sauté for a further minute. Remove from the heat and place in a bowl. Add the octopus, marjoram and thyme, and mix well.

Soak the bread in the milk, squeeze dry, chop finely and add to the octopus. Add the ricotta, parsley, eggs and olives. Season with salt and pepper, mix thoroughly and set aside.

Brush the base and sides of a 35-cm (14-inch) pie dish with olive oil.

Flour the work surface, take the larger ball of dough and, first with your fist and then with a rolling pin, flatten it out until very thin and even. Line the pie dish with the dough, allowing a little overhang to enable the pie to be sealed. Spread the octopus and mussel mixture evenly on top. Roll out the second ball of dough until very thin, and place on top. Fold the overhanging dough from the bottom sheet towards the centre and seal the pie by pinching the two together. Brush the top with olive oil and prick holes in the surface with a fork.

Bake in an oven preheated to 180°C (350°F/gas 4) for 35 minutes or until golden brown. Serve warm. **SERVES 4**

Crostatina di moscardini e sedano

Octopus tartlet

FOR THE PASTRY
125 g (4 oz) plain (all purpose)
  flour
pinch of salt
75 g (2½ oz) butter, diced
2 egg yolks

FOR THE FILLING
2 kg (4 lb) baby octopus about
  1.2 kg (2½ lb) cleaned
1 carrot, cut in half
1 white onion, cut in half
2 bay leaves

4–5 celery hearts, with the
  yellow leaves attached, finely
  chopped, reserving some of
  the leaves for garnish
100 ml (3½ fl oz) olive oil
juice of 1 lemon
1 tbsp oregano leaves,
  finely chopped
sea salt
black pepper

To make the pastry, combine the flour, salt and butter in a blender and pulse until you have achieved a breadcrumb consistency. Transfer to a bowl and add the eggs. Knead until the dough just comes together. Wrap in plastic wrap and rest for 1 hour.

Preheat the oven to 180°C (350°F/gas 4).

On a floured board, roll out the dough until thin. Cut out four 8-cm (3¼-inch) discs. Line four 5-cm (2-inch) tart shells with the dough. Press the dough into each shell, and bake in the oven for 25 minutes or until golden brown. Set aside to cool a little.

To make the filling, rinse the octopus under cold water and place in a large saucepan with enough water to cover by 5 cm (2 inches). Add the carrot, onion and bay leaves, bring to the boil, reduce the heat to low and simmer for 45 minutes, or until the octopus is tender. Cool in the broth and drain. Place the octopus on a chopping board and cut into 2-cm (¾-inch) pieces. Set aside in a bowl, and add the celery.

Whisk together the olive oil, lemon juice, oregano and a sprinkle of salt. Pour over the octopus and celery mixture and toss well. Allow to marinate for at least 20 minutes, tossing from time to time to incorporate all the flavours.

Place a tartlet case in the centre of each plate, divide the octopus and celery mixture between each one and top with some of the reserved celery leaves. Grind a little pepper and serve immediately.
SERVES 4

Pasta e risotto

Pasta and risotto

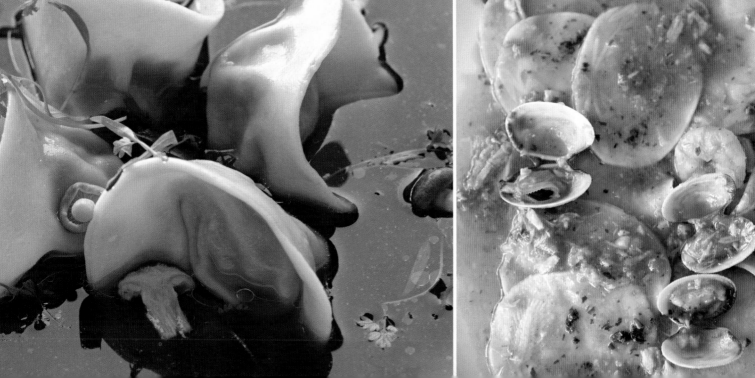

Pasta and risotto

Ravioli, an umbrella term for stuffed pasta that might also go by such names as *tortelli,* *agnolotti* and *pansotti,* seem to have been around since the Middle Ages. A book called *Libro Per Cuoco* (literally *Book for Cook*), written in the 1300s, contained a recipe for ravioli, which were stuffed with chopped herbs mixed with cheese and egg, cooked in a beef broth and sprinkled with a spice mixture that included pepper, cinnamon, ginger, cloves and saffron.

The town of Gavi, in Liguria's neighbouring region of Piemonte, claims the dish was invented there 800 years ago by an innkeeper named Raviolo. The scholar Waverly Root, in his book *The Food of Italy*, offers a more plausible explanation. He says the name comes from the word *rabiole*, which is a Genoese dialect word meaning things of little value—in the kitchen, leftovers.

'On shipboard, at least in the days of sail, making use of leftovers was important; if they were thrown away, a ship might risk running out of food if the voyage were unexpectedly prolonged. The story is that on Genoese ships anything left over at one meal was chopped up together, whatever it might be, stuffed into envelopes of pasta, and served at the following meal.'

Now ravioli are the symbol of celebration, festivity and family companionship. Ligurians all over the world remember their mothers making ravioli for a special occasion—a wedding, an anniversary, a saint's day—with the sauce bubbling gently on the fire, and the whole family round the table reaching for seconds from the large dish in the centre.

They have become a regional obsession: fried, sweet (filled with rice and sprinkled with sugar), stuffed with meat, fish or vegetables (potato, spinach, artichoke, asparagus, leeks), served with *tocco* (meat sauce) or tomato or walnuts or mixed herbs and pine nuts. In 800 years, Ligurians have had plenty of time to think up permutations.

The favourite sauce to go with Ligurian pasta is of more recent origin: pesto. Although it is sometimes claimed that Christopher Columbus would have taken dried noodles and the makings of pesto sauce on his voyages of discovery, it's unlikely that his ingredients included basil. More likely, he carried some of the wild herbs that grew around his home town of Genoa, and crushed them with the implement from which the sauce gets its name—what the English call a pestle.

The first published recipe, from 1844, says the sauce can be made with garlic, oil, cheese and basil or parsley or marjoram, but by the early twentieth century basil had become the core ingredient, guaranteed by law. In 1992 a group of Ligurian gourmets formed The Confraternity of Pesto, designed to protect the dish from bastardisation, and in 2001 the European Union issued a DOP (Denomination of Origin Protected) certificate for pesto which specified that it must contain basil, oil, garlic, salt, pine nuts, parmesan and pecorino.

That's how seriously we Ligurians take our pasta and our sauces. You'll understand why when you try these recipes.

The basic dough

The fresh pasta in this book is made by hand and rolling pin. It's easy and fairly quick (most of the time is taken up letting the dough rest, and during the waiting period you can be making your sauce). Putting your shoulder muscles into the kneading is very rewarding and you can taste the difference.

Once you have rolled out your thin sheets of pasta, called *sfoglie* (leaves), you can make them into any shape: *pappardelle, fazzoletti, tagliatelle, tagliolini, gasse* (also called *farfalle*), lasagne and all kinds of ravioli and *tortelli*.

In most of northern Italy, the usual pasta-making ratio is 100 g (3½ oz) of flour to 1 egg. In Liguria we make our pasta with less egg, but we take extra care to make the sheets very thin and silky.

What you need is a flat work bench, preferably made of wood, a knife, a rolling pin with no handles, a bowl of flour to keep sprinkling on the dough, and a pasta-cutting wheel.

Of course, if you have a pasta machine, you could use that, but be sure to run the dough through many times to get that fine springiness.

300 g (10 oz) plain
(all purpose) flour
2 pinches of salt
2 eggs, at room temperature
3 tsp water

Place the flour in a mound on a clean flat work surface, sprinkle on salt, and form a well in the middle, not too deep. Break the eggs into the well. The first operation is to combine the eggs and flour. Beat the eggs with a fork and when the yolks and white are combined, start incorporating the flour into the egg mixture a bit at a time, still using the fork. Mix until the eggs are no longer runny. At this point, when the dough starts to form, use your palms and fingers to work the mixture until you have a smooth and elastic dough, adding a bit of water if it seems too dry. This should take about 8 minutes.

Cover the dough with a tea towel and rest for 10 minutes in a warm place with no draughts.

Wash and dry your hands well, scrape off any remaining flour on the bench. You are now ready for the last knead. Sprinkle some fresh flour on the work bench, take the dough and start kneading. Put it close to you and, with the heel of your palm and your fingers bent, push it away from you, pressing down against the surface. Then fold the dough in half, turn it around and repeat the operation. Knead like this for about 10 minutes, when you will see bubbles appearing on the surface. Cover with a tea towel and rest for 30 minutes. Cut the dough in two and form into two balls. Now you are ready to flatten the dough into thin sheets.

Put a bit more flour on the work bench and taking one ball at a time, flatten it with the palm of your hand. Gently run a rolling pin forwards and backwards over the dough, adding a bit of flour if it gets sticky. With that motion, applying a little more pressure each time and continuing to turn it around, flatten the dough into a very thin and even round shape about 2-mm (¹⁄₁₆-inch) thick.

Now you are ready to cut out the pasta shapes you need. **FEEDS 4–6**

Ravioli di magro al burro e salvia

Spinach ravioli with sage butter

Ligurian cooking has three great characteristics: simplicity, poverty and originality. *Raviolo* is a classic example. The use of aromatic herbs is the result of sailors returning home after their long stints at sea craving the perfumed herbs of the Ligurian hillsides as well as fresh vegetables.

FOR THE PASTA
300 g (10 oz) plain
   (all purpose) flour
2 pinches of sea salt
2 eggs
45 ml (1½ fl oz) warm water

FOR THE FILLING
500 g (1 lb) English spinach,
   trimmed and washed
4 eggs
4 tbsp freshly grated
   parmesan cheese

100 g (3½ oz) ricotta cheese
pinch of freshly grated nutmeg
sea salt and freshly ground
   black pepper

FOR THE SAUCE
60 g (2 oz) butter
20 sage leaves
4 tbsp freshly grated
   parmesan cheese

First, make the pasta dough as explained in the Basic dough recipe on page 146, using the quantities provided for this recipe.

While the dough is resting prepare the filling. Toss the spinach over a medium heat, with only the water left on the leaves after washing, until soft, about 3 minutes. Squeeze dry and finely chop. Break 3 of the eggs into a bowl and lightly beat. Add the spinach, 2 tablespoons of the parmesan, ricotta and nutmeg. Season with salt and pepper and mix with a wooden spoon until amalgamated.

Now, make the ravioli. Divide the dough into two balls and with a rolling pin flatten them into very thin sheets, sprinkling more flour on both the rolling pin and the bench should they become sticky. Both sheets should be about the same size.

Place one sheet on the bench. Lightly beat the remaining egg and brush over the pasta. Place spoonfuls of the filling at even and aligned intervals at least two fingers—about 4 cm (1½ inches)—apart and not less than 2 cm (¾ inch) from the edge of the sheet. The rows of filling should be at least 2 cm (¾ inch) apart.

Place the second sheet of pasta on top of the first and with your fingers press gently around each mound of filling, taking care not to leave air bubbles inside. Cut along the rows with a pastry cutter and finish each *raviolo* with a final press of your fingers to seal around the edges. Let the ravioli rest, not touching each other, for 30 minutes. Cook the ravioli in plenty of boiling salted water for 3–4 minutes.

In the meantime, make the sauce. Melt the butter in a large non-stick frying pan over a low heat and add a few sage leaves. Lift out the ravioli, a few at a time, with a slotted spoon and put them in the pan with the butter and sage. Add the rest of the sage leaves and the other half of the parmesan. Toss gently for a minute or so. Place the ravioli on a serving platter and serve immediately.

The sauce for these ravioli should not be too dry, so if you think you need a bit more butter, add it to the pan before serving. You can also add more cheese to your liking. **SERVES 4–6**

Ravioli di carne al tocco di carne

Meat ravioli with meat sauce

FOR THE MEAT SAUCE

500 g (1 lb) lean beef or veal

5 ripe tomatoes, peeled, seeded and diced

30 g (1 oz) dried porcini mushrooms, soaked in warm water for 10 minutes and drained

60 ml (2 fl oz) olive oil

20 g (¾ oz) butter

45 g (1½ oz) bone marrow

1 celery stalk, chopped

1 small carrot, chopped

1 white onion, chopped

1 garlic clove, peeled

3 bay leaves

sea salt and freshly ground black pepper

60 ml (2 fl oz) white wine

125 ml (4 fl oz) water

FOR THE FILLING

45 ml (1½ fl oz) olive oil

1 garlic clove

1 tbsp flat-leaf parsley, finely chopped

200 g (6½ oz) minced (ground) beef

200 g (6½ oz) minced (ground) pork (or pork sausage, minced)

sea salt

200 g (6½ oz) silverbeet, stalks removed, washed

2 thick slices Italian bread, crusts removed, weighing no more than 60 g (2 oz)

45 g (1½ oz) mortadella, finely chopped

4 eggs

pinch of freshly grated nutmeg

freshly ground black pepper

90–120 g (3–4 oz) freshly grated parmesan cheese

FOR THE PASTA

300 g (10 oz) plain (all purpose) flour

2 eggs, at room temperature

45 ml (1½ fl oz) warm water

1 egg, lightly beaten, to brush over pasta

You'll need to get started at least 90 minutes before you want to serve the ravioli. First make the meat sauce, which benefits from long slow cooking.

Cut the beef or veal into small pieces and set aside. Pass the tomatoes through a mouli and set aside. Roughly chop the porcini mushrooms.

Heat the oil in a saucepan (a terracotta pan if you have one) over a low heat. Add the butter and the marrow and cook until melted. Add the celery, carrot, onion, garlic and bay leaves. Cook for 8–10 minutes, stirring occasionally with a wooden spoon. Add the mushrooms, mix them in, add the meat, and season with salt and pepper. Increase the heat to medium-high and cook for 10 minutes, stirring regularly. Add the white wine and simmer until the alcohol evaporates, about 3 minutes. Finally, add the tomatoes and water, and mix thoroughly. Remove the garlic and bay leaves and discard. Reduce the heat to low, cover the pan and simmer for at least an hour, stirring regularly. The meat should be almost melted. If it looks a little dried out you can add some water a little at a time. Remove the pan from the heat and cool a little. Pass through a mouli into a bowl. Set aside.

While the sauce is simmering, make the filling. Heat the oil in a heavy-based saucepan over a low heat. Add the garlic and parsley and fry for 3 minutes, mixing with a wooden spoon. Add the minced beef and pork, sprinkle with salt, mix thoroughly and brown for 10 minutes, stirring frequently.

Wilt the silverbeet in a hot frying pan, with just the water from washing clinging to the leaves. Wrap in a tea towel, squeeze out the moisture and chop finely.

Dip the bread in the meat sauce and combine it in a bowl with the mortadella, silverbeet, eggs and nutmeg. Season with salt and pepper, then add the meat and 45 g (1½ oz) of the parmesan. Mix well to amalgamate and set aside.

Now, make the pasta. Prepare the dough using the method described in the Basic dough recipe on page 146. It will take about 50 minutes, including time for it to rest and you to rest. Divide the dough into two balls and with a rolling pin flatten them into very thin sheets, sprinkling more flour on both the rolling pin and the bench should they become sticky. Both sheets should be about the same size.

Place one pasta sheet on the bench and brush with the beaten egg. Place spoonfuls of the filling at even and aligned intervals at least two fingers—about 4 cm (1½ inches)—apart and not less than 2 cm (¾ inch) from the edge of the sheet. The rows of filling should be at least 2 cm (¾ inch) apart.

Place the second sheet of pasta on top of the first and with your fingers press gently around each mound of filling, taking care not to leave air bubbles inside. Cut along the rows with a pastry cutter and finish each *raviolo* with a final press of your fingers to seal the edges together. Rest the ravioli for 30 minutes.

Bring a large saucepan of salted water to the boil over a high heat. Warm the meat sauce over a low heat. Put the ravioli into the boiling water and cook for 4–5 minutes. Remove a few at a time with a slotted spoon.

Cover the bottom of a serving plate with a layer of sauce, place the ravioli on top and cover with the rest of the sauce. Sprinkle the remaining parmesan on top, and take the platter to the table with a big spoon so guests can help themselves. **SERVES 4**

Ravioli di carciofi alle erbe

Artichoke ravioli with herb sauce

All the Ligurian vegetables are excellent in ravioli, especially artichokes. To make the filling they are cut thinly and pan-fried with garlic, onion and white wine. This type of cooking can also be used for zucchini (courgettes) or peas (cooked and mashed first). We use a herb and butter sauce because its simplicity and perfume complement the filling.

FOR THE PASTA
300 g (10 oz) plain
  (all purpose) flour
2 pinches of sea salt
2 eggs, at room temperature
45 ml (1½ fl oz) warm water

FOR THE RAVIOLI FILLING
6 globe artichokes
45 ml (1½ fl oz) olive oil
½ white onion, finely chopped
60 ml (2 fl oz) white wine
sea salt and freshly ground
  black pepper
1 tbsp, flat-leaf parsley,
  finely chopped

1 garlic clove, finely chopped
75 g (2½ oz) ricotta cheese
2 eggs
45 g (1½ oz) freshly grated
  parmesan cheese
1 small sprig marjoram, leaves
  picked and chopped
pinch of freshly ground nutmeg

FOR THE SAUCE
60–75 g (2–2½ oz) butter
2 tbsp finely chopped mixed
  herbs such as thyme, marjoram,
  sage, mint
parmesan cheese, to grate over
  the top

First make the pasta dough as shown in the Basic dough recipe on page 146, with the quantities provided for this recipe.

While the dough is resting prepare the filling.

Remove the tough outer leaves of the artichokes, cut in half, remove the hairy choke and slice the heart very thinly.

Heat the oil in a heavy-based saucepan over a medium heat. Add the onion and sauté for about 3 minutes, or until soft, stirring with a wooden spoon. Add the artichokes and mix in with the onion. Pour in the white wine, stir, reduce the heat to low and cook for 15 minutes, stirring occasionally. Season with salt and pepper, sprinkle with the parsley and garlic, stir, and cook for 10 minutes. Remove the artichokes from the cooking liquid, place on a board and chop finely. Place the chopped artichokes in a bowl, add the ricotta, eggs, parmesan and marjoram. Season with salt and pepper and nutmeg, and work this mixture with a wooden spoon to amalgamate.

Now, make the ravioli as per the Meat ravioli recipe on page 150, using the artichoke mixture instead of the meat filling. Rest for half an hour.

Cook the ravioli in plenty of boiling salted water for 3–4 minutes. In the meantime, melt the butter in a frying pan over a low heat. Transfer to a large bowl. Add the herbs and mix well. Remove the ravioli, a few at a time, with a slotted spoon. Toss delicately into the butter and herb mixture and sprinkle on some parmesan.

Place the ravioli in a serving dish and serve with the rest of the parmesan on top. **SERVES 4**

Pansotti alla salsa di noci

Round ravioli with walnut sauce

The name for this dish comes from *pancia*, which means belly. It is difficult to give one classic recipe as there are many different shapes and fillings, from square to round to rectangular, from tortellini parcels to half moons, as long as they honour the name and are fat. The filling originally was made with the *preboggion*, a selection of wild greens also called *erbi*.

Because it is difficult, even in Italy, to get the *preboggion* and because the bitter greens have a short season, we prepare this version with silverbeet. The walnut sauce is an ancient one which, over the years got gentler, losing a lot of the strong flavour of the garlic. But in true Ligurian style, we still thicken it with white bread.

FOR THE PASTA
300 g (10 oz) plain
 (all purpose) flour
2 pinches of sea salt
2 eggs, at room temperature
45 ml (1½ fl oz) warm water

FOR THE FILLING
800 g (1 lb 10 oz) silverbeet,
 stalks removed, washed
60 g (2 oz) parmesan cheese,
 freshly grated, plus extra, to
 serve
100 g (3½ oz) ricotta cheese
2 eggs
1 tbsp chopped marjoram leaves
15 ml (½ fl oz) olive oil
pinch of freshly grated nutmeg

sea salt
60 g (2 oz) butter

FOR THE SAUCE
20 walnut kernels or 250 g
 shelled walnuts
2 slices Italian bread, crusts
 removed, weighing no more
 than 45 g (1½ oz)
60 ml (2 fl oz) milk
30 g (1 oz) pine nuts
1 garlic clove, peeled
75 g (2½ oz) ricotta cheese
45 ml (1½ fl oz) olive oil
sea salt
1 tbsp marjoram leaves, finely
 chopped

First make the pasta dough as shown in the Basic dough recipe on page 146, using the quantities provided for this recipe.

While the dough is resting prepare the walnut sauce. Blanch the walnuts in boiling water for a few seconds, drain and peel. Place a few at a time in a mortar and start pounding. Soak the bread in the milk, squeeze and add to the walnuts. Continue pounding, then add the pine nuts and garlic. Keep pounding until you achieve a homogenous paste. Transfer to a bowl, add the ricotta and mix with a wooden spoon to amalgamate. Add the oil and a few pinches of salt, mix, add the marjoram and mix well to incorporate. Set aside.

Now prepare the filling for the *pansotti*. Place the silverbeet in a frying pan, with only the water from washing left on the leaves, and cook until soft (about 5 minutes). Squeeze dry, place on a chopping board and chop finely. Transfer to a bowl, add the parmesan, ricotta, eggs, marjoram, olive oil, nutmeg and a few pinches of salt and work this mixture well to amalgamate. Now make the *pansotti* by rolling out two sheets of dough and placing spoonfuls of the filling between them, as explained in the Meat ravioli recipe on page 150. Instead of cutting into square shapes, make the parcels circular by pressing a glass over each mound, and using it to cut the dough. Set aside to rest for 30 minutes. Bring a large saucepan of salted water to the boil and cook the *pansotti* for 3–4 minutes.

Melt the butter and place it in a large bowl. Fish out the *pansotti*, a few at a time, with a slotted spoon and place them in the bowl with the melted butter. Sprinkle some grated parmesan on the *pansotti* and toss delicately. Add the walnut sauce, toss some more.

Place the *pansotti* on a platter or on individual plates, sprinkle with some more parmesan and serve. You can also sprinkle the *pansotti* with some fresh marjoram leaves.

Never heat the walnut sauce or it will lose the fragrance of raw preparation. **SERVES 4**

Tortellini di quaglia
Quail tortellini with quail broth

The shortage of space in Liguria means there is a shortage of large meat animals; so the locals like to hunt the small birds of the area, and use the tiny quantities of meat as filling for their favourite pasta parcels. Here we have substituted quail for the *tordi* of the area, and serve it with a clear, full-flavoured broth.

FOR THE PASTA
300 g (10 oz) plain
  (all purpose) flour
2 pinches of sea salt
2 eggs
45 ml (1½ fl oz) water

FOR THE BROTH
30 ml (1 fl oz) olive oil
1 carrot, roughly chopped
1 celery stalk, roughly chopped
½ white onion, cut in half
3 bay leaves
6 quail
30 ml (1 fl oz) white wine
sea salt and freshly ground
  black pepper
3 litres (96 fl oz) chicken stock

FOR THE FILLING
quail meat, from the quail
  cooked in the broth
1 egg, lightly beaten
45 g (1½ oz) ricotta cheese
45 g (1½ oz) freshly grated
  parmesan cheese
½ bunch English spinach,
  blanched and chopped
pinch of freshly grated nutmeg
sea salt and freshly ground
  black pepper
1 egg, lightly beaten,
  to assemble the tortellini

freshly grated parmesan
  cheese, to serve

Make the pasta dough as described in the Basic dough recipe on page 146. While the dough is resting, prepare the broth.

Heat the oil in a large saucepan over a low-medium heat. Add the carrot, celery, onion and bay leaves, and fry for 5 minutes, stirring with a wooden spoon. In the meantime, cut the quail in half, wash them and pat dry with paper towel.

When the *soffritto* is ready, increase the heat, add the quail and brown quickly on both sides. Sprinkle in the white wine and let it evaporate, about 3 minutes. Season with salt and pepper, pour in the chicken stock, mix gently and cook over a low heat for 25 minutes.

Remove the quail with a slotted spoon and separate the meat from the bones, it should come off easily. Put the bones back into the stock and cook for 10 minutes. Chop the quail meat very finely using a knife or a mezzaluna. Strain the broth through a fine sieve and set aside.

Now, to make the filling, place the quail meat in a bowl. Add the egg, ricotta, parmesan, spinach and nutmeg. Season with salt and pepper, and mix thoroughly with a wooden spoon.

To make the tortellini, cut the sheets of pasta dough into 10-cm (4-inch) squares. Place a teaspoon of filling in the centre of each square and brush the edges with the egg. Take one corner of the square, fold over the filling to the opposite corner to form a triangle, and seal the edges with your fingers. Fold the tip of the triangle back over so the point extends slightly past the base of the triangle. Now fold the other two points behind the filling so they overlap each other. Squish them together to make a ring around the filling. Place the tortellini on a floured surface or a tea towel, making sure they do not touch each other.

Bring the broth to the boil, add the tortellini and cook for 4–5 minutes. Fish them out with a slotted spoon and divide among four soup bowls. Pour the broth into a jug and pour it over the tortellini at the table. Serve with a sprinkle of grated parmesan. **SERVES 4**

Ravioli alle melanzane
Eggplant ravioli on eggplant

Northern Italians think of eggplants (aubergines) as exotic vegies from the sunny south, and we use them sparingly. But in this three-layer recipe, eggplant appears twice—as the base on which the ravioli rest, and as part of the stuffing. Also making a double appearance is a delicious mix of Ligurian herbs, which enhance both the stuffing and the sauce that tops off the dish.

FOR THE PASTA
300 g (10 oz) plain
  (all purpose) flour
2 pinches of sea salt
2 eggs, at room temperature
45 ml (1½ fl oz) warm water

FOR THE HERB MIXTURE
1 tbsp finely chopped
  mint leaves
1 tbsp finely chopped
  thyme leaves
1 tbsp finely chopped basil leaves
2 small garlic cloves,
  finely chopped
1 pinch of sea salt
1 pinch of freshly ground
  black pepper

FOR THE FILLING
2 large eggplants (aubergines),
  peeled and chopped
half of the herb mixture

75 (2½ oz) parmesan cheese,
  freshly grated
100 g (3½ oz) ricotta cheese
3 eggs

FOR THE BASE
1 large eggplant (aubergine),
  sliced into 12 discs
75 ml (2½ fl oz) olive oil,
  for frying

FOR THE SAUCE
60 ml (2 fl oz) olive oil
half of the herb mixture
5 ripe tomatoes, peeled, seeded
  and diced

45 g (1½ oz) pecorino cheese
2 tbsp freshly grated parmesan
  cheese
12 basil leaves, to garnish

First make the pasta dough as shown in the Basic dough recipe on page 146, using the quantities provided for this recipe.

While the dough is resting, mix together all the ingredients in the herb mixture in a bowl, and set aside.

Now prepare the ravioli filling. Peel and chop the two eggplants and place the pieces in a colander. Sprinkle with salt and set aside to sweat for 10 minutes.

Heat the oil in a large frying pan over a medium heat and fry the eggplant, in batches, for 5 minutes, adding more hot oil if necessary. Tip the eggplants onto a wooden board and chop them finely. Place the chopped eggplant into a bowl and add half the herb mixture, plus the parmesan, ricotta and eggs. Mix well until everything is amalgamated. Use this filling to make ravioli as shown in the Meat ravioli recipe on page 150.

Now prepare the base. Slice the eggplant into 12 discs, sprinkle on a little salt and let them sweat for 10 minutes in a colander. Heat ½-cm depth of the oil in a non-stick frying pan over medium heat. Add the eggplant slices and fry them, in batches, for 2 minutes each side, or until golden brown. Add more hot oil if it all disappears halfway through. Scoop the pieces out and set aside.

To make the sauce, heat the olive oil in a heavy-based frying pan over low heat. Add the remaining herb-garlic mixture and sizzle for 2 minutes. Increase heat to medium, add the tomatoes, season with salt and pepper and cook for 5 minutes, mixing often with a wooden spoon. Take off the heat.

Cook the ravioli in plenty of boiling salted water for 3–4 minutes (if they rise to the surface too soon gently push them back to the bottom).

To serve, place a thin layer of sauce at the base of the serving plates, arrange the eggplant slices (which you have divided into four) on top, brush with oil and sprinkle with some pecorino. Place a *raviolo* on top of each eggplant slice. Sprinkle a little more pecorino on top of the ravioli then cover with more sauce. Serve at once sprinkled with a little parmesan and topped with the basil leaves, if you like. **SERVES 4**

Ravioli bianchi e neri di salmone con crema di granturco

Black and white salmon ravioli with sweet-corn sauce

This recipe is not easy but it's very rewarding. It presupposes you have a pasta machine; so if you don't, read it for amusement. It's not traditional (the fishermen's wives had other things to do than play with pasta colours), but dishes like it came about because of the recent influx of visitors into the Riviera, wanting something new and elegant.

It tastes as fine as it looks—the subtle flavour of the squid ink is in harmony with the fish filling, for which we bake the fish whole in *cartoccio* (wrapped in foil) because it achieves a better texture and flavour than poaching in stock.

FOR THE PASTA

WHITE

300 g (10 oz) plain
  (all purpose) flour
pinch of sea salt
2 eggs
45 ml (1½ fl oz) warm water

BLACK

1 egg
1 tsp squid ink (available
  from your fishmonger)
pinch of sea salt
150 g (5 oz) plain
  (all purpose) flour
15 ml (½ fl oz) warm water

FOR THE FILLING

500 g (1 lb) salmon fillet
  with skin on
60 ml (2 fl oz) olive oil
1 garlic clove, finely chopped
½ small onion, finely chopped
1 celery stalk, chopped

a few sage leaves, finely chopped
1 handful flat-leaf parsley leaves,
  finely chopped
45 ml (1½ fl oz) white wine
sea salt and freshly ground
  black pepper
2 eggs
30 g (1 oz) freshly grated
  parmesan cheese
100 g (3½ oz) ricotta cheese
pinch of freshly ground nutmeg
1 tbsp breadcrumbs
1 egg, lightly beaten,
  to assemble the ravioli

FOR THE SAUCE

2 corn cobs
500 ml (16 fl oz) fish stock
vegetables from the filling
  used to cook the fish
100 ml (3½ fl oz) cream
1 tsp chopped thyme leaves
4 tsp salmon roe

First make the white dough as described in the Basic dough recipe on page 146, and divide into three balls. Set them aside to rest.

Now make the black dough. First beat the egg with the squid ink. Put a mound of flour on a wooden board, make a well in the middle and pour in the squid ink and egg mixture, kneading it in the same way as for the white dough. Make it into a ball and let it rest for half an hour.

... **Recipe continued on page 163**

To make the filling, preheat the oven to 180°C (350°F/gas 4). Place some foil on a baking tray, leaving enough foil to cover and seal the salmon. Brush the salmon with a little oil and place the fish in the centre of the foil. Then, on top of the fish and all around, place the garlic, onion, celery, sage and parsley. Add the rest of the oil and the wine. Season with salt and pepper. Seal the salmon in the foil and bake for 30 minutes. Remove from the oven and open the foil. Transfer the fish to a chopping board, remove and discard the skin, remove any remaining bones and with a sharp knife, then chop the fish finely. Take the vegetables that were in the parcel and pass them through a fine mouli or a sieve. Set aside for the sauce.

Place the fish in a bowl, add the egg, parmesan, ricotta and nutmeg. Season with salt and pepper, sprinkle with the breadcrumbs and mix thoroughly with a wooden spoon to amalgamate. Set aside while rolling out the pasta.

With a rolling pin, roll out two of the white balls of dough into thin sheets and set them aside.

For the third white ball and the black ball, you will need a pasta machine, because you are turning them into ribbons. Place the pasta machine on your benchtop and flour the bench just in front of the machine. Set the rollers to the widest spacing. Flatten the ball of white dough with the heel of your hand into a strip that will fit between the rollers (about 1 cm, ½ inch, thick). Run the dough through the machine four times, folding it in half and turning it back on itself each time.

Then, reducing the pasta machine setting one notch at a time, keep feeding the dough through the rollers until it is a long rectangular sheet about 3 mm thick. This will involve at least 8 pressings.

Repeat this process with the black dough.

Allow the sheets to dry for 10 minutes. Attach the cutters for ribbon pasta (*fettucine or tagliatelle*) to the machine and feed each sheet through so you have two sets of ribbons about 2 cm (1 inch) wide. Separate and spread the ribbons to dry on a tea towel for 5 minutes.

You are now ready to assemble the black and white top part of the ravioli. Place one of the sheets of white dough you rolled out earlier onto a floured surface, and starting from the outside edge, lay alternate black and white ribbons across it (using our photograph as a guide). When the entire sheet is covered, flour it lightly and flatten the ribbons into the sheet. Set aside.

Now make the ravioli, using the other white sheet as the base and placing spoonfuls of the fish mixture in rows across it, at intervals of about 5 cm (2½ inches).

Paint a little of the beaten egg around each lump of filling. Cover with the sheet of black and white dough, gently press down around each lump, removing any air bubbles. Cut along the rows with a pastry cutter and seal the edges with your fingers. Set aside for 15 minutes while you prepare the sauce.

To make the sauce, scrape the corn kernels from the cob. Pour the fish stock into a saucepan, add the corn and bring to the boil. Lower the heat and simmer for 20 minutes, or until the corn is soft. Add the vegetable paste reserved from the filling, the cream and thyme, and simmer for 5 minutes. Transfer the sauce to a blender and puree.

Boil the ravioli in plenty of salted water for 3–4 minutes. Drain and place on four serving plates. Top with a few tablespoons of the sauce and a teaspoon of salmon roe. **SERVES 4**

Lasagne tordellate

Open lasagne

Ligurian cuisine is poor and family oriented but every now and then we come across a refined dish like this lasagne which is served with a sauce that normally functions as the filling for ravioli or *tordelli* dishes—hence the name *tordellate* which means *tordelli*-style.

The most important thing in the ravioli is the filling—proven by the original habit of eating ravioli with no sauce and a sprinkle of cheese. Here,, we bring the filling to the outside. You can use very cheap cuts of beef and pork because they are slow-cooked, but trim the fat.

Lasagne in Liguria differs from the well-known baked version of Emilia-Romagna, and instead is the name of a shape of pasta—square and so thin as to be almost transparent. I would not like to state a heresy, but I suspect the great Milan chef Gualtiero Marchesi got the inspiration for his amazing open *raviolo* from this Ligurian classic. In fact, this dish is served in layers—pasta, sauce, pasta, sauce, like an open *raviolo*.

FOR THE PASTA
500 g (1 lb) plain
  (all purpose) flour
2 pinches of sea salt
2 eggs
warm water, as needed

FOR THE SAUCE
30 ml (1 fl oz) olive oil
30 g (1 oz) butter
1 white onion, finely chopped
1 carrot, chopped
1 celery stalk, chopped
1 handful flat-leaf parsley, finely
  chopped
300 g (10 oz) lean beef, roughly
  chopped

300 g (10 oz) lean pork,
  roughly chopped
sea salt and freshly ground
  black pepper
3 bay leaves
pinch of freshly grated nutmeg
30 ml (1 fl oz) dry white wine
500 g (1 lb) tomatoes, peeled,
  seeded and diced

1 bunch silverbeet,
  white stalks removed
inner soft part of 1 white
  Italian bread roll
milk
60 g (2 oz) freshly grated
  parmesan cheese
2 eggs

To make the pasta, follow the Basic dough recipe on page 146. Set aside to rest.

To make the sauce, first make a *soffritto*. Heat the oil and butter in a heavy-based saucepan over a low heat. Add the onion, carrot, celery and parsley. Mix with a wooden spoon and cook for a few minutes until the vegetables are soft and the onion translucent. Add the beef and pork, turn up the heat to medium-high to brown the meat on all sides. Season with salt and pepper, add the bay leaves and nutmeg. Mix thoroughly, fry for 8–10 minutes, then add the white wine. When the wine has evaporated, turn the heat to low, stir in the tomatoes, and cook for 30 minutes, stirring regularly, adding water if it dries out. The sauce should be fairly thick.

In the meantime, wash the silverbeet. Place in a large saucepan and cook until the leaves are wilted, using only the water that clings to the leaves after washing. Allow to cool, squeeze dry, chop finely and set aside in a bowl.

Place the bread in a small saucepan and add just enough milk to cover the bread. Cook on a low heat for 3–4 minutes, stirring constantly. Add to the silverbeet.

Take the meat sauce off the heat, and transfer the pieces of meat to a chopping board. Chop finely with a mezzaluna or a sharp knife and combine with the silverbeet and bread. Add 30 g (1 oz) of the parmesan, the eggs and some pepper. Mix thoroughly to amalgamate.

Reheat the sauce over a low heat, add the chopped meat and silverbeet mixture, stir gently and cook for 30 minutes, adding a little water if it seems to be drying out. The sauce should be thick but able to flow.

Cut the pasta sheets into 8-cm (3-inch) squares. Bring a large saucepan of salted water to the boil. Add a little oil to stop the pasta from sticking and cook the lasagne squares, a few at a time, for 5 minutes. Remove one at a time with a slotted spoon, and put them in a bowl.

Working very quickly, build the lasagne on individual plates using 4–5 sheets of pasta on each. Start with a little sauce on the plate, place a square of pasta on top, add sauce, sprinkle on parmesan, add another layer of pasta and so on. End with sauce and a sprinkle of parmesan. Serve immediately.

SERVES 4

Ravioli di gamberi e pomodori secchi

Oven-dried tomato ravioli with prawns

FOR THE PASTA
300 g (10 oz) plain
  (all purpose) flour
sea salt
2 eggs
45 ml (1½ fl oz) water

FOR THE FILLING
6 large tomatoes (4 for the
  filling and 2 for the sauce)
sea salt and freshly ground
  black pepper
olive oil
500 g (1 lb) green medium
  prawns (shrimp), peeled
  and deveined
2 eggs, lightly beaten
45 g (1½ oz) ricotta cheese
1 tbsp pine nuts

1 tsp marjoram leaves,
  finely chopped

FOR THE SAUCE
olive oil from the oven-dried
  tomatoes
2 garlic cloves, peeled and
  crushed a little with the
  blade of a knife
4 of the oven-dried tomato
  halves, roughly chopped

10 basil leaves, chopped
12 green medium prawns
  (shrimp), peeled and
  deveined with tails intact
sea salt and freshly ground
  black pepper

To make the filling, you need to prepare the oven-dried tomatoes the day before you want to eat these ravioli.

Preheat the oven to 70°C (150°F/gas ¼). Cut the tomatoes in half lengthwise and place, cut-side up without overlapping, on a baking tray. Sprinkle with salt, place in the oven and bake for 6 hours. Allow to cool, place in a container and cover with the oil. They will keep for 6 months like this.

On the day, prepare the pasta dough as described in the Basic dough recipe on page 146. While the dough is resting, prepare the filling.

Heat 30 ml (1 fl oz) olive oil in a non-stick frying pan over a medium heat. Add the prawns and quickly cook for 1 minute on each side. Transfer to a chopping board, pat dry with paper towel and chop finely with a sharp knife or a mezzaluna. Set aside in a bowl.

Finely chop 8 oven-dried tomato halves and add to the prawns. Add the eggs, ricotta, pine nuts and marjoram. Season with salt and pepper, and mix well with a wooden spoon to amalgamate everything. Using this filling, make the ravioli as described in the Meat ravioli recipe on page 150.

To prepare the sauce, heat 100 ml (3½ fl oz) of the oil in a frying pan over a medium heat. Add the garlic and sauté until a light golden colour. Discard immediately. Add the oven-dried tomatoes and cook for 2 minutes, mixing with a wooden spoon. Transfer to a large bowl.

Cook the ravioli in plenty of boiling salted water for 4–5 minutes. Remove with a slotted spoon and add to the sauce. Sprinkle with the basil and toss gently. Keep warm in a very low oven.

Preheat the grill to high. Grill the prawns for 2 minutes on each side, and season with salt and pepper to taste.

To serve, place the sauce around the ravioli, not on top. Place the prawns in a line on top of the ravioli and serve immediately. **SERVES 4**

Ravioli di triglia
Red mullet ravioli

FOR THE PASTA
300 g (10 oz) plain
  (all purpose) flour
2 pinches of sea salt
2 eggs, at room temperature
45 ml (1½ fl oz) warm water

FOR THE SAUCE
5 large red mullets, cleaned
2 bay leaves
½ onion, cut in half
1 carrot, cut in half
1 celery stalk, cut in three
30 ml (1 fl oz) white wine
sea salt
100 ml (3½ fl oz) olive oil
30 g (1 oz) butter
1 garlic clove, finely chopped
1 tbsp finely chopped flat-leaf
  parsley leaves

30 ml (1 fl oz) dry white wine
3 ripe tomatoes, peeled,
  seeded and diced
10 basil leaves

FOR THE FILLING
45 g (1½ oz) butter
5 red mullet fillets
  (reserved from the sauce)
3 tbsp freshly grated
  parmesan cheese
100 g (3½ oz) ricotta cheese
2 eggs
1 tbsp marjoram leaves,
  finely chopped
sea salt and freshly ground
  black pepper

First, make the pasta dough as explained in the Basic dough recipe on page 146, using the quantities provided for this recipe.

While the dough is resting, prepare the sauce. Wash and fillet the red mullet with a sharp knife. Remove any bones with tweezers, if necessary. Reserve the fillets for the filling and the sauce.

Put the red mullet heads and bones in a saucepan. Add the bay leaves, onion, carrot, celery and white wine. Cover with water and bring to the boil. Add a few sprinkles of salt and stir with a wooden spoon. Reduce heat to low and cook for 30 minutes. Strain the stock, return to the pan and cook for 5 minutes. The stock is now ready to use, keep it handy for the sauce.

Now prepare the filling. Melt the butter in a frying pan over a medium heat. Add half the red mullet fillets reserved from the stock and cook for 3–4 minutes, stirring with a wooden spoon. Drain off the butter and place the fillets in a bowl. Mash with a fork then add the parmesan, ricotta, eggs and the marjoram. Season with salt and pepper and mix properly to amalgamate. Set aside.

Make the ravioli as described in the Meat ravioli recipe on page 150. While the ravioli are resting for half an hour, continue with the sauce. Heat the oil and butter in a heavy-based saucepan over a low heat. Add the garlic and parsley, and fry for 3 minutes, mixing with a wooden spoon. Add the remaining fillets of red mullet and cook them for 1 minute on each side. Add the white wine and let the alcohol evaporate for 1 minute. Mix in the tomatoes, cook for 2 minutes, then add 75 ml (2½ fl oz) of fish stock. Break up the fillets with a fork, mix well to combine, and cook for 3–5 minutes. Season with salt and pepper to taste and take off the heat.

Cook the ravioli in salted boiling water for 3–4 minutes. Fish them out, a few at a time, with a slotted spoon. Spoon some sauce into each serving dish, place the ravioli on top and cover with the rest of the sauce. Serve steaming with basil scattered over the top. **SERVES 4**

Gasse ai piselli
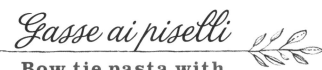

Bow tie pasta with prosciutto and peas

FOR THE PASTA
400 g (13 oz) plain
  (all purpose) flour mixed
  with 30 g (1 oz) freshly
  grated parmesan cheese
pinch of sea salt
2 eggs
warm water, as needed

FOR THE SAUCE
30 ml (1 fl oz) olive oil
1 onion chopped

100 g (3 ½ oz) prosciutto,
  finely chopped
1 kg (2 lb) freshly
  shelled peas
sea salt and freshly
  ground black pepper
500 ml (16 fl oz)
  chicken stock
60 g (2 oz) butter
45 g (1 ½ oz) freshly grated
  parmesan cheese

Make the pasta as described in the Basic dough recipe on page on page 146. When you have your two very thin sheets, cut them into 4-cm (1 ½-inch) ribbons with a pasta-cutting wheel. Then cut the ribbons at 6-cm (2 ½-inch) intervals so that you obtain pasta rectangles. Squeeze these rectangles in the centre using your thumb and index fingers to form a bow tie shape. Cover with a tea towel and set aside to dry for an hour.

To make the sauce, heat the oil in a heavy-based saucepan over a low heat. Fry the onion for 5 minutes, or until softened, stir well. Add the prosciutto, mix well, and sauté for 5 minutes. Then add the peas, mix, season with salt and pepper (keeping in mind that the prosciutto is quite salty) and mix. Pour in one ladle of stock and cook for 4 minutes, or until the peas are tender. Add more stock if necessary.

Cook the bow ties in plenty of boiling salted water. They are ready when they float to the surface. Remove a few at a time with a slotted spoon and place them in a large serving bowl. Stir in the butter. Pour the sauce over the pasta, sprinkle on 30 g (1 oz) of the parmesan, add a little more pepper, and toss gently and thoroughly. Sprinkle the last of the parmesan on top and serve steaming hot. **SERVES 4**

Sua maestá il pesto

His majesty the pesto

Basil seems to have originated in the Middle East and was seen as a symbol of fertility by the ancient Romans, but it found its ideal habitat in the climate and soil of Liguria. The people learnt quickly how to use it in the most noble way—as a sauce for pasta.

The great debate along the Italian Riviera is about the strength of the sauce, the amount of garlic used and the sharpness of the pecorino. Near the Tuscan border (where I come from), it is quite mild, using little garlic and small basil leaves, and it is traditionally served with a hard wheat pasta, such as *trenette* or spaghetti, and green beans and potatoes.

Other types of pasta that work with pesto include *troffie* (little twists of wheat and chestnut flour, without egg); *mandilli de sea* (silk handkerchiefs—very fine fresh rag pasta) and *gnocchi* (potato dumplings).

The purists may insist on using a stone mortar and a wooden pestle, but today almost everybody uses a blender. The purists assert that when using the mortar and pestle the basil leaves are crushed to release maximum flavour, whereas with the blender, the cutting of the leaves closes up their capillaries and impedes the release of their full aroma.

I prefer the mortar but the blender works perfectly well, as long as you don't let it overheat the oil, as this ruins the flavour of the basil. So minimum blender speed and frequent pauses for cooling are necessary.

And remember that pesto is a sauce used only *a crudo*, that is, not cooked, so when you add the sauce to the pasta, it must be done off the heat.

1 garlic clove, peeled
pinch of sea salt
40 small basil leaves, carefully
 washed and patted dry
1 tbsp pine nuts
2 tbsp freshly grated
 parmesan cheese

1 tbsp freshly grated mild
 Sardinian pecorino
6 tbsp extra virgin olive oil,
 or as much as needed to give
 the required consistency

MORTAR AND PESTLE METHOD

Place the garlic, salt (which helps to keep the basil green) and basil leaves in the mortar and start crushing with the pestle. You're not pounding but pressing the pestle around the sides in a rotary motion so the ingredients melt smoothly together. Add the pine nuts (raw, not toasted) and the two cheeses and keep pressing until everything is blended to a paste. Transfer to a larger bowl and add the oil, mixing with a wooden spoon.

BLENDER METHOD

Place all of the ingredients in a blender, and process on the lowest speed with intermittent pulsing until the sauce is creamy, and transfer to a bowl.

If you're not using the sauce immediately, pour a layer of olive oil over the sauce to prevent discolouration. **MAKES ENOUGH SAUCE TO DRESS 400 G (13 OZ) PASTA**

Mandilli de saea con pesto

Silk handkerchief pasta with pesto sauce

FOR THE PASTA
400 g (13 oz) plain (all
  purpose) flour
pinch of salt
2 eggs
warm water, as needed

FOR THE COOKING OF THE PASTA
water
pinch of salt
1 tsp olive oil
Pesto sauce, see page 170
freshly grated parmesan cheese,
  to serve

Make the pasta as per the recipe for Basic dough on page 146, but when you roll out the dough make it into very, very thin sheets (hence the name). This will be easier if the dough is divided into four balls instead of two. Cut your sheets of pasta into 10-cm (4-inch) squares with a sharp knife (the sides of the mandilli have to be smooth).

Cover the squares with a tea towel and let them dry for half an hour. Cook the mandilli, three at a time, in plenty of boiling salted water to which you have added a splash of olive oil. Scoop out one at a time with a slotted spoon, being careful not to break them. Arrange delicately in a serving dish in layers of 2 or 3 mandilli. Add some of the pesto sauce then another layer of pasta, then sauce. Finish with a sprinkle of parmesan, and serve. Instead of pesto, you could use the tocco (ravioli meat sauce) on page 150. **SERVES 4**

Trenette al pesto con fagiolini e patate

Trenette with pesto, potato and green beans

This recipe is not just pasta with sauce—it's a meal in itself, because you cook the vegetables with the pasta. It's as vegetarian as anybody could ask.

Remember that pesto is a sauce used only *a crudo*, that is, not cooked, so when you add it to the pasta it must be done off the heat.

3 litres (96 fl oz) water
1 large waxy potato, such as
  desiree, peeled and diced
300 g (10 oz) green beans,
  sliced
400 g (13 oz) *trenette* pasta
  (or linguini if you can't
  find *trenette*)

Pesto sauce, see page 170
1 knob butter
freshly grated parmesan
  cheese, to serve

Bring the water to the boil in a large saucepan. Throw in the potatoes and cook for 5 minutes. Add the beans and pasta and cook for 7 minutes. Strain the pasta, beans and potatoes, and reserve 2 tablespoons of the cooking water.

Put half of the pesto in a large bowl. Add the reserved water, the pasta, beans, potatoes and butter, and toss well to coat. Spoon the rest of the pesto on top, sprinkle on some parmesan, and serve immediately. **SERVES 4**

Trofie di farina di castagne al pesto di Castelnuovo

Pasta twists with basil and walnut sauce

Trofie is a classic pasta of the Riviera di Levante, originating in the town of Recco, near Genoa. It can be made with just wheat flour but the original recipe has chestnut flour as well, giving it a slightly sweet flavour.

Trofie twists are not difficult to make, but it does take a little practice and patience to give this pasta its spiral shape. The trofie are usually served with pesto or walnut sauce and sometimes they are accompanied (that is, cooked together with, before dressing) zucchini (courgettes), cannellini beans or green beans and potatoes.

We suggest tossing them with the version of pesto made in the village of Castelnuovo Magra which is at the opposite end of the Levante from Recco. It's very different from the versions made closer to Genoa. Walnuts are used instead of pine nuts and the villagers add marjoram and parsley. It is a perfect match for the chestnut flavour.

FOR THE PASTA
200 g (6½ oz) chestnut flour
200 g (6½ oz) plain
  (all purpose) flour
pinch of sea salt
45 ml (1½ fl oz) water

FOR THE SAUCE
30 g (1 oz) walnuts,
  roughly chopped

1 garlic clove, peeled
1 small handful flat-leaf parsley
  leaves, finely chopped
1 small handful basil leaves
1 tbsp marjoram leaves
75 g (2½ oz) freshly grated mild
  pecorino cheese
90 ml (3 fl oz) olive oil

To make the pasta, combine the two flours in a bowl with the salt, then, adding a few drops of water at a time, work with your hands until you have a firm dough. Leave the dough in a ball to rest for 30 minutes. Then you can start making your trofie. Tear off little pieces of dough the size of a chickpea and with your index and middle fingers quickly roll them backwards and forwards on a floured surface, so that they develop a spiral shape. When finished let the trofie dry on a floured surface for 30 minutes.

To make the sauce, place the walnuts in a mortar and start pounding with a pestle. Add the garlic, parsley, basil and marjoram. Pound everything really well, and add the pecorino a bit at a time. If using a blender, process all ingredients on the lowest speed with intermittent pulsing until the sauce is creamy.

When you obtain a smooth paste, add the olive oil, and mix well with a wooden spoon to amalgamate all the ingredients.

Add a splash of olive oil to a large saucepan of boiling salted water, add the trofie and cook for 3–4 minutes. They are ready when they float to the surface. Drain, place in a bowl and toss gently with the pesto of Castelnuovo and serve immediately. Serve with extra grated pecorino, or if you prefer, with a sprinkle of parmesan. **SERVES 4**

Corzetti

Medal pasta with green beans and tomato

There are two types of *corzetti* in Liguria. In the Riviera di Ponente, near France, the pasta is made into little balls the size of borlotti beans and is flattened between the thumb and index finger so that they take the shape of a figure eight. They are then left to dry before cooking.

In the Riveria di Levante, where they are also called *corsetti* or *croxetti* or *cruset*, they are made into a medallion shape. The sheet of pasta is flattened to 3 mm (⅛ inch) thick, cut and stamped with a special wooden utensil—if the utensil is not available a glass is used to cut the pasta into discs which are then 'signed' in the middle with a thumb or a cross. The wooden stamps were once engraved with the coat of arms of the noble families. There were many artisans carving these stamps by hand.

Corzetti are dressed typically with extra virgin olive oil, pine nuts and herbs; a runny pesto; tomato and basil; sometimes with a meat sauce (*tocco di carne*); and occasionally with seafood and pesto, as in the picture on the opposite page.

We make our *corzetti* medallions plain and smooth. Feel free to put your own imprint on them.

FOR THE PASTA
300 g (10 oz) plain
  (all purpose) flour
sea salt
2 eggs
45 ml (1½ fl oz) water

FOR THE SAUCE
60 ml (2 fl oz) olive oil
2 anchovy fillets
1 garlic clove, finely chopped

1 tbsp mixed herbs, such as
  oregano, thyme, marjoram,
  finely chopped
3 tomatoes, peeled, seeded
  and diced
150 g (5 oz) green beans,
  halved and cut into julienne
45 g (1½ oz) freshly grated
  parmesan cheese
sea salt

Prepare the pasta dough and make the sheets as thin as possible (see page 146). Then press a strong glass or a biscuit cutter 6 cm (2½ inches) in diameter into the dough and cut out the discs. Spread them out to dry on a floured board for about 30 minutes.

In the meantime, prepare the sauce. Heat the oil in a heavy-based saucepan over a low heat. Melt the anchovies into the oil by pressing them with a wooden spoon. Add the garlic and fry for 1 minute (you want to leave a bit of the raw taste in this sauce). Add the herbs, mix and cook for 30 seconds. Add the tomatoes, season with salt, mix through to flavour and cook for 5 minutes on medium heat, mixing frequently.

Bring a large saucepan of salted water to the boil, add a splash of oil and the green beans. Cook for 6 minutes, then add the *corzetti* and cook them for another 2–3 minutes. Drain and place the *corzetti* and green beans in a large bowl. Pour the sauce on top, mix delicately, sprinkle with the parmesan, mix again and serve immediately. **SERVES 4**

Opposite: Medal pasta with pesto.

Tagliolini ai Calamari
Ribbon pasta with calamari and chilli

As with all simple recipes this requires quality ingredients and fine execution. For this dish we decided to cut the pasta with the machine as the *tagliolini* are very thin and they have to have a square shape. But if you don't have a pasta machine you could slice a sheet of pasta into the finest ribbons you can manage. Or you could make the classic Ligurian pasta called *piccagge*, which is a ribbon with one straight edge and one crinkly edge, by alternating knife and pasta-cutting wheel.

The oven-fried bread is a very Ligurian ingredient and gives a pleasant crunchiness. It is important that in this preparation you do not use bought breadcrumbs!

FOR THE PASTA
300 g (10 oz) plain
 (all purpose) flour
pinch of sea salt
2 eggs
45 ml (1½ fl oz) water

FOR THE SAUCE
1 loaf Italian bread (½ if large)
75 ml (2½ fl oz) olive oil

2 garlic cloves, finely chopped
500 g (1 lb) fresh small
 calamari, cleaned, washed
 and cut into rings
sea salt and freshly ground
 black pepper
60 ml (2 fl oz) white wine
3 large red chillies, thinly sliced
15 small basil leaves, roughly
 chopped

Prepare the pasta dough as described in the Basic dough recipe on page 146, and divide it into four balls.

While the dough is resting, prepare your bread pieces. Preheat the oven to 180°C (350°F/gas 4). Cut the crust off the bread, leaving a bit of the soft part attached. Dice the crust and place on a baking tray, sprinkle on some olive oil and about one-third of the garlic. Place in the hot oven, turning the bread and shaking the tray two or three times so the bread browns on all sides, for 30 minutes or until golden brown. Cool a little, then place the bread on a tea towel, place another tea towel on top and crush the bread with your hands. Set aside.

Place the pasta machine on a workbench. Sprinkle flour onto the bench in front of the pasta machine. Set the rollers to the widest spacing. Flatten each ball of dough with the palm of your hand. Run the dough through the pasta machine three or four times, folding in half and turning each time. Then, reducing the pasta machine setting, one notch at a time, continue feeding the pasta sheet through the rollers until you reach the desired thinness, in this case about 3 mm (⅛ inch).

Place each sheet of dough on a tea towel, and leave to dry for about 10 minutes. Attach the ribbon cutters to the pasta machine and feed the sheets through to give the desired shape. Separate and spread the *tagliolini* to dry on a tea towel for 20 minutes.

In the meantime, prepare the sauce. Heat the oil in a heavy-based saucepan over a low heat. Add the remaining garlic and fry for 2 minutes, mixing with a wooden spoon. Add the calamari, increase the heat to medium-high and cook for 5 minutes. Season with salt and pepper. Add the wine, mix and reduce for 3 minutes. Mix in the chillies, and cook for 8 minutes, so the calamari becomes tender and coated with specks of chilli.

Cook the *tagliolini* in plenty of boiling salted water, with a splash of olive oil added, for 2 minutes. Drain, combine with the sauce in the pan, sprinkle with 4 tablespoons of the bread pieces and the basil, and toss gently.

Should the sauce seem too dry, add a splash of olive oil and a few spoonfuls of the cooking water. Serve on individual plates with a sprinkle of the bread pieces. **SERVES 4**

VARIATION

To make this dish even more Ligurian you can add 20 g (¾ oz) of pine nuts at the same time as the chillies and 45 g (1½ oz) of pitted and chopped small black olives in the last 5 minutes.

Gnocchi verdi ai battibá

Spinach gnocchi with Balmain bug

The small lobster known as *battibá* in Liguria (because batti-batti is the sound it makes when it wriggles in the bottom of the boat) is similar to the crustaceans called Balmain bug and Moreton Bay bug in Australia. The meat from any of them makes an elegant accompaniment for gnocchi.

FOR THE GNOCCHI
1 kg (2 lb) desiree potatoes, scrubbed
1 bunch English spinach
250 g (8 oz) plain (all purpose) flour
1 egg
pinch of sea salt

FOR THE BATTIBÀ SAUCE
3 large Balmain bugs
½ white onion, cut in half
1 small carrot, cut in half
1 celery stalk, cut in half
1 bay leaf

60 ml (2 fl oz) olive oil
1 garlic clove, crushed a little with the blade of a knife
1 leek, trimmed to just the yellow centre and thinly sliced
1 tbsp chopped marjoram leaves
30 ml (1 fl oz) dry white wine
sea salt and freshly ground black pepper
8 small zucchini (courgettes), with flowers attached (when in season)
45 g (1½ oz) freshly grated parmesan cheese

To make the gnocchi, place the potatoes in a saucepan of salted cold water. Bring to the boil, reduce heat and cook gently until just soft. Drain and when cool enough to handle, peel. Return them to the pan and mash.

While the potatoes are cooking, clean and wash the spinach, place in a saucepan with just the residual water, and cook until wilted. Squeeze out as much water as possible, place on a chopping board, chop finely and set aside.

To make good gnocchi, you should start with mash that is very dry, otherwise you need too much flour and the gnocchi become rubbery and heavy. Place the potato mash over a low heat and stir constantly for about 3 minutes, until it doesn't stick to the side of the pan. Cool the mash and transfer to a floured work bench. Mix in the flour, egg, spinach and salt, and knead until the dough is smooth and slightly sticky to the touch.

Keeping your hands and the work surface well floured, tear off small pieces of the dough and roll into cylinders the thickness of a finger (the length does not matter). Cut these cylinders into 2-cm (¾-inch) pieces. When they are all done, press each *gnoccho* with your index finger to make the centres of the gnocchi thinner. Place in a single layer, without touching each other, on a floured tray until you are ready to cook them.

To make the *battibà* sauce, first make a stock. Detach the heads from the bugs, put the heads in a saucepan and squash them with a wooden spoon. Add the onion, carrot, celery and bay leaf. Cover with water (do not add salt) and simmer for 20 minutes. Strain through a fine sieve and set aside.

Shell the bug tails so you are left with only the meat. Cut into pieces the same size as the gnocchi and set aside.

Put a large saucepan of salted water on to boil so you can quickly cook the gnocchi when the sauce is almost complete.

Heat the oil in a heavy-based frying pan over a low heat. Add the garlic and gently fry for 2 minutes, stirring constantly with a wooden spoon to flavour the oil, until a light golden colour. Remove the garlic and discard.

Add the leek slices and sauté gently for 5 minutes. Add the bug meat, mix delicately, add the marjoram and wine, and season with salt and pepper. Add the zucchini, delicately mix again and cook for 4 minutes. Add 2 tablespoons (1½ fl oz) of the reserved stock, mix well and cook for another 2 minutes then remove from the heat.

Cook the gnocchi in the saucepan of boiling salted water—until they float to the surface. Allow to float for about 10 seconds, then remove with a slotted spoon. Place the gnocchi into the pan with the *battibá*, put it back on low heat and toss gently for 1 minute to mix the gnocchi with the sauce. Pour into a large bowl and serve. **SERVES 4**

Conchiglioni con muscoli
Shell pasta with mussels

Now we move from the homemade pasta, which is most common in Liguria, to bought dried pasta. Ligurians believe dried pasta, like spaghetti and *conchiglioni* (cooked only long enough to be *al dente*), works best with seafood sauces, because of the texture contrasts. We are not going to argue.

100 ml (3½ fl oz) extra virgin
  olive oil
1 small onion, finely chopped
1 small celery stalk,
  finely chopped
1 small carrot, finely chopped
500 g (1 lb) tinned Italian
  tomatoes
sea salt and freshly ground
  black pepper

1.5 kg (3 lb) black mussels,
  scrubbed and de-bearded
1 garlic clove, lightly crushed
  with the blade of a knife
20 ml (¾ fl oz) dry white wine
a few marjoram and thyme leaves
350 g (11 oz) shell-shaped pasta
1 handful chopped flat-leaf
  parsley

Heat half the olive oil in a heavy-based saucepan over a low heat. Add the onion, celery and carrot and sauté until the onion starts to colour, about 5 minutes. Add the tomatoes, season with salt and pepper, stir, and cook for about 30 minutes. If possible, pass the mixture through a mouli or puree briefly in a blender. Transfer to a bowl.

Place the mussels in a large saucepan over a high heat (the larger the pan the more even the opening process). As soon as each mussel opens, remove it to a bowl. Strain the mussel liquid into a bowl and keep to one side. Remove the mussels from the now cooled shells and roughly chop half of them, keeping the rest whole.

Heat the remaining oil in the mussel pan, over a low heat. Add the garlic and simmer for about 1 minute, being careful not to burn it. Remove and discard the garlic. Add all the mussels, sprinkle on the white wine and let it evaporate. Add 3 tablespoons of the mussel liquid and the tomato puree. Stir in the thyme and marjoram, and season to taste.

Meanwhile cook the pasta in plenty of boiling salted water for 1 minute less than the packet recommends. Drain, add the pasta to the mussel mixture in the pan and stir gently for 1 minute.

Sprinkle with the parsley and serve immediately. **SERVES 4**

Spaghetti a freddo

Spaghetti with a cold tomato dressing

3 large tomatoes, peeled, seeded and diced
12 black olives, pitted and chopped
12 green olives, pitted and chopped
1 tbsp salted capers, rinsed and dried
6 marinated anchovy fillets, finely chopped
90 ml (3 fl oz) olive oil
2 garlic cloves, finely chopped
1 tbsp white wine vinegar
2 sprigs oregano, leaves picked
2 sprigs marjoram, leaves picked
2 sprigs thyme, leaves picked
10 basil leaves, finely chopped
sea salt and freshly ground black pepper
500 g (1 lb) spaghetti

Put the oil into a large bowl that later will hold the pasta. Add all the ingredients except the spaghetti, and season with salt and pepper. Mix well and rest for about 30 minutes.

In the meantime, cook the spaghetti in plenty of boiling salted water, following the cooking time recommended on the packet. Drain when *al dente* and toss in the bowl with the marinade. Serve immediately. **SERVES 4**

Spaghetti allo scoglio
Spaghetti reef style

The word *scoglio* means the rocks along the shoreline.

The details that make this recipe outstanding are: first, the seafood is cooked without tomato, unlike many so-called 'marinara' sauces; secondly, the different cooking times of the various seafood are important to preserve flavour; thirdly, the spaghetti is crucial for texture, so buy an imported Italian version and cook it *al dente*; and finally, the quality of the olive oil is vital, so try to use mild Ligurian, as the southern oils are too strong.

500 g (1 lb) *vongole* (clams)
500 g (1 lb) mussels, scrubbed
  and de-bearded
200 g (6½ oz) baby calamari
60 ml (2 fl oz) dry white wine
90 ml (3 fl oz) olive oil
2 garlic cloves, finely chopped
2 small red chillies, finely
  chopped

8 green medium prawns
  (shrimp), peeled and deveined
  with heads and tails intact
4 medium scampi, cut in half
500 g (1 lb) spaghetti
1 handful flat-leaf parsley,
  finely chopped

Soak the *vongole* in fresh water to filter out any sand. Drain and set aside with the mussels.

For the calamari, separate the tentacles from the body by holding the body in one hand and pulling away the tentacles with the other. Cut the tentacles straight across below the eyes and discard everything from the eyes up. Squeeze out the bony beak and cut the tentacles in two. Remove and discard the bone and everything else from the hood and wash under running water. Peel off the skin under running water and cut the body into thin rings. Wash the rings and the tentacles one more time under running water, pat dry with paper towel and set aside.

Place the mussels and *vongole* in a heavy-based pan over a high heat. Add the white wine and cook until the shells open. Remove from the pan one at a time as soon as they open. Strain the cooking liquid into a large bowl and reserve. Remove the mussel and *vongole* meat from the shells, leaving some in the shell for presentation, and return to the cooking liquid so they don't dry out.

Heat the oil in the same pan over a low heat. Add the garlic and chillies and sauté for 3 minutes. Add the calamari and cook for another 5 minutes. Add the prawns and scampi. Detach the prawn heads and squash them into the pan to release the flavour. Cook for 3 minutes, then add all the mussels and *vongole* with 4 tablespoons of their cooking liquid and cook for a further 3 minutes, mixing well to combine all the flavours. Remove the prawn heads and discard.

Cook the spaghetti until *al dente* in plenty of boiling salted water. Drain and add to the sauce. Sprinkle on the parsley, toss gently and serve immediately. **SERVES 4**

Spaghetti acciughe e basilico

Spaghetti with anchovies and basil

This is the Ligurian version of the classic *Spaghetti aglio e olio*, which serves as a speedy late-night snack and hangover cure. Liguria's cooking is all about oil, garlic and herbs. We find here, with the addition of anchovies, that the basil and oregano replace the parsley used all over Italy for the same dish.

You have to work quickly with this one. Ideally the sauce should be ready just before the spaghetti, certainly not after, because the spaghetti must be eaten as soon as it's cooked.

4 salted anchovies
500 g (1 lb) spaghetti
90 ml (3 fl oz) Ligurian olive oil
1 garlic clove, finely chopped
sea salt

2 sprigs oregano, leaves
  picked and chopped
10 basil leaves, finely chopped
freshly grated parmesan cheese,
  if desired

Clean and fillet the anchovies. Wash well under running water and chop into little pieces. Set aside.

While you are cooking the spaghetti in plenty of boiling salted water, prepare the sauce.

Heat the oil in a large frying pan over a low heat. Add the garlic and fry for about 1 minute, or until fragrant. Add the anchovies and a pinch of salt. Squash the anchovies with a fork until they melt into the oil, mix well with a wooden spoon and cook for another minute or so. Add the oregano and stir.

When the spaghetti is cooked *come Dio comanda* (as God intended, that is, *al dente*), drain and tip immediately into the pan with the sauce. Toss briefly over the heat to coat all the strands and turn out into a large serving bowl. Sprinkle the basil on top, toss again and serve. **SERVES 4**

Spaghetti ai muscoli e vongole

Spaghetti with mussels and clams

400 g (13 oz) mussels,
   scrubbed and de-bearded
400 g (13 oz) *vongole* (clams),
   scrubbed
30 ml (1 fl oz) dry white wine
90 ml (3 fl oz) olive oil
2 garlic cloves, finely chopped

1 tbsp chopped oregano leaves
3 large tomatoes, peeled, seeded
   and diced
freshly ground black pepper
500 g (1 lb) spaghetti
1 handful flat-leaf parsley leaves,
   finely chopped

Combine the mussels, *vongole* and wine in a heavy-based saucepan over a medium-high heat. Cook until the shells open. Remove them from the pan as soon as they do so. Strain the cooking liquid and pour into a large bowl. Take half of the *vongole* and all but 8 of the mussels out of their shells.

Heat the oil in the same pan over a low heat. Add the garlic and sauté for 2 minutes, mixing well with a wooden spoon. Add the mussels, *vongole*, oregano and 2 or 3 tablespoons (1½–2 fl oz) of the reserved liquid, stir, and cook for 2 minutes. Add the tomatoes and some pepper to taste (you should not need any salt), mix thoroughly and cook for 5 minutes.

In the meantime, cook the spaghetti until *al dente* in a large saucepan of boiling salted water. Drain and add to the sauce. Sprinkle with parsley and toss vigorously, adding a little more of the reserved liquid if necessary. Serve immediately. **SERVES 4**

Risotto al radicchio e basilico

Radicchio and basil risotto

1 litre (32 fl oz) white veal
   (or vegetable) stock
60 g (2 oz) butter, diced
2 onions, finely chopped
300 g (10 oz) arborio rice

1 radicchio, washed and thinly
   sliced
½ bunch basil, finely sliced
150 g (5 oz) freshly grated
   parmesan cheese

Heat the stock in a saucepan over a low heat and keep at a simmer.

Melt half the butter in a large heavy-based saucepan over a low heat. Add the onions and cook for 3–5 minutes, or until translucent. Add the rice to the onions and stir for at least 3 minutes to ensure all the grains are coated. Increase the heat slightly and add just enough of the simmering stock to cover the rice. Stir the rice with a wooden spoon until all the stock is absorbed. Add more of the simmering stock and stir until absorbed. Repeat this process for 15–18 minutes, or until all of the stock has been absorbed by the rice.

Add the radicchio and basil, leave to wilt for 1 minute then add the remaining butter and the parmesan. Stir vigorously to incorporate and serve immediately. **SERVES 4**

Risotto allo zafferano e fiori

Saffron and zucchini-flower risotto

30 zucchini (courgette) flowers
1 litre (32 fl oz) chicken (or
  vegetable) stock
60 g (2 oz) butter diced
2 onions, finely chopped
½ tsp saffron threads
300 g (10 oz) arborio rice
150 g (5 oz) freshly grated
  parmesan cheese

Remove and discard the stigma and stems from the zucchini flowers. Chop the flowers roughly.

Pour the stock into a saucepan, bring to the boil, reduce heat to low and keep at a simmer.

Melt half the butter in a large heavy-based saucepan. Add the onions and cook over a low heat for 3–5 minutes, or until translucent. Add the saffron and rice, and stir for at least 3 minutes to ensure all the rice is coated. Increase the heat slightly and add just enough of the simmering stock to cover the rice. Stir the rice with a wooden spoon until all the stock is absorbed. Add more of the simmering stock and stir again until absorbed. Repeat this process for 15–18 minutes until all the stock has been absorbed by the rice, which is now a wonderful yellow colour from the saffron and still a little *al dente*. Add the zucchini flowers and leave to wilt for 1 minute. Remove the risotto from the heat, add the remaining butter and the parmesan, and mix vigorously. (This last step of risotto making is called *mantecare* and is what gives the risotto its luscious creaminess.)

Serve immediately. **SERVES 4**

Pesce

Seafood

Seafood

It's natural to assume that seafood has always been central to the cooking of the Riviera, but that wasn't entirely true. Yes, the ocean provided a livelihood for the majority of the population, who worked on cruise ships, trading vessels or fishing boats, but most of them couldn't afford to eat the best of the bounty caught off their shore. Until the 1970s the most luscious seafood went to wealthier parts of Europe, and only the smallest and ugliest creatures stayed to be eaten where they were caught.

As Ligurians grew richer in recent decades, they've come to experience the full range of seafood that lay at the end of their lines. The newfound wealth of the coast dwellers is symbolised in the renaissance of one extraordinary dish—*cappon magro*, and that is how we begin this chapter. We should say right away that we don't expect you to cook this every week. Or even every month.

Yes, it is over the top—as much a work of architecture as of gastronomy—because it's the food of festivity, to be consumed once a year, at most. *Cappon magro*, theoretically a seafood salad, is actually the most fantastic and monumental creation of Italian cooking, harmoniously combining the produce of the sea with all the colours, flavours and aromas of the land.

Its origin is probably from the more modest dish the sailors called *capponada* (see page 268 for the recipe)—gradually enriched over time. But of course there are those who think the opposite—that the *capponada* comes from the *cappon magro*. One legend suggests this dish was invented by the wives of sailors leaving for a long trip, so they would remember them.

There is some debate about the origin of the name as well. Some say it comes from the main ingredient—a fish called *cappone*, and because there is no meat, it is *magro* (lean). Others say that, being a Christmas dish, it takes its name from the rooster (*capon*) that would be eaten in regions further inland.

Some of the ingredients are difficult to get—like the hard ships' biscuits called *gallette*. It is a long preparation—maybe a full day for one person plus the shopping time. It would be fun to build a Sunday lunch party for eight people around it, involving your guests in the cooking and construction, and maybe even the shopping.

Don't be put off by the enormity of preparing *cappon magro*. The recipes become a lot simpler from then on, as we deconstruct the bounty of Liguria.

Cappon magro
Seafood pyramid

One element of the traditional *Cappon magro*, as recently as the 1950s, was *mosciame*—dried fillets of dolphin. The dolphins used to play in the wakes of the fishing boats, and the fishermen saw no reason to treat them differently from any other fish.

Nowadays dolphin has been replaced by tuna. The fishermen select the biggest tuna, cut out the fillets and put them under salt. After 24 hours the fillets are washed and hung to dry in well-ventilated places and moulded by hand every day for 15 days to achieve the classic cylinder shape. We don't recommend attempting that—there are serious health risks for the amateur *mosciame* maker. In the recipe we recommend seared tuna instead.

Bear in mind that the quantities we give here are approximate. This is not a chemistry experiment, where a small deviation ruins the whole thing, it's a construction, according to your taste. So if you feel like putting in 15 *vongole* (clams) and 9 oysters and 7 slices of Italian bread, go for it.

FOR THE SAUCE
1 thick slice Italian bread,
  crusts removed
45 ml (1½ fl oz) white wine
  vinegar, to soak the bread
1 bunch flat-leaf parsley,
  roughly chopped
2 garlic cloves
20 g (¾ oz) pine nuts
30 g (1 oz) salted capers,
  rinsed and dried
2 hard-boiled egg yolks
4 anchovy fillets marinated in oil
8 green olives
sea salt
125 ml (4 fl oz) olive oil

FOR THE SEAFOOD
6 slices Italian bread
sea salt
1 garlic glove, cut in half
300 g (10 oz) sashimi-grade tuna,
  cut into 5-mm (¼-inch) thick slices
olive oil
1 small carrot, peeled
1 celery stalk
1 white onion, cut in half
20 ml (½ fl oz) white wine vinegar
8 peppercorns
1.5 kg (3 lb) whole snapper,
  cleaned and gutted

lemon juice
1–1.5 kg (2–3 lb) lobster
8 green king prawns (shrimp)
8 scampi
16 mussels, scrubbed and de-bearded
16 *vongole* (clams), scrubbed
8 oysters on the half shell

FOR THE VEGETABLES
300 g (10 oz) green beans, trimmed
  and cut into 5-cm (2-inch) pieces
1 small cauliflower, cut into florets
6 small globe artichokes, trimmed
  and quartered (see page 130)
2 medium potatoes, peeled
  and cut into 2-cm (¾-inch) thick
  slices
2 carrots, peeled and cut into julienne
2 celery hearts, cut into julienne
8 baby beetroot

FOR THE GARNISH
8 black olives
8 green olives
8 anchovy fillets
4 hard-boiled eggs, peeled
  and quartered
16 marinated champignon
  mushrooms

Opposite, top: toast and mosciame. Bottom: ingredients.

To make the sauce, soak the bread in half the vinegar, then squeeze dry. Place the bread, parsley, garlic, pine nuts, capers, egg yolks, anchovies and olives in a mortar or blender, and pound or pulse until everything is combined. Add the remaining vinegar and a generous pinch of salt and mix well. Transfer this mixture to a bowl and slowly add the olive oil, while stirring with a wooden spoon. The sauce should not be too runny, because it partly serves to hold the ingredients together. Set aside until you are ready to use it.

To prepare the seafood, season the bread with salt and toast it, rub it with garlic and let it get cold so it hardens.

Brush both sides of the tuna with a little olive oil and sprinkle with salt. Heat a non-stick frying pan over a high heat, add the tuna and sear for 30 seconds on each side. Thinly slice and set aside.

To cook the seafood, fill a large saucepan with water, add the carrot, celery, onion, vinegar and peppercorns. Bring to the boil, add the snapper and poach for 15–20 minutes. Lift out the fish, keeping the water in the pan; the flesh should be falling away from the bone. Skin and carefully debone the fish. Break up into small pieces and dress while still warm with some olive oil and a squeeze of lemon juice. Set aside.

In the same pan, boil the lobster for 10 minutes. Lift out, remove the shell and slice the flesh into medallions. Reserve the head if you want to use it to garnish. Set aside.

… Recipe continued on page 200

In the same water, still over a high heat, immerse the prawns and scampi and simmer for 3 minutes. Drain and shell, leaving the heads and tails intact, and dress with a little olive oil and lemon juice. Set aside.

In a large saucepan over a medium heat, combine the mussels and *vongole*, and as soon as they open, remove from the heat (one by one if necessary). Snap off the top shells and discard. Place the mussels and *vongole* in their half shells in a large dish and cover with the liquid they released during cooking, so they do not dry out.

To cook the vegetables, simmer each vegetable separately in salted water until tender. Leave the beetroot until last if using the same pot. Keeping each vegetable separate, dress with a little olive oil and lemon juice and a pinch of salt, and set aside.

Now we are ready to start building the *cappon magro*. It has been a long time since we started this recipe, so let's double check that we have all the ingredients in separate containers in front of us on our work bench: the sauce, the seafood and the garnish.

Place a large platter (big enough to hold your pyramid of food) in front of you and take a few seconds to think about the way you want to build up your *cappon magro*. Look at the ingredients, look at the platter, and try to picture in your mind the end result.

Make each successive layer a bit smaller than the one beneath so you can see what is in each layer. Prepare the base by placing the toasted bread, one slice next to the other, on the platter. Sprinkle some olive oil and vinegar on top. Cover the bread with the tuna slices, and spread some of the sauce over the tuna. Now make a layer of one of the vegetables (cauliflower is a good start) and on top of that add a layer of snapper.

Spread some sauce on top of the snapper and top with a different type of vegetable. Continue with the layers, alternating vegetables and fish, spreading some sauce on each layer. Finish the pyramid with a layer of lobster.

Garnish the top and sides with the scampi.

Garnish the base of the pyramid with the oysters, mussels, *vongole*, olives, egg quarters and anchovies. Spread some more sauce on the walls of the *cappon magro*.

Now to finish take 8 wooden skewers and on each one thread as follows: champignon, prawn, champignon. Plant the skewers carefully into the centre of the *cappon magro*, making sure they are secure.

Serve this amazing multi-coloured tower in the middle of the table and take a photo to remember the occasion. Enjoy it with your family and friends and you will understand why we call *cappon magro* 'the king of conviviality'. **SERVES 6–8**

Pesce in crosta di mandorle

Almond-crusted fish fillets

The beauty of this dish is that, having scaled the fish, you then replace the silver scales with golden ones made of almond flakes. It looks great, it has interesting texture contrasts of crunchy and slippery, and the flavours are dramatic—nutty, fishy and aniseedy.

4 x 150 g (5 oz) fillets
  blue-eye trevalla (or other
  meaty fish), skin on

FOR THE CRUST
45 g (1½ oz) butter
1 onion, finely chopped
1 garlic clove, finely chopped
1 tbsp chopped thyme leaves
200 g (6½ oz) flaked almonds,
  toasted
1 egg

FOR THE BASE
1 celeriac, peeled and
  thinly sliced
½ handful dill
½ handful fennel fronds
75 ml (2½ fl oz) olive oil
15 ml (½ fl oz) lemon juice

To make the crust, melt the butter in a saucepan over a medium heat, add the onion and sizzle for 2 minutes. Add the garlic and simmer for another 2 minutes. Add the thyme and cook for 1 minute. Crush two-thirds of the almonds and toss into the pan. Remove the pan immediately from the heat and when the mixture is cool, add the egg and mix well.

Place the blue-eye, skin-side up, on a chopping board. Remove skin and pat a thin layer of the nut mixture on the surface. Place the remaining almonds on top in a scale pattern.

Preheat the oven to 180°C (350°F/gas 4). Splash a little oil into a baking dish, add the blue-eye, and bake in the oven for 10 minutes.

Toss the celeriac with the dill and fennel and arrange on four plates. Whisk the oil and lemon juice until emulsified. Splash a little of this dressing on the celeriac. Place a piece of blue-eye on top of the celeriac and serve immediately. **SERVES 4**

Tagliata di tonno in crosta d'erbe con salsa verde

Herb-crusted tuna with salsa verde

People from the Middle East were frequent visitors to the Riviera over the centuries, once bringing weapons to obtain what they wanted, more recently bringing money. In return, we've borrowed a classic Middle Eastern mixture—*chermoulah*—to coat our tuna in this recipe.

600 g (1 lb 3½ oz)
  tuna fillet

FOR THE BASE
300 g (10 oz) dried
  cannellini beans
1 onion, cut in half
3 bay leaves
1 celery stalk, cut in half
4 baby leeks,
  trimmed
2 red capsicums
  (bell peppers), roasted
  (see page 295)
  and cut into strips
45 ml (1½ fl oz) olive oil
juice of ½ lemon
sea salt and freshly
  ground black pepper

FOR THE SALSA VERDE
20 g (¾ oz) pine nuts
2 or 3 anchovy fillets

1 bunch flat-leaf parsley,
  leaves picked
75 ml (2½ fl oz) olive oil
45 ml (1½ fl oz) white
  wine vinegar
20 g (¾ oz) salted capers,
  rinsed and dried

FOR THE HERB CRUST
1 tbsp ground cumin
1 tbsp ground coriander
½ tbsp dried chilli flakes
1 tbsp sweet paprika
2 garlic cloves, peeled
½ red onion, roughly chopped
juice of ½ lemon
60 ml (2 fl oz) extra
  virgin olive oil
1 bunch flat-leaf parsley,
  leaves picked and chopped
1 bunch basil, leaves
  picked and chopped
45 g (1½ oz) breadcrumbs

To make the base, soak the beans in cold water for 12 hours. Drain and place in a saucepan of fresh cold water. Add the onion, bay leaves and celery, and bring to the boil. Reduce heat to low and simmer for 45 minutes. Strain and place the beans in a bowl. Set them aside. Boil the leeks in salted water for 3 minutes. Drain and set aside. Add the strips of roasted capsicum to the cannellini beans. Pour on the olive oil and lemon juice, sprinkle with salt and ground pepper, and mix thoroughly with a wooden spoon.

To make the salsa verde, combine the pine nuts, anchovies and parsley in a blender, pulse to mix well, then add the oil, vinegar and capers and pulse—it should not be too fine. This salsa will keep for 1 week in the refrigerator if stored, covered by a little more oil, in a glass container.

To make the herb crust, toast the cumin, coriander, chilli and paprika in an oven preheated to 150°C (300°F/gas 2) for 5 minutes. Crush in a mortar, then transfer to a blender. Add the garlic, onions, lemon juice and oil, and puree for 1 minute. Add the parsley and basil and puree for

2 minutes, or until you get a coarse pesto-like consistency. Pour the mixture into a bowl, add the breadcrumbs and stir.

Press a thin layer of the herb mixture onto the tuna, completely covering it. Marinate for 15 minutes. Preheat oven to 180°C (350°F/gas 4).

Heat a large ovenproof frying pan over a medium heat, add the tuna and sear on all sides for 90 seconds. Transfer to the oven for 5 minutes. Remove.

Make a bed of bean mixture in the centre of four plates. Wind one baby leek around the base of the bean mound on each plate.

Slice the tuna into 12 portions and place 3 on each mound of beans. Spoon the salsa verde on top in any quantity you fancy. **SERVES 4**

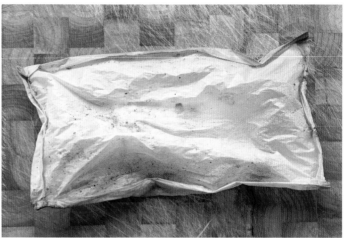
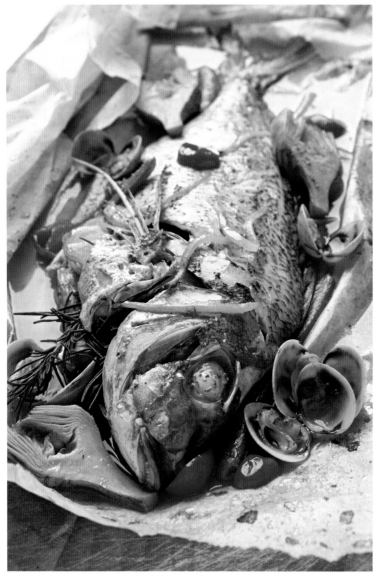

Pesce al cartoccio
Whole fish baked in parchment

This is a spectacular way to cook fish, with all the flavours trapped inside a parchment parcel where, instead of escaping, they go back into the fish. I suggest that when you serve this dish you open it at the table, so that your guests can enjoy: first, the surprise and the mystery of a closed parcel; second, the fantastic aroma that is liberated when the parcel is opened; and third your skilful filleting and composition.

1.5 (3 lb) whole snapper
  or bream
4 globe artichokes, cleaned and
  cut in half (see page 130)
90 ml (3 fl oz) olive oil
4–6 sprigs tender rosemary
½ head garlic, cut in half
sea salt

8 *vongole* (clams), rinsed
12 snow peas (mange tout),
  trimmed
8 cherry tomatoes, cut in half
zest of ½ lemon, thinly sliced
juice of ½ lemon
30 ml (1 fl oz) white wine

Wash the snapper and pat it dry with paper towel.

Bring a large saucepan of salted water to the boil, reduce heat to low, add the artichokes and simmer for 10 minutes. Drain and set aside.

Preheat the oven to 200°C (400°F/gas 6). Lay some parchment paper on an oven tray large enough to hold the fish and brush with a little of the olive oil.

Place the rosemary, garlic and some salt in the cavity of the fish and transfer to the prepared oven tray. Arrange the *vongole*, snow peas, cherry tomatoes, artichokes and the lemon zest over and around the fish.

Whisk together the remaining oil, lemon juice and wine and pour over the snapper. Place another piece of parchment paper over the top and roll the edges together to seal the fish and the juices inside. Bake in the oven for 20 minutes.

To serve, at the table, tear open the parchment, move the vegetable garnish to the side, and remove the skin by inserting the prong of a fork into the skin at the back of the head and lifting it away.

Fillet the fish at the table as follows: when the skin is removed, the bones along the top of the fish are very easy to see and can be removed by pushing them away from the fish using a spoon and fork. Slide the spoon under the top two fish fillets down the spine and lift them off and divide them between four plates. These two fillets should be completely free of bones.

Don't turn the fish over. You need to lift the spine and head of the fish away from the lower flesh and discard them, but first use a teaspoon to take out the fish cheeks—the sweetest part. Scrape off the stomach bones from the remaining fish, paying particular attention to get them all. Add the remaining flesh to the other fillets on the four plates. Distribute the vegetable garnish between the plates and spoon a little of the cooking juices over the top. **SERVES 4**

Triglie piccanti al pomodoro e basilico

Red mullet with tomato and basil

16 medium red mullet fillets
sea salt and freshly ground black
  pepper
75 ml (2½ fl oz) olive oil
1 garlic clove, thinly sliced

8 roma (plum) tomatoes,
  skinned, seeded and diced
1 tsp finely chopped red chilli
1 handful baby basil leaves

Preheat the oven to 70°C (150°F/gas ¼). Season the fillets with salt and pepper. Heat half the oil in a non-stick frying pan over a medium heat. Add the fish and pan-fry for 1 minute on each side, starting with the skin side.

Remove the fish from the pan and keep warm in the oven.

Heat the remaining oil in the clean pan over a medium heat. Add the garlic and cook, stirring occasionally, for 2 minutes. Add the tomatoes and chilli, and simmer for about 2 minutes, or until the mixture starts to thicken. Throw in the basil and cook for 1 minute. Taste and season if necessary with salt and pepper.

Arrange the fillets on the plates. Start with a layer of sauce, put two fillets on it, top them with more sauce, then top with two more fillets, skin side up. Serve immediately. **SERVES 4**

Fritto misto di mare

Fried mixed seafood

300 g (10 oz) baby calamari

300 g (10 oz) small prawns (shrimp)

2 fennel bulbs, trimmed and tough outer leaves removed

4 medium red mullet, filleted

plain (all purpose) flour, for coating the seafood

1 litre (32 fl oz) canola oil, for deep-frying

sea salt

lemon wedges, for serving

FOR THE GARLIC MAYONNAISE

2 eggs

4 egg yolks

2 tsp Dijon mustard

1 garlic clove, finely chopped

juice of 1 lemon

400 ml (13½ fl oz) olive oil

60 ml (2 fl oz) sherry vinegar

sea salt and freshly ground black pepper

60 g (2 oz) natural yoghurt

Clean and wash the calamari (see page 224). Leave the tentacles whole and cut the body into pieces. Do not peel the prawns because when they are small you can eat them whole. Slice the fennel into eighths.

Coat the seafood and fennel with the flour, shaking off the excess. Heat the canola oil to 180°C (350°F) in a heavy-based saucepan. If you don't have a thermometer, you can tell the oil is ready if it starts sizzling as soon as you drop in a piece of bread. Add the seafood and fennel, and fry in very small batches for 3–5 minutes, or until golden and floating on the surface. Remove with a slotted spoon and drain on paper towel to absorb the excess oil.

Divide the fritto between four plates, sprinkle with the salt and serve with a lemon wedge and a side bowl of garlic mayonnaise.

To make the garlic mayonnaise, whisk the eggs, egg yolks, mustard, garlic and lemon juice in a large bowl until combined. Slowly pour a thin steam of olive oil into the bowl, whisking vigorously until all the oil is incorporated. Add the vinegar and salt and pepper, and fold in the yoghurt. Place the mayonnaise in an airtight container and it will keep for up to 1 week in the fridge. **SERVES 4**

Insalata di scampi e rucola

Scampi and rocket salad

On Ligurian menus these days you'll often find lobster, scampi and prawn (shrimp) dishes described as *alla catalana*, which literally means Catalan style. They don't seem to have originated in Barcelona (the capital of Catalonia, in Spain) or any place where the Catalan language is spoken. The term has come to mean simply 'served with raw vegetables'.

It was probably invented in the Sardinian town of Alghero and quickly took over the Ligurian coast. Alghero was settled in 1354 by Catalonians, after they had defeated and then exiled the Sardinians and the Genoese.

The following two recipes are seafood salads done *alla catalana* in our interpretation. They are simple and require a mild Ligurian olive oil as dressing. The first dish can be decorated with bright orange *bottargá* (mullet roe) but you can skip this if you don't like the bitter taste.

1 onion, peeled and cut in half
2 carrots, peeled and cut in half
2 celery stalks, washed and cut into quarters
4–5 sprigs flat-leaf parsley
4–5 white peppercorns
60 ml (2 fl oz) white wine vinegar
sea salt
16 scampi

FOR THE SALAD
2 bunches baby rocket (arugula) leaves, washed and picked
juice of ½ lemon
30 ml (1 fl oz) olive oil
5 thin slices of *bottargá* per person (optional)
freshly ground white pepper

First, prepare the stock (which French chefs would call a *court-bouillon*). Fill a saucepan large enough to hold the scampi with water. Add the onion, carrots, celery, parsley, peppercorns, vinegar and salt, and bring to the boil. Reduce the heat to low and simmer for 20 minutes. Drop in the scampi and simmer for 5–6 minutes. Drain the scampi and set aside to cool. Discard the stock.

Place the rocket in a bowl and dress it with a little olive oil and salt. Shell the scampi, place the flesh in a bowl and toss lightly with the lemon juice and some olive oil.

To serve, cover four plates with the rocket, arrange the scampi on top and if using *bottargá*, add a few thin slices. Sprinkle with pepper and serve. **SERVES 4**

Scampi con insalata di pomodori

Scampi with tomato salad

1 onion, peeled and cut in half
2 carrots, peeled and cut in half
2 celery stalks, washed and cut
 into quarters
4–5 sprigs flat-leaf parsley
4–5 white peppercorns
60 ml (2 fl oz) white wine
 vinegar
sea salt
16 scampi

juice of ½ lemon
30 ml (1 fl oz) olive oil
4 large tomatoes, thinly sliced
sea salt
2 cucumbers, peeled and
 thinly sliced
1 red onion, thinly sliced
2 basil leaves, roughly chopped

First, prepare the stock (or *court-bouillon*). Fill a saucepan large enough to hold the scampi with water. Add the onion, carrots, celery, parsley, peppercorns, vinegar and salt, and bring to the boil. Reduce the heat to low and simmer for 20 minutes. Drop in the scampi and simmer for 5–6 minutes. Drain the scampi and set aside to cool. Discard the stock. Shell the scampi, place the flesh in a bowl and toss with the lemon juice and olive oil.

To serve this dish, arrange the tomatoes, overlapping a little in a circular shape, on four plates. Season with salt.

Arrange the cucumber slices on the tomatoes, and top with the onions. Scatter on the basil leaves, drizzle with a little extra olive oil and place the dressed scampi on top. **SERVES 4**

Pesce spada con purè di olive verdi

Grilled swordfish with green olive salsa

150 g (5 oz) large green olives,
 pitted and finely chopped
8 French shallots, finely
 chopped
75 ml (2½ fl oz) extra virgin
 olive oil

15 ml (½ fl oz) red wine
 vinegar
4 swordfish steaks
olive oil, for grilling
sea salt and freshly ground
 black pepper

To make the green olive salsa, combine the olives, shallots, olive oil and vinegar in a large bowl and mix well.

Brush the swordfish steaks with a little olive oil, sprinkle with salt and pepper and grill on high for 3–5 minutes on each side, according to thickness.

Serve with the olive salsa on the side. **SERVES 4**

Filetti di aguglie con fagiolini e noci

Grilled garfish with beans and walnuts

Ask the fishmonger to fillet the garfish for you, but you may need to go over them with tweezers.
We're suggesting green and yellow beans for visual effect, but green beans alone are fine.

200 g (6½ oz) green beans,
  topped and tailed
200 g (6½ oz) yellow wax
  beans, topped and tailed
100 g (3½ oz) walnut pieces
juice of 4 lemons

300 ml (10 fl oz) olive oil,
  plus extra
sea salt and freshly ground
  black pepper
12 garfish, filleted

Cook the beans in boiling salted water for 4 minutes. Drain, allow to cool a little and place in a
bowl with the walnuts.

Whisk together the lemon juice, olive oil and salt and pepper. Add to the bean and walnut
mixture and toss lightly.

Preheat the grill on high. Brush the fish fillets with a little olive oil and grill for 2–3 minutes.
Place the beans and walnuts on a serving plate and arrange the fish on top. **SERVES 4**

Dentice al forno con patate e olive nere

Snapper with potatoes and black olives

4 desiree potatoes, scrubbed
60 g (2 oz) black olives,
  pitted and chopped
30 ml (1 fl oz) olive oil
2 sprigs rosemary
sea salt and freshly ground
  black pepper

45g (1½ oz) unsalted
  butter, diced
4 x 200 g (6½ oz) snapper fillets
30 ml (1 fl oz) dry white wine
juice of ½ lemon

Parboil the potatoes in boiling salted water until just soft enough to slice without breaking. Peel
and slice as thinly as possible. Toss in a bowl with the olives, half the olive oil and 1 sprig of
rosemary and season with salt and pepper. Place on an oiled baking tray and dot with the butter.
Place the snapper fillets on the potato mixture. Sprinkle the wine, the rest of the olive oil and the
lemon juice over the top of the fish, top with the remaining sprig of rosemary and bake in an oven
preheated to 220° (425°F/gas 7) for 15 minutes, or until the fish is cooked. **SERVES 4**

Dentice con muscoli e capperi

Snapper with mussels and capers

1.2 kg (2½ lb) mussels,
 scrubbed and de-bearded
30 ml (1 fl oz) extra
 virgin olive oil
1 French shallot finely chopped
2 anchovy fillets
3 ripe tomatoes, peeled,
 seeded and diced
sea salt and freshly ground
 black pepper

1 sprig oregano, leaves picked
 and finely chopped
1 tbsp tiny salted capers,
 rinsed and dried
2 garlic cloves, whole, peeled
 and crushed slightly
6 x 250 g (8 oz) snapper fillets
60 ml (2 fl oz) dry white wine
1 small handful young basil
 leaves

Place the mussels in a large saucepan over a high heat and remove from the pan as they open. Place in a bowl. Strain the remaining liquid from the pan and set aside. Remove the mussels from their shells, chop roughly and pour over some of the filtered liquid to keep them moist.

Heat the oil in a heavy-based frying pan over a medium heat. Add the shallot and sauté until just starting to change colour. Add the anchovies and stir them into the *soffritto* with a fork. Add the tomatoes and cook over a medium heat for 5 minutes, mixing with a wooden spoon. Add 20 ml (½ fl oz) of the mussel liquid and the mussels and stir well. Remove from the heat immediately. Season to taste and add oregano and capers and mix delicately.

In the meantime, heat the olive oil in a large non-stick frying pan over a low heat. Add the garlic and sauté gently until the garlic starts to change colour. Remove the garlic with a slotted spoon and discard. Place the fish fillets in the pan, increase the heat to medium, and cook for 2 minutes on each side. Add the white wine and cook for about 3 minutes, until evaporated. Season to taste.

To serve, place the fish on individual plates, cover with the mussel mixture and top with basil leaves. **SERVES 4**

Filetti di rombo in padella

Flounder with celery and pine nuts

1 celery heart
1 tbsp sultanas (seedless
  white raisins)
75 ml (2½ fl oz) olive oil
1 small white onion, finely
  chopped
4 tomatoes, peeled, seeded
  and finely chopped

sea salt and freshly ground
  black pepper
1.5 kg (3 lb) flounder fillets
1 tbsp pine nuts
3–4 sprigs thyme, leaves picked

Cut the celery into 5-cm (2-inch) pieces, then cut each piece into thin strips. Blanch for 2 minutes in boiling water, drain and set aside.

Revive the sultanas in warm water, drain, squeeze dry and chop finely. Set aside.

Heat the 60 ml (2 fl oz) of the oil in a heavy-based frying pan over a medium heat. Add the onion and sauté for 5 minutes, stirring with a wooden spoon. Add the tomatoes, season with salt and pepper, and cook for 10 minutes, stirring frequently. Add the flounder fillets, pine nuts and sultanas, shaking the pan to let them sink into the sauce. Cook the fillets for 5 minutes on each side, being careful not to break them when you turn them over. Carefully remove the flounder fillets from the sauce with a fish slice (2 egg slices can do the trick if you don't have one) and set aside. Turn the heat up for 20 seconds and give the sauce a really good stir.

Heat the remaining olive oil in a non-stick frying pan. Add the celery and thyme and sauté for 3 minutes.

Divide the sauce between four plates and place the fillets on top. Spoon over the fried celery and thyme, and serve immediately. **SERVES 4**

Sardine in padella con pomodoro fresco

Pan-fried sardines with tomato, capers and parsley

12 new potatoes
200 ml (7 fl oz) olive oil
800 g (1 lb 10 oz) sardine fillets
100 g (3½ oz) cornflour
  (cornstarch)
6 ripe tomatoes, peeled
  and diced

½ bunch flat-leaf parsley,
  chopped
4 tbsp salted capers,
  rinsed and dried
45 ml (1½ fl oz) extra virgin
  olive oil

Parboil the potatoes in salted water until soft enough to slice without breaking (at least 10 minutes). Let them cool then cut them into thick slices.

Heat half the olive oil in a large frying pan over a medium heat, add the potatoes and sauté until cooked, about 3 minutes. Remove and drain on paper towel.

Trim any small fins off the sardine fillets. Coat the sardines in the cornflour, shaking off any excess. Heat the remaining oil in a frying pan over a medium heat, add the sardines and pan-fry for 2 minutes on each side.

Combine the tomatoes, parsley, capers and extra virgin olive oil in a bowl and toss well.

To serve, place the fried potatoes on four plates, top with the sardines and arrange the tomato mixture around the sardines. **SERVES 4**

Pesce in umido bianco

Pan-fried whiting

20 g (¾ oz) dried porcini
  mushrooms
30 g (1 oz) pine nuts
1 tbsp salted capers, rinsed and
  dried
1 tbsp plain (all purpose) flour
sea salt and freshly ground black
  pepper
90 ml (3 fl oz) dry white wine
90 ml (3 fl oz) olive oil
4 anchovy fillets
1 celery stalk, finely chopped

2 tbsp finely chopped flat-leaf
  parsley
1 carrot, finely chopped
2 garlic cloves, finely chopped
1 small white onion, finely
  chopped
800 g (1 lb 10 oz) white fish
  fillets, such as King George
  whiting

Soak the porcini mushrooms in warm water for 20 minutes. Drain, squeeze dry, chop roughly and set aside.

Place the pine nuts, mushrooms and capers in a mortar, sprinkle in a little flour and some salt. Pound to obtain a uniform paste, then place in a bowl. Add the wine, stir, and set aside.

Heat the oil in a large heavy-based frying pan over a low heat. Add the anchovies and stir into the oil with a fork until melted.

Now, make the *soffritto* by adding the celery, parsley, carrot, garlic and onion. Mix well and sauté for 5 minutes. Increase the heat to medium, and pour in the mushroom and wine mixture. Cook for 3 minutes, stirring from time to time. Add the fish and cook gently, turning the fish once for 5–10 minutes, being careful not to break the fillets. The cooking time will depend on the thickness of the fillets. Shake the pan regularly to avoid sticking.

Place the fillets on four plates, give a final good stir to the sauce, spoon over the fish and serve immediately. **SERVES 4**

Seppie in zimino
Cuttlefish with silverbeet

Zimino means lightly stewed with tomato and spinach. It is a way of cooking reserved only for cuttlefish, chickpeas and *stoccafisso* (dried cod). The Italian name *zimino* comes from the Ligurian dialect *zemin*, which in turn comes from the Arab word *semin*, meaning a rich sauce.

The *seppie in zimino* that we are presenting here is another of those dishes that benefit from the anarchic Ligurian way of dealing with food. The cuttlefish and the silverbeet are cooked sometimes with tomato, sometimes without. Where I come from near the Tuscan border, they add dried porcini and pine nuts.

Occasionally you may even see aromatic herbs used, sometimes only onion, never only garlic. In our recipe we hope to tame the anarchy and combine the best of what we saw.

1 kg (2 lb) cuttlefish (the smaller the better)
75 ml (2½ fl oz) olive oil
1 garlic clove, finely chopped
1 small white onion, finely chopped
1 small carrot, finely chopped
1 celery stalk, finely chopped
sea salt
1 tbsp chopped flat-leaf parsley leaves

45 ml (1½ fl oz) dry white wine
20 g (¾ oz) dried porcini mushrooms
1 tbsp pine nuts
3 tomatoes, peeled, seeded and diced
2 bunches silverbeet, white stalks removed, shredded
freshly ground black pepper

Clean the cuttlefish in the same way as the calamari in the Stuffed calamari recipe on page 224. Cut the cleaned cuttlefish into 1-cm (½-inch) strips, leaving the tentacles intact.

Heat the oil in a terracotta or heavy-based saucepan over a low heat. Add the garlic, onion, carrot and celery, mix with a wooden spoon, and sauté for 3 minutes. Add the cuttlefish, season with salt, sprinkle with parsley and mix well. Add the wine, increase the heat to medium-high, mix well, and cook for 12 minutes.

In the meantime, soak the mushrooms in warm water for 10 minutes, drain, squeeze dry and chop finely. Add the mushrooms and pine nuts, mix, add the tomatoes, mix again, and cook for 3 minutes. Add the silverbeet, mix thoroughly, reduce the heat to low and cook for 30–40 minutes. It should be moist and glossy, not dried out. Serve hot. **SERVES 4**

Seppie e piselli

Cuttlefish and peas

1 kg (2 lb) medium cuttlefish
60 ml (2 fl oz) olive oil
1 garlic clove, finely chopped
1 small white onion, finely chopped
½ carrot, finely chopped
1 tbsp chopped flat-leaf parsley leaves

1 sprig marjoram, leaves picked
1 sprig oregano, leaves picked
sea salt and freshly ground black pepper
90 ml (3 fl oz) dry white wine
500 g (1 lb) fresh peas, shelled

Clean the cuttlefish in the same way as the calamari in the Stuffed calamari recipe on page 224. It is a dirtier job because of the ink, but can be simplified by cutting the sac open (you don't need to keep it whole, as you would if you were stuffing it). Cut the cleaned cuttlefish into 1-cm (½-inch) strips, leaving the tentacles intact.

Heat the oil in a terracotta or heavy-based saucepan over a low heat. Add the garlic, onion, carrot, parsley, marjoram and oregano, mix with a wooden spoon, and sauté for 3 minutes.

Add the cuttlefish, season with salt and pepper, mix well, and cook for 8–9 minutes, stirring frequently. Add the wine and cook until evaporated, then add the peas. Mix well, cover, and cook for 30 minutes, checking and stirring from time to time. If it dries out add a little water. Serve hot.

SERVES 4

Totani ripieni

Stuffed calamari

This classic dish of the Riviera di Levante is prepared in many different ways from village to village along the coast. These variations all have one thing in common—the combination of the flavours of the sea with aromatic herbs and vegetables, and sometimes meat. In fact, we see stuffings for fish made with mortadella, prosciutto or ham; lettuce, radicchio or spinach; the herbs vary from oregano to marjoram to rosemary to basil.

Here we prepare our stuffing without meat. We cut up parts of the calamari to go in the stuffing. The herbs we use are parsley, marjoram and basil and we finish the dish with a handful of Taggiasca black olives.

4 large (not monsters)
  or 8 small calamari
100 ml (3½ fl oz) olive oil
2 garlic cloves, finely chopped
½ onion, finely chopped
1 handful flat-leaf parsley leaves,
  chopped
sea salt
90 ml (3 fl oz) dry white wine
1 small butter lettuce, endive or
  radicchio, washed and dried
45 g (1½ oz) freshly grated
  parmesan cheese
2 eggs

3 sprigs marjoram, leaves picked
3 thick slices Italian bread,
  crusts removed
60 ml (2 fl oz) milk
freshly ground black pepper
pinch of freshly grated nutmeg
1 garlic clove, peeled
1 small carrot, chopped
1 celery stalk, chopped
4 large tomatoes, peeled, seeded
  and diced
6 basil leaves, roughly chopped
1 handful small black olives

First, prepare the calamari. Hold the body in one hand and with the other hand pull away the tentacles (they will come off with some of the insides attached). Cut the tentacles horizontally below the eyes and discard the eyes and everything above. Remove the beak from the centre of the tentacles, and with your fingers pull away the bone and everything else inside the sac. Peel off the skin and wash the tentacles and inside the sac under running water. Cut off the wings on the side of the sac and combine with the tentacles. Drain and pat dry with paper towel. Chop the tentacles roughly.

Heat 60 ml (2 fl oz) olive oil in a frying pan over a low heat. Add the garlic and one-third of the onion and sauté until they start to change colour, stirring with a wooden spoon. Add the chopped tentacles, sprinkle with parsley, season with salt, and cook for 4 minutes, stirring regularly.

Add 30 ml (1 fl/oz) of the white wine, mix, and let the alcohol evaporate for 3 minutes. Put this *soffritto* into a large bowl and set aside. Shred the lettuce and add to the *soffritto*. Stir in the parmesan, eggs and marjoram.

Soak the bread in the milk, squeeze dry and add to the bowl. Season with salt, pepper and nutmeg, and mix to amalgamate. Using a spoon half-fill each *calamaro* sac with this mixture (they will shrink while cooking). Close the calamari sacs with toothpicks.

In a large heavy-based, preferably terracotta, saucepan, heat the remaining olive oil over a low heat. Add the garlic, the rest of the onion, the carrot and celery and sauté for 2 minutes, stirring with a wooden spoon. Discard the garlic, add the stuffed calamari and cook for 4 minutes, turning gently and cooking on all sides. Add the rest of the wine and cook until the alcohol evaporates. Add the tomatoes and basil, mix gently and cook for 40 minutes, adding a little hot water, about 3 tablespoons (2 fl oz), if drying out.

To serve, place the calamari on a chopping board, cut into slices about 2 cm (¾ inch) thick, being careful not to let the stuffing fall out. Arrange on a serving dish and pour the sauce on top.

SERVES 4

Polpo con le patate

Octopus and potatoes

This is a wonderful antipasto, but given the hard work involved in cooking the octopus, it should be a main course or a *piatto unico* (one course) lunch, particularly in summer. The quality of the olive oil is very important here, as it locks the main ingredients together.

Today, octopus is sold already tenderised but I remember, as a child, seeing the women in the late morning after the fishermen had returned, holding the octopus by the head and bashing them against the rocks. The perfectionists would only touch the octopus with a fig-tree branch, so as to enhance the flavour.

1 celery stalk, cut in half
1 carrot, peeled and cut in half
1 white onion, peeled
  and cut in half
3 bay leaves
1 cork*
125 ml (4 fl oz) white
  wine vinegar
sea salt and freshly ground
  black pepper

1.5 kg (3 lb) octopus,
  cleaned
600 g (1 lb 3½ oz) desiree
  potatoes, peeled and
  thickly sliced
90 ml (3 fl oz) olive oil
juice of ½ lemon
1 garlic clove, finely chopped
1 tbsp finely chopped
  flat-leaf parsley leaves

*The tradition in the Levante is to cook the octopus with a cork to make it tender.

Place the celery, carrot, onion, bay leaves and the cork in a large saucepan. Fill with water, add the vinegar and a few pinches of salt and bring to the boil. Add the octopus, reduce heat to low and simmer for 1½ hours, or until the octopus is tender. Skim the surface with a slotted spoon to remove any foam or small particles. The octopus is ready when a fork goes into it without resistance. Remove from the heat and allow the octopus to cool in the stock.

In the meantime, cook the potatoes in boiling salted water for 20 minutes, or until just tender. Drain well and place in a bowl.

Strain the octopus while it is just warm and discard the stock. You can skin the body leaving only the white flesh if you think that looks better, although the skin is edible. Cut into bite-sized pieces and add to the potatoes.

Whisk together the olive oil, lemon juice, garlic, parsley, and some salt and pepper in a separate bowl. Pour this dressing over the octopus and potatoes, toss gently and serve on a large platter in the middle of the table. Make sure the pepper grinder is nearby! **SERVES 4**

Polipetti brasati alla salsa piccante

Spicy braised octopus with black olives

45 g (1½ oz) unsalted butter
2 onions, finely chopped
2 small red chillies, chopped
800 g (1 lb 10 oz) baby
  octopus, cleaned

4 large tomatoes, peeled,
  seeded and diced
60 ml (2 fl oz) dry white wine
¼ cup black olives
½ bunch basil, picked leaves

Melt the butter in a large saucepan over a low heat. Make a *soffritto* by adding the onions and chillies and simmering for 10 minutes. Add the octopus and tomatoes, splash in the white wine, stir well and bring to a gentle simmer. The baby octopus will let out some water as it cooks but you can add more if necessary. Simmer gently, mixing with a wooden spoon from time to time, for 1 hour, or until the octopus is tender.

Add the olives and basil, mix well, and serve. **SERVES 6**

Stoccafisso in umido

Dried cod with tomatoes and walnuts

Stoccafisso and *baccalà* are dried versions of the cod which swim in the cold northern seas of Europe and the Canadian east coast. To make *stoccafisso*, the cod is cleaned, hung by the tail, and air-dried. In markets throughout Italy the dried cod stand up like wooden boards—indeed, the word *stocca* means stick. To make *baccalà*, the cod is filleted and layered with salt.

Both forms of cod first arrived in the port of Genoa in the twelfth century and from there the dried fish were embraced all over the north of Italy. It was appreciated inland in the mountain villages because it was a cheap, non-perishable and highly portable protein. The shepherds and farmers quickly learned how best to cook it and match it with vegetables, olives and olive oil. Later they found it was a perfect match with tomatoes and potatoes.

As a child I remember dried cod being sold not in the fish shop but in the delicatessen where buckets full of *stoccafisso* and *baccalà* would greet you at the front door. In our cellar at home there was always a big bucket of fresh water where one or the other was soaking. Following are two ways my mother used to cook these dried fish.

800 g (1 lb 10 oz) *stoccafisso* (dried cod)
10 g (⅓ oz) dried porcini mushrooms
5 sage leaves
1 sprig rosemary, leaves picked
½ small white onion
1 garlic clove, peeled
90 ml (3 fl oz) olive oil
90 ml (3 fl oz) dry white wine
2 medium tomatoes, peeled, seeded and diced
sea salt
600 g (1 lb 3½ oz) potatoes, peeled and thinly sliced
2 anchovy fillets, chopped
10 g (⅓ oz) pine nuts, chopped
20 g (¾ oz) walnuts, chopped
30 g (1 oz) black olives

Soak the cod for 4 days in a large saucepan of cold water, changing the water twice a day. Remove the cod from the water, peel off the skin, and remove all the bones with tweezers. Cut the flesh into bite-sized pieces.

Soak the porcini mushrooms in warm water for 20 minutes, drain and squeeze dry. Chop finely and set aside.

Combine the sage, rosemary, onion and garlic on a chopping board and mince finely with a very sharp knife or a mezzaluna.

Heat the oil in a heavy-based saucepan over a low heat. To make the *soffritto*, add the herb and onion mixture, stirring regularly with a wooden spoon, and sauté until the onion is soft. Add the cod and brown on all sides. Add the white wine, stir, and let the alcohol evaporate for 2 minutes. Add the tomatoes and mushrooms, season with salt, and shake the pan to mix delicately.

Continue to cook for 30 minutes. Add the potatoes, anchovies, pine nuts, walnuts and olives. Gently shake the pan again and mix delicately, making sure the contents don't stick to the bottom. Turn the cod twice during the cooking process and this must be done delicately so as not to break the pieces. If the sauce becomes a little too dry you can add a couple of tablespoons of warm water as needed. Serve hot. **SERVES 4**

Baccalà con cipolle e patate

Salt cod with onions and potatoes

This simple way to prepare *baccalà* was a favourite of the workers in the olive mills, where they did not have the luxury of a kitchen, but simply an open fire and a pot. They'd carry slabs of dried cod and leave them to soak overnight in water from the nearby river. They could top the dish off with the first pressing of extra virgin olive oil.

800 g (1 lb 10 oz) *baccalà* (salted cod)
4 large potatoes, peeled and cut in half
4 medium white onions, peeled and trimmed
1 tbsp chopped flat-leaf parsley leaves
125 ml (4 fl oz) olive oil

Leave the cod to soak for 24 hours in fresh water, changing the water at least four times.

Cook the potatoes and onions in boiling salted water for 20 minutes, or until tender. Drain well.

Rinse the cod, remove any bones with tweezers, and cook in unsalted boiling water for 10 minutes. Drain the cod and place on a serving platter. Add the potatoes and onions, sprinkle with parsley, pour the olive oil over everything and serve. **SERVES 4**

This picture shows a version of baccalà as made in Due Corone restaurant, Lerici.

Carne

Meat

Meat

236 QUAGLIE CON SPINACI E FICHI ~ *Quail with spinach and figs*

238 CONIGLIO FARCITO CON FINOCCHI ~ *Rolled rabbit with pistachio stuffing*

240 CONIGLIO AL VINO BIANCO E OLIVE TAGGIASCHE ~ *Rabbit with white wine and Taggiasca olives*

241 POLLO IN TEGAME CON BARBE ~ *Chicken casserole with salsify*

243 ANATRA ALLE OLIVE ~ *Duck with olives*

245 BRACIOLE DI MAIALE CON PATATE E SALSA VERDE ~ *Pork chops with potatoes and salsa verde*

247 CARRÉ D'AGNELLO IN CROSTA DI ERBE CON SPADELLATA DI CARCIOFI E MENTA

     ~ *Herb-crusted rack of lamb with artichokes and mint*

248 TOMAXELLE ~ *Veal parcels*

250 MEDAGLIONI DI VITELLO IN SALSA PICCANTE ~ *Veal medallions in spicy sauce*

250 SPEZZATINO CON OLIVE ~ *Veal stew with olives and potatoes*

252 CIMA ALLA GENOVESE ~ *Stuffed shoulder of veal*

254 TRIPPA AL POMODORO ~ *Tripe with tomato sauce*

255 STECCHI ~ *Veal skewers*

256 BOLLITO ALLA LIGURE ~ *Beef stew with anchovy sauce*

257 FEGATO ALL'AGLIATA ~ *Veal liver with garlic sauce*

258 VITELLO TONNATO ~ *Roast veal with fresh tuna mayonnaise*

259 VITELLO ALL'UCCELLETTO ~ *Veal pan-fried in white wine and bay leaves*

259 STRACOTTO ~ *Braised beef*

Meat is rare in Liguria, so it's highly valued and carefully cooked. Because the region is mostly mountains and seashore, our food animals tend to be small—chickens, rabbits, game birds, with the occasional pig or sheep (which also provides milk for pecorino cheese).

In the past, when Ligurians wanted beefier treats, we had to trade with our neighbours in Tuscany and Emilia-Romagna, where the farmers know how to breed and feed cattle. And once we got the big animals, we used every part of them.

In this chapter, we start with the smallest creatures and work our way up, adapting Ligurian approaches to Australian availability. Thus we're substituting quail for the tasty birds known as *tordi*. The great advantage you have is that you won't need to pick the little pieces of buckshot out of the quail, as many a Ligurian cook must do with the hunter's catch.

We've included two rabbit recipes, in the full knowledge that Australians have not yet warmed to rabbit as a dish they want to cook at home. We're urging you to be adventurous, because it's a delicacy. We'll explain how to debone a rabbit and roll it round a delicious pistachio nut stuffing— a dish we kept encountering up and down the Riviera. We hope ours—and yours—can come close to the signature dish at Trattoria Armanda in the town of Castelnuovo Magra.

When we finally reach the biggest animal, we'll show how Ligurians made the best out of the parts richer regions never bothered to reach. And don't forget to keep all the leftovers to put into your pies and ravioli the following day.

Quaglie con spinaci e fichi

Quail with spinach and figs

8 quail
175 ml (6 fl oz) olive oil
1 tbsp chopped flat-leaf
  parsley leaves
16 sage leaves
1 garlic clove, finely chopped
2 small red chillies, finely
  chopped
8 large figs

30 ml (1 fl oz) balsamic vinegar
1.5 kg (3 lb) English spinach
45 g (1½ oz) sultanas
  (seedless white raisins)
45 g (1½ oz) pine nuts
pinch of freshly grated nutmeg
sea salt
freshly ground black pepper

Split the quails in half down the backbone leaving the two halves connected. Cut off the tips of the wings and discard. Place the quail on a large dish.

Combine 45 ml (1½ fl oz) of the olive oil, the parsley, sage, garlic and chilli in a bowl and whisk to amalgamate. Pour over the quail and marinate for 10 minutes.

Chop off the top part of the figs and cut into thick slices. Heat 15 ml (½ fl oz) of olive oil in a non-stick frying pan over a medium heat. Add the figs and cook for 1 minute on each side, sprinkling with balsamic vinegar. Remove the figs and set aside.

Wash the spinach leaves thoroughly, then wilt for 2 minutes in a saucepan over a medium heat. Delicately squeeze out the water.

In the meantime revive the sultanas in warm water and dry well with paper towel.

Heat 60 ml (2 fl oz) of the oil in a frying pan over a low heat. Add the spinach, sultanas, pine nuts, nutmeg, a pinch of salt and freshly ground pepper to taste. Mix well with a wooden spoon and sauté for 10 minutes, mixing from time to time. Set the pan aside.

Heat the remaining oil in another pan large enough to hold the quail. Add the quail, skin-side down, and cook for 7 minutes each side, brushing them from time to time with the marinade and shaking the pan so they don't stick. Season with salt.

Warm the spinach for 1 minute and divide it between four plates. Surround the spinach with the fig slices and place 2 quail on top of the spinach. Pour some of the cooking juices on each quail and serve. **SERVES 4**

Coniglio farcito con finocchi
Rolled rabbit with pistachio stuffing

There may be a way to convince your butcher to debone the rabbit for you, but if he or she won't, enjoy the challenge. Imagine you're doing fine surgery—only there's no life and death involved. However you slice it, it will taste magnificent.

1.5 kg (3 lb) rabbit, dressed

FOR THE STUFFING
100 g (3½ oz) pistachio
  nuts, toasted and chopped
½ bunch thyme,
  leaves picked
¼ bunch rosemary,
  leaves picked
3 garlic cloves, finely sliced
sea salt and freshly ground
  black pepper

10 slices prosciutto
3 fennel bulbs
1 garlic clove, crushed
  with the blade of a knife
5 sprigs thyme
100 ml (3½ fl oz)
  chicken stock
75 ml (2½ fl oz) olive oil
20 g (¾ oz) butter

Place the rabbit on a large chopping board. Cut off the legs and slice the meat off them. Cut the meat off the shoulders and set aside. Slice along the ribs on each side towards the spine, and slice around the hips. Once you've separated as much flesh from the spine as you can, pull away the spine and ribs. The idea is to end up with a single sheet of belly flesh, which can be rolled up. Reserve the bones for making stock.

The sheet of belly flesh will be thinner in the middle, so that's the spot where you place the meat from the legs and shoulders, with the aim of creating a roll of even thickness.

To make the stuffing, simply combine all the ingredients in a bowl. Spread the stuffing along half the rabbit meat. Working from one side of the belly to the other, roll up to make a cylinder shape. It should stick together in such a way that you won't need to tie it up with string.

Place the strips of prosciutto side by side and slightly overlapping on the chopping board. Place the rolled rabbit on top on the side closest to you, and wrap the prosciutto around the rabbit. Wrap the cylinder tightly in plastic wrap, going round four times, then seal the cylinder in foil. Place the cylinder in a saucepan of simmering water and cook for 30 minutes. Remove the rabbit from the water and rest for 10 minutes before unwrapping.

Preheat the oven to 200°C (400°F/gas 6). Trim the tops and bottoms of the fennel bulbs and chop each one into eight. Place the fennel in a baking tray, add the garlic, thyme, salt, pepper and chicken stock. Cover with foil and bake in the oven for 30 minutes. Reduce the oven temperature to 180°C (350°C/gas 4).

Heat the olive oil and butter in a large flameproof baking dish and when the butter is foaming, add the rabbit and brown on all sides for 5 minutes. Toss in the braised fennel, and transfer to the oven for 5 minutes.

Carry the baking dish to the table, lift out the rabbit, place on a chopping board and slice into discs. Distribute the rabbit and the fennel between the plates. **SERVES 4**

Coniglio al vino bianco e olive taggiasche

Rabbit with white wine and Taggiasca olives

This typically Ligurian way to cook rabbit—with very few ingredients that are easy to source—is a classic example of farming life, showing the simplicity of the peasant gastronomy, which, when well executed, brings an exquisite experience. The essential flavours in this recipe come from the aromatic herbs and olives that give the rabbit an intriguing bitterness. I recommend Taggiasca olives from my area, but if you can't find them, any small black olives will do.

1.5 kg (3 lb) white rabbit, dressed
60 ml (2 fl oz) olive oil
1 small onion, thinly sliced
3–4 garlic cloves, peeled and crushed with the blade of a knife
1 small bunch herbs, such as rosemary, thyme, bay leaves
1 small red chilli, finely chopped
375 ml (12 fl oz) dry white wine
sea salt
75 g (2½ oz) black Taggiasca olives

Wash and pat dry the rabbit. Cut into 16 even-sized pieces.

Heat the olive oil in a frying pan large enough to accommodate the rabbit in a single layer. Add the onion, garlic, herbs and a little of the chilli, and sauté, stirring occasionally with a wooden spoon, for 5 minutes, or until the onion is lightly coloured. Increase the heat to high, add the rabbit to the *soffritto* and brown, stirring occasionally for 10 minutes, or until the rabbit is golden. Add the wine and salt, cover, reduce the heat to low and simmer, mixing gently every now and then, for 1 hour or until the meat falls easily off the bone. In the last 10 minutes add the olives and mix. If the cooking juices become dry, add a little water as needed.

This rabbit dish is enhanced by rosemary roasted potatoes and a salad of radicchio and fennel with an olive oil and red wine vinegar dressing. **SERVES 4**

Pollo in tegame con barbe

Chicken casserole with salsify

Salsify is a root vegetable, a bit like parsnip, which is only in season for a short time of the year. To make this dish when it's not in season you can either avoid the salsify altogether (the result will still be excellent!) or replace it with celeriac, treated in the same way.

1.5 kg (3 lb) chicken
  (free-range preferably)
125 ml (4 fl oz) olive oil
½ onion, finely chopped
2 garlic cloves, finely chopped
3 sprigs rosemary, leaves picked
5 sage leaves, roughly chopped
sea salt

125 ml (4 fl oz) dry white wine
4 tomatoes, peeled,
  seeded and diced
600 g (1 lb 3½ oz) salsify,
  peeled and trimmed
20 black olives (Ligurian,
  Taggiasca or any small olives)

Chop the chicken in half, and then cut each half into four or five pieces. Heat the oil in a large heavy-based frying pan over a medium heat. Make a *soffritto* by adding the onion, garlic, rosemary and sage. Sauté for 5 minutes, mixing with a wooden spoon. Add the chicken, season with salt, and brown the chicken on all sides. Pour in the wine, mix well, and let it evaporate. Stir in the tomatoes, and taste for seasoning. Reduce the heat to low and cook for 40 minutes, covered, mixing every so often.

In the meantime, cook the salsify in plenty of boiling salted water for 5 minutes. Drain them and cut into 6-cm (2½-inch) pieces. Add the salsify and black olives to the pan, mix properly to combine all the ingredients and cook for another 15–20 minutes. Serve hot. **SERVES 4**

Anatra alle olive

Duck with olives

1.5 kg (3 lb) duck
2 tbsp chopped flat-leaf parsley
  leaves
1 tbsp sage leaves, finely chopped
2 bay leaves, roughly chopped
sea salt and freshly ground black
  pepper
100 ml (3½ fl oz) olive oil
1 lemon, thinly sliced

1 garlic head, cut in half
3 sprigs rosemary
1 white onion, chopped
½ celery stalk, chopped
1 carrot, chopped
20 black olives
250 ml (8 fl oz) chicken stock
juice of 1 lemon

Wash and dry the duck. Combine the parsley, sage, bay leaves, salt and pepper and a little of the olive oil, and rub into the skin of the duck. Place the sliced lemon, the garlic and rosemary in the duck's cavity. Transfer the duck to a bowl, pour a little more olive oil on top, sprinkle with salt and marinate for 1 hour, turning a few times.

Heat the remaining olive oil in a large ovenproof frying pan, that is big enough to hold the duck, over a medium heat. To make a *soffritto*, add the onion, celery and carrot and sauté for 3 minutes, mixing with a wooden spoon. Add the duck and brown on all sides. Transfer the pan to an oven preheated to 180°C (350°F/gas 4) and bake for 45 minutes, basting from time to time with a little stock as necessary. Place the duck on a chopping board and cut into about 8 pieces, discarding the stuffing.

In the meantime take one-third of the olives, pit them, crush them in a mortar and pestle and set the resulting paste aside. Wash another one-third of the olives, and pit and chop. Leave the remaining third whole.

Pass the leftover juices from the pan and *soffritto* through a mouli and return this sauce to the pan. Add the duck, lemon juice and all the olives. Mix gently and return to the oven for 30 minutes, stirring from time to time.

Serve hot accompanied by spinach, roast potatoes, beans or silverbeet. **SERVES 4**

Braciole di maiale con patate e salsa verde

Pork chops with potatoes and salsa verde

4 thick cut pork chops,
  with fat left on
sea salt and freshly ground
  black pepper
500 g (1 lb) waxy potatoes,
  such as desiree, scrubbed
90 ml (3 fl oz) olive oil
15 ml (½ fl oz) white wine
  vinegar
8 garlic cloves, unpeeled and
  lightly crushed with the
  blade of a knife
16 sage leaves

8 sprigs rosemary

FOR THE SALSA VERDE
20 g (¾ oz) pine nuts
2–3 anchovy fillets
1 bunch flat-leaf parsley,
  leaves picked
75 ml (2½ fl oz) olive oil
45 ml (1½ fl oz) white wine
  vinegar
20 g (¾ oz) salted capers,
  rinsed and dried

To make the salsa verde, place the pine nuts, anchovies and parsely in a blender and blitz. Add the oil, vinegar and capers and process until well combined. The consistency should not be too fine. This salsa will keep for 1 week in the refrigerator if stored, covered by a little more oil, in a glass container.

Make cuts into the pork skin so that the meat won't curl while cooking. Season the pork with salt and pepper. Place the unpeeled potatoes in a saucepan, cover with cold water, bring to the boil and cook until tender but not too soft. Drain, return to the pan and cook, shaking the pan now and then, over a low heat for a few minutes to remove all moisture. Set aside until cool enough to handle, then peel and slice. Place in a bowl, sprinkle with a little of the oil, a touch of vinegar and some salt. Set aside.

Heat the remaining oil in a heavy-based saucepan over a high heat. Add 3 garlic cloves and cook until coloured a little. Add the pork chops, the remaining garlic, the sage and rosemary and cook the chops, taking care not to let them stick to the pan, for 5 minutes on each side, or until golden brown and the fat looks like crackling. Serve hot topped with the garlic, sage and rosemary and accompanied by the potatoes and salsa verde. **SERVES 4**

Carré d'agnello in crosta d'erbe con spadellata di carciofi e menta

Herb-crusted rack of lamb with artichokes and mint

sea salt and freshly ground
  black pepper
4 x 4-cutlet racks of lamb,
  trimmed of fat
90 ml (3 fl oz) olive oil
75 g (2½ oz) butter, softened
2 egg yolks
2 tbsp mixed herbs, such as
  rosemary, thyme, oregano, sage,
  mint, very finely chopped

10 small black olives, pitted
  and finely chopped
1 tbsp dried breadcrumbs
1 tbsp freshly grated
  parmesan cheese
8 medium globe artichokes
1 tbsp finely chopped mint

Preheat the oven to 220°C (425°F/gas 7).

Rub a little salt and pepper into the lamb.

Heat 45 ml (1½ fl oz) of the oil in a heavy-based frying pan over a medium-high heat and sear the lamb on all sides.

To make the herb crust, place the butter, egg yolks, herbs, olives, breadcrumbs and parmesan in a bowl. Mix well and rub onto the lamb, pressing firmly into place with your fingers. Place on an oven tray, sprinkle on a little of the remaining olive oil and roast in the oven for 15 minutes, to cook the lamb to medium.

In the meantime prepare the artichokes. Discard the tough outer leaves, cut in half as described on page 130, scrape out the hairy choke, and slice each artichoke heart very thinly. Heat the remaining oil in a heavy-based frying pan over a medium heat. Add the artichokes and sauté for 5 minutes, add the mint, mix with a wooden spoon, and cook for a few more minutes to allow the flavours to develop.

Just before serving, place the lamb back in the oven for 4 minutes.

To serve, arrange the artichokes on four plates. Cut each of the lamb racks into two double cutlets and arrange on top of the artichokes. **SERVES 4**

Tomaxelle
Veal parcels

Here's another example of the Ligurian *cucina di recupero*, or not wasting anything. This dish was created for utilising leftovers from roasts, which would be chopped up to go into the veal filling. It is similar to the recipe for *involtini* of other regions, but the filling is very Ligurian.

The name comes from a Latin word for little sausages. The veal rolls entered the Riviera gastronomic repertoire when they were served to Austrian officers held prisoner during the siege of Genova in 1800. What the locals thought was common sense was viewed as a delicacy by the prisoners, who took the legend back home with them.

We're offering two recipes: one traditional (where the *tomaxelle* look a bit like stretched sausages), one a modern variation (where the meat is in a roll to be sliced).

TRADITIONAL METHOD

500 g (1 lb) veal loin, cut into 8 thin slices of about 60 g (2 oz) each
30 g (1 oz) dried porcini mushrooms
75 ml (2½ fl oz) olive oil
½ white onion, finely sliced
200 g (6½ oz) minced (ground) veal
sea salt
60 ml (2 fl oz) dry white wine
1 thick slice Italian bread, crusts removed
60 ml (2 fl oz) milk
30 g (1 oz) pine nuts
2 tbsp marjoram leaves, roughly chopped
1 tbsp flat-leaf parsley, finely chopped
pinch of freshly grated nutmeg
45 g (1½ oz) freshly grated parmesan cheese
2 eggs, lightly beaten
freshly ground black pepper
2 garlic cloves, finely chopped
3 tomatoes, peeled, seeded, chopped and pureed

Pound the veal with a meat mallet to flatten until very thin.

Soak the dried porcini mushrooms in warm water for 8 minutes, drain, squeeze dry and chop finely.

To make the stuffing, heat 45 ml (1½ fl oz) of the oil in a heavy-based frying pan over a low heat. Add the onions, and sauté for 5 minutes, or until soft and translucent. Add the ground veal and porcini, season with salt and mix well with a wooden spoon. Increase the heat to medium and sauté for a few minutes until the veal is light brown. If the meat releases a lot of water, drain by tipping the pan over the sink and holding the meat with a wooden spoon. Add the wine, mix, and cook for 3 minutes or so to let it evaporate. Remove the pan from the heat and transfer the mixture to a large bowl. Allow to cool for a few minutes.

Soak the bread in the milk and add to the veal. Add the pine nuts, marjoram, parsley, nutmeg, parmesan, eggs and salt and pepper. Mix thoroughly to amalgamate.

To make the *tomaxelle*, place the slices of veal on a workbench and top with the stuffing. Flatten the stuffing over the surface of the veal with a knife, roll up the slices and secure with a toothpick.

Heat the remaining oil in the same pan over a low heat. Add the garlic and gently sauté for 2 minutes, then increase the heat to high. Add the tomatoes and a pinch of salt and cook for 3–4 minutes, stirring occasionally. Add the *tomaxelle* to the sauce. Reduce the heat to low and cook for 20 minutes, turning from time to time.

To serve, place 2 *tomaxelle* on each plate and pour the sauce on top.

MODERN METHOD

75 g (2½ oz) butter
1 onion, finely chopped
2 garlic cloves, finely chopped
½ bunch thyme, leaves picked
  and chopped

120 g (4 oz) pine nuts,
  toasted and finely chopped
800 g (1 lb 10 oz) veal fillet
olive oil

To make the filling, melt the butter in a heavy-based frying pan over a medium heat. Add the onion and sauté for 3 minutes. Add the garlic and sauté for 2 minutes. Add the thyme and pine nuts and stir for 1 minute to mix all the flavours. Set aside.

Make an incision along the veal fillet and slice, so you end up with a single rectangular sheet about 1 cm (½ inch) thick. Lay out flat on a chopping board, spread the filling on top, and roll into a cylinder. Tie securely with string.

Preheat the oven to 180°C (350°F/gas 4). Splash a little olive oil into a heavy-based pan over a high heat. Add the *tomaxelle* and seal the outside until golden brown, for about 2 minutes on each side. Place the pan in the oven and roast for 10 minutes. Allow to rest in a warm place for 5 minutes before slicing into discs and serving. We suggest spinach and canellini beans as an accompaniment—see the Beans sautéed with silverbeet recipe on page 277). **SERVES 4**

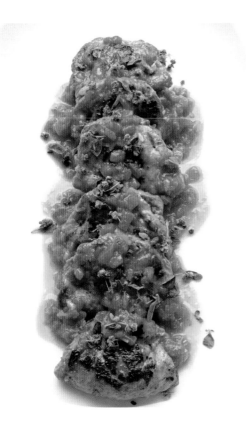

Medaglioni di vitello in salsa piccante

Veal medallions in spicy sauce

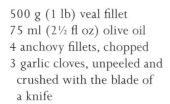

500 g (1 lb) veal fillet
75 ml (2½ fl oz) olive oil
4 anchovy fillets, chopped
3 garlic cloves, unpeeled and
  crushed with the blade of
  a knife

1 tbsp salted capers, rinsed
  and dried
1 small red chilli, finely chopped
2 sprigs rosemary, leaves picked
sea salt
60 ml (2 fl oz) white wine

Cut the veal into 12 medallions. Heat the oil in a non-stick frying pan, over a low heat. Add the anchovies and stir with a wooden spoon, until melted into a paste. Add the garlic, mix around a little, then add the veal medallions. Sprinkle with the capers and chilli, top with the rosemary and season with salt. Cook the meat for 3–5 minutes per side. Add the wine, shake the pan and cook until the wine has evaporated. Serve the medallions on a platter with the sauce on top. **SERVES 4**

Spezzatino con olive

Veal stew with olives and potatoes

60 ml (2 fl oz) olive oil
400 g (13 oz) butter
1 onion, finely chopped
1 large carrot, finely chopped
1 celery stalk, finely chopped
800 g (1 lb 10 oz) boned veal
  shoulder, trimmed and cut into
  5-cm (2-inch) cubes
125 ml (4 fl oz) dry white wine
120 g (4 oz) tinned Italian

tomatoes, pureed
250 ml (8 fl oz) water
sea salt and freshly ground
  black pepper
2 sprigs rosemary
5 sage leaves
4 medium potatoes, peeled and
  cut into 5-cm (2-inch) cubes
24 Ligurian (or small) black
  olives

Heat the oil and butter in a large heavy-based saucepan over a low heat. Add the onion, carrot and celery, and cook, stirring frequently, for 3 minutes, or until softened and lightly coloured. Increase the heat to high, add the veal and brown evenly on all sides. Add the wine, stir, and cook until evaporated, for a minute or so. Add the tomatoes and water, mix, and season with a few pinches of salt and pepper. Add the rosemary, sage and potatoes and mix thoroughly. Reduce the heat to low, cover, and gently simmer for 1 hour, or until the meat is soft enough to cut with a fork. Check and stir occasionally, adding more water if necessary.

Add the olives, mix well and cook for another 5 minutes. Serve hot. **SERVES 4**

Cima alla Genovese

Stuffed shoulder of veal

Cima, a dish now made for festive celebrations (particularly Easter), was originally made mostly with leftovers and included very little meat. With time this dish has been transformed into one of the richest examples of Liguria's food. It varies a little along the coast. In the La Spezia province it is made mainly with vegetables; from Chiavari to Genova mainly offal (sweetbreads, brains and udders) is used. Constant ingredients are eggs and parmesan cheese.

The piece of meat should be thin and long. Ask your butcher to cut a pocket into it, ready for the stuffing. The cut should be parallel to the grain and go almost from one end to the other.

The filling that we propose is a lovely combination of meat, vegetables, nuts and herbs (and no scary offal), which we think will maintain the characteristics of cima while looking inviting, light and tasty. It is best enjoyed warm or cold, but not hot.

1 kg (2 lb) boneless breast of
  veal, with a pocket cut into
  one side
20 g (¾ oz) porcini mushrooms
1 bunch silverbeet
3 slices Italian bread, crusts
  removed
60 ml (2 fl oz) milk
45 g (1½ oz) butter
1 onion, finely chopped
300 g (10 oz) minced
  (ground) veal
100 g (3½ oz) minced
  (ground) pork
sea salt and freshly ground
  black pepper

60 g (2 oz) shelled fresh peas
1 tbsp pine nuts
1 tbsp unsalted pistachio nuts
1 garlic clove, finely chopped
1 tbsp marjoram leaves,
  finely chopped
3 eggs
60 g (2 oz) freshly grated
  parmesan cheese
4 hard-boiled eggs, peeled
1 onion, cut in half
1 carrot, cut in half
1 celery stalk, cut in half
1 bay leaf

Wash the veal breast under running water, drain and pat dry with paper towel. Soak the porcini mushrooms in warm water for 10 minutes, squeeze dry, chop finely and set aside.

Remove the stems of the silverbeet and wash the leaves well. Place in a large heavy-based saucepan with just the water left after washing, and wilt over a medium heat. Chop finely and squeeze out excess liquid. Soak the bread in the milk for 10 minutes and squeeze lightly.

Melt the butter in a heavy-based saucepan over a medium heat. Add the finely chopped onion and cook for 7–8 minutes, stirring frequently with a wooden spoon. Add the minced veal and pork, season with salt and pepper, mix well and cook until the meat is well browned all over. Drain any excess liquid and transfer to a large bowl. Add the peas, silverbeet, pine nuts, pistachio nuts, garlic, marjoram and bread. Beat the eggs and parmesan and add to the mixture. Season with salt and pepper, and mix gently with a wooden spoon until all the ingredients have amalgamated into a smooth and fluffy mixture.

Spread about half of the stuffing into the veal breast pocket. Arrange the hard-boiled eggs lengthwise on top, and place the rest of the stuffing inside the veal pocket, covering the eggs completely. Keep in mind that the veal pocket should be only two-thirds full because the meat will shrink and the stuffing will puff up during cooking. Sew the opening of the pocket closed with strong cotton thread and a needle or skewer. Make about a dozen little holes in both sides of the *cima* to allow air to escape and prevent bursting during cooking.

Combine the onion halves, carrot, celery and bay leaf in a large heavy-based saucepan. Place the *cima* on top and cover with plenty of cold water, add a few pinches of salt and bring to the boil over a medium heat. Reduce the heat to low and simmer gently for 2 hours, checking every now and then and skimming off the fat if necessary.

Remove from the heat, cool down a little then take the *cima* out of the stock (which, by the way, is excellent!) and place on a plate. Cover the *cima* with an upside-down plate and place a 2-kg (4-lb) weight on top to squeeze out the broth absorbed and allow the *cima* to take on the classic oval shape.

To serve, use a very sharp knife to slice the *cima* as thinly or thickly as you like. Just as good eaten cold. **SERVES 4**

Trippa al pomodoro

Tripe with tomato sauce

Tripe is one of those dishes that have almost completely disappeared from our tables and restaurant menus. It is a pity because when well prepared, the softness and flavour of tripe cannot be matched by more expensive cuts of meat. So, we suggest that you don't think about where it comes from, but just buy it, wash it well, cook it the Ligurian way and enjoy!

In the beautiful village of Castelnuovo Magra, in the hills at the beginning of the Levante, there was an unusual tradition. The day before Easter, early in the morning, the local peasants would go to the village of Castelnuovo Magra and present chickens, eggs and vegetables to their landlords living in the elegant mansions. Then they would meet in what was an *osteria*, now a great restaurant called Armanda, and eat tripe from the early hours of the morning.

The sign 'Saturday Tripe' was once a common sight outside *trattorie* and *osterie*. Because it is impossible to preserve tripe by drying or salting, it has to be eaten very fresh. So for the rich the roasts, and for the poor, the tripe. We think the poor got the better experience.

1 kg (2 lb) honeycomb tripe, washed
sea salt
60 ml (2 fl oz) olive oil
45 g (1½ oz) butter
1 garlic clove, finely chopped
1 onion, finely chopped
1 celery stalk, finely chopped
1 carrot, finely chopped
1 small red chilli, finely chopped
1 sprig rosemary, leaves picked and roughly chopped
2 tbsp chopped flat-leaf parsley
4 bay leaves, torn
20 g (¾ oz) dried porcini mushrooms, soaked for 10 minutes, squeezed dry and chopped
60 ml (2 fl oz) dry white wine
400 g (13 oz) tinned Italian tomatoes, pureed
freshly ground black pepper
100 g (3½ oz) freshly grated parmesan cheese

Place the tripe in a large heavy-based saucepan, cover with water, add salt and bring it to the boil, then reduce heat and simmer for 1 hour. Drain and reserve 250 ml (8 fl oz) of the stock. When the tripe is cool enough to handle cut it into strips 8 mm (⅜ inch) thick, the length doesn't matter.

Heat the oil and the butter in a heavy-based saucepan over a medium heat. To make a *soffritto* add the garlic and onion and cook for 3 minutes, mixing with a wooden spoon, then add the celery and carrot and sauté for 1 minute. Add the chilli, rosemary, parsley, bay leaves and porcini mushrooms. Mix well, and cook for 1 minute. Add the tripe and cook for 8–10 minutes, stirring frequently. Add the wine and simmer until evaporated, for about 1 minute. Add the tomatoes and the reserved stock, season with salt and pepper and mix well. Cover, reduce the heat to low and simmer for 2 hours, checking and stirring regularly. The tripe is cooked when it is tender enough to be cut with a fork. Taste, and if it needs more cooking to tenderise, do so. It should not be as liquid as soup, but if during the cooking it dries out too much, add a few spoonfuls of water. Serve the tripe very hot, topped with plenty of parmesan cheese. **SERVES 4**

Stecchi
Veal skewers

60 g (2 oz) butter
120 g (4 oz) sweetbreads
  (optional)
300 g (10 oz) veal fillet, cut into
  24 x 3-cm (1¼-inch) cubes
12 button mushrooms
2 zucchini (courgettes), trimmed
  and cut into 12 pieces the size
  of the mushrooms
sea salt and freshly ground
  black pepper

3 eggs
150 g (5 oz) breadcrumbs
3 tbsp freshly grated
  parmesan cheese
1 tbsp marjoram leaves,
  finely chopped
oil, for frying
12 skewers, about 25 cm
  (10 inches) long

Melt the butter in a heavy-based frying pan over a low heat. Add the sweetbreads if you like them, and cook for 10 minutes, or until browned well on all sides. Remove from the pan and set aside. Add the veal, mushrooms and zucchini to the pan, season with salt pepper and sauté over a medium heat, mixing gently with a wooden spoon, for 5 minutes, or until the veal is browned on all sides. Remove from the heat and set aside.

Beat the eggs in a dish wide enough to hold the skewers horizontally. Combine the breadcrumbs, parmesan and marjoram on a plate and place near the eggs.

Thread a piece of zucchini, then a cube of veal, a sweetbread, a mushroom and another cube of veal onto a skewer and repeat until all the skewers and ingredients are used.

Dip each skewer in the egg, then roll in the breadcrumb mixture. Pour the oil to a depth of 2.5 cm (1 inch) into a deep frying pan and heat until a small piece of bread thrown in sizzles immediately. Fry the *stecchi* for 3 minutes on each side, or until golden brown. Drain on paper towel and serve with a very proud look on your face. **SERVES 4**

Bollito alla Ligure

Beef stew with anchovy sauce

600 g (1 lb 3½ oz) shoulder
  of beef, boned and trimmed
3 small tomatoes, cut into
  quarters
1 carrot, chopped
1 onion, peeled and quartered
1 celery stalk, chopped
sea salt

FOR THE *ACCIUGATA* SAUCE
1 tbsp salted capers, rinsed
  and dried

4 anchovy fillets
1 garlic clove, chopped
2 sprigs parsley, leaves
  picked and chopped
2 hard-boiled egg yolks
pinch of sea salt
30 ml (1 fl oz) white wine
  vinegar
60 ml (2 fl oz) olive oil,
  plus extra

Place the beef in a large saucepan. Add the tomatoes, carrot, onion and celery. Cover with abundant cold water, season with salt and bring to the boil over a high heat. Reduce the heat to low and cook very gently, skimming the surface with a slotted spoon every now and then, for 2 hours, or until the meat is tender.

While the meat is cooking prepare the sauce. Place the capers, anchovies, garlic and parsley in a mortar and pound with a pestle into a paste. Add the egg yolks and pound a little to amalgamate. (You could do all this in a blender, but it's less fun.) Transfer to a bowl, season with salt, add the vinegar and mix with a wooden spoon. Add the oil a little at a time while still mixing. The amount of oil used determines the thickness of the sauce; if you prefer it to be thinner, add more oil. Pour into a bowl or jug.

When the meat is ready, place on a chopping board and slice. Arrange on a platter, sprinkle with a little extra oil and serve with the sauce on the side, so the diners can help themselves.

SERVES 4

Fegato all'agliata
Veal liver with garlic sauce

This dish has very quick preparation, because prolonged cooking will make the liver tough and dry. It differs from *Fegato alla Veneziana*—the liver prepared in the other marine republic—by the strong use of garlic instead of onions and the way the liver is cut. Here it is cut into thin strips, while in Venice it is cut into thick squares. The presence of bread in the sauce mellows the sharpness of the garlic, and the vinegar complements the natural flavour of the liver.

700 g (1 lb 6 oz) veal liver,
  ask the butcher to cut it
  into thin slices
4 garlic cloves, peeled
2 slices Italian bread,
  crusts removed

60 ml (2 fl oz) white wine
  vinegar
sea salt and freshly ground
  black pepper
60 ml (2 fl oz) olive oil

Cut across the grain of the liver with a sharp knife to make thin strips.

To make the sauce, place the garlic in a mortar and pound with the pestle to form a paste. Transfer to a bowl. Soak the bread in a little of the vinegar and combine with the garlic paste. Add the rest of the vinegar and a pinch of salt. Mix well with a wooden spoon until creamy.

Heat the oil in a heavy-based frying pan over a medium heat. Add the liver, season with salt and pepper, and sauté, stirring with a wooden spoon, for 3 minutes. Push the liver to one side of the pan, pour the sauce into the other side and combine the two, mixing with the spoon. Simmer, stirring constantly, for 4 minutes, being careful not to burn the garlic. Remove from the heat and serve hot. **SERVES 4**

Vitello tonnato

Roast veal with fresh tuna mayonnaise

800 g (1 lb 10 oz) veal fillet,
  trimmed of sinew and fat
30 ml (1 fl oz) olive oil
capers (optional), to serve
black olives, chopped
  (optional), to serve

FOR THE TUNA MAYONNAISE
2 eggs
4 egg yolks
2 tsp Dijon mustard

juice of 1 lemon
400 ml (13½ fl oz) olive oil
200 g (6½ oz) tuna fillet,
  grilled and chopped
20 g (¾ oz) anchovy fillets,
  chopped
60 ml (2 fl oz) sherry vinegar
3 tbsp natural yoghurt
sea salt and freshly ground
  black pepper

Preheat the oven to 220°C (425°F/gas 7). Heat the oil in a large heavy-based ovenproof frying pan over a high heat. Add the veal and seal on all sides. Transfer to the oven and roast for 9 minutes. Remove and cool on a wire rack for 20–30 minutes, or until at room temperature.

To make the tuna mayonnaise, whisk the eggs, yolks, mustard and lemon juice in a large bowl until combined. Slowly pour in a thin stream of olive oil, whisking vigorously until all the oil is incorporated. Add the tuna, anchovies, vinegar and salt and pepper, then fold in the yoghurt.

To serve, place 2 spoonfuls of the mayonnaise on each serving plate. Slice the veal, arrange on top of the mayonnaise, then spoon some more mayonnaise on top. Sprinkle with capers and black olives, if desired. **SERVES 4**

Vitello all'Uccelletto

Veal pan-fried in white wine and bay leaves

75 ml (2½ fl oz) olive oil
45 g (1½ oz) butter
3 bay leaves, torn
6 sage leaves
700 g (1 lb 6 oz) veal fillet,
  thinly sliced

sea salt and freshly ground
  black pepper
60 ml (2 fl oz) dry white wine

Heat the oil and butter in a heavy-based frying pan over a low heat. Add the bay leaves and sage, and cook, stirring with a wooden spoon, until fragrant. Increase the heat to medium, add the veal, season with salt and pepper and cook for 3 minutes, turning the veal once. Sprinkle in the white wine and cook, shaking the pan a few times to prevent sticking, until evaporated.

Remove the veal and place on individual plates or a large platter. Reduce the sauce for a few seconds, pour over the veal and serve hot. **SERVES 4**

Stracotto

Braised beef

45 ml (1½ fl oz) olive oil
60 g (2 oz) bacon or
  pancetta, chopped
1 white onion, finely chopped
1 celery stalk, finely chopped
1 garlic clove, finely chopped
600 g (1 lb 3½ oz) boned
  shoulder of beef, trimmed of fat

60 ml (2 fl oz) white wine
4 tomatoes, peeled, seeded
  and diced
sea salt
1 clove
4 sprigs flat-leaf parsley,
  whole with the stems

Heat the oil in a large heavy-based frying pan over a medium heat. To make a *soffritto*, add the bacon or pancetta, onion, celery and garlic and sauté for 5 minutes, mixing with a wooden spoon. Add the beef and cook, turning a few times, until browned on all sides. Add the wine and simmer until evaporated. Add the tomatoes, salt, clove and parsley. Cover the meat completely with water and bring to the boil. Reduce the heat to low, cover, and simmer for 1 hour, or until the meat is very soft, turning the meat a few times, and adding more water if necessary. Place the meat on a chopping board, cut into thick slices, and arrange the slices on a large dish. Strain the sauce, pour over the meat, and serve. **SERVES 4**

Contorni

Vegetables and salads

Vegetables and salads

Now we come to the heart of the matter. This is what Liguria was created for. The climate is perfect for vegetables and salad ingredients, and over the centuries the locals have delighted in finding new ways of combining them to taste even better.

The Slow Food movement, concerned to preserve and encourage the world's most special foodstuffs, has included eleven Ligurian ingredients as unique and essential in its 'Ark of Taste'. Of course the list includes two types of anchovy, a sheep's cheese, a focaccia and sciacchetrà, the rare dessert wine of the Cinque Terre. But after that it's all fruit or veg: asparagus from Albenga; garlic from Vessalico; pigna beans; chestnuts; a kind of rose syrup; and a variety of orange. To that list we would want to add artichokes, eggplants (aubergines), potatoes, zucchini (courgettes), tomatoes, spinach, peas, cauliflower and many kinds of mushrooms.

Some of these foodstuffs didn't reach Liguria until the seventeenth century, after being discovered in the Americas. But Ligurians were happy to embrace them, on the principle that if it tastes good with our olive oil—and especially, if we can stuff it—we'll give anything a try.

For home cooks, the great news is that most of the favourite Ligurian leaves, herbs and vegetables are available in high quality and quantity in Australia. That's why this is one of the longest chapters in the book.

In the recipes you'll find we sometimes list 'olive oil' or 'vinegar' at the end of the ingredients without giving a quantity. That's because we're talking about a little splash of oil and a smaller splash of vinegar at the end of the salad- or vegetable-making process. The size of the splash is up to you. As long as you have a big bottle of extra virgin olive oil and a bottle of vinegar to hand, you can judge how much to sprinkle over your dish to give it a healthy gleam and a Ligurian flavour just before serving.

Insalata di pere, rucola e parmigiano

Pear, rocket and parmesan salad

2 punnets (tubs) baby rocket
  (arugula)
4 firm pears
juice of 2 lemons

150 g (5 oz) shaved parmesan
  cheese
olive oil

Wash and dry the rocket.

Peel and quarter the pears, remove the core and stalk, and slice thinly. Place in a bowl and toss with the lemon juice to prevent them from discolouring. Add the rocket and the parmesan. Drizzle with extra virgin olive oil, toss well and serve. **SERVES 4**

Fichi con endivia e funghi

Marinated figs with witlof and shiitake mushrooms

12 ripe figs
60 ml (2 fl oz) red wine vinegar, plus extra
300 ml (10 fl oz) olive oil, plus extra
2 garlic cloves, thinly sliced
1 tbsp finely chopped marjoram leaves
1 tbsp finely chopped thyme leaves
2 witlof (Belgian endive)
16 shiitake mushrooms, cut in half
8 slices Italian bread, toasted
2 garlic cloves, peeled
sea salt

Wash and carefully dry the figs, remove the stalks and slice in half lengthwise.

To make the marinade, combine the vinegar, oil, the sliced garlic, marjoram and thyme in a bowl. Whisk to emulsify, add the figs, mix gently and set aside for 30 minutes.

In the meantime, remove the outer leaves from the witlof and cut off the base. Cut into 2-cm (¾-inch) slices and place in another bowl. Lightly dress with some oil, vinegar and salt.

Heat 60 ml (2 fl oz) of the marinade in a heavy-based frying pan over a medium heat. Add the mushrooms and quickly sauté for 1–2 minutes. Add the figs and cook for 2 minutes. Remove from the heat and mix half in with the witlof.

Rub one side of each slice of bread with the garlic cloves and brush with a little olive oil. Arrange the slices of bread on four plates.

Divide the witlof mixture between the four plates leaving most of the toasted bread in view. Place the remaining fig and mushroom mixture on the bread. Serve immediately. **SERVES 4**

Capponada

Tuna and tomato salad

This is a nineteenth-century invention prepared on board the sailing ships that followed the Ligurian coastline. Often the only meal of the day, it was ideal because the strong flavours and hearty ingredients satisfied the needs of working men.

Capponada is yet another combination of produce from the land and the sea, with two ingredients in common with the *cappon magro* (see page 198)—the *mosciame* (preserved tuna) and the *gallette* (ships' biscuits). It is based on food that can be preserved for a long time. The most basic recipe used only toasted bread, capers, anchovies, green olives and oregano—which struck me as a possible accompaniment for *carpaccio* (see Carpaccio with anchovy salad, page 75).

Instead of tuna, you could use *bottargà*—the preserved roe of the mullet. This has a strong bitter taste which would give a zing to the salad. About 90 g (3 oz) would be enough.

4 ripe tomatoes
4 hard-boiled eggs, peeled
250 g (8 oz) tinned tuna
6 slices Italian bread
1 garlic clove, peeled
75 ml (2½ fl oz) olive oil
20 ml (¾ fl oz) red wine
  vinegar
12 anchovy fillets
1 tbsp salted capers,
  rinsed and dried

1 tbsp oregano leaves
½ red onion, finely chopped
2 celery stalks, thinly sliced
20 black olives, such as
  kalamata, pitted and
  roughly chopped
sea salt and freshly ground
  black pepper
1 handful basil leaves,
  roughly chopped

Cut a cross in the base of each tomato and plunge into boiling water for about 1 minute. Immediately remove and immerse in iced water until the skin starts to wrinkle. Drain and when cool, peel off the skin. Cut in half and remove the seeds with a spoon. Dice, drain off excess liquid and put to one side.

Cut the eggs into thick slices.

Drain the tinned tuna, break it up with a fork and dress with a splash of olive oil.

Toast the bread, rub with garlic and place on a serving dish. Whisk the oil with the vinegar and sprinkle most of it over the toast. Arrange 2 anchovy fillets on each piece of toast and add the capers and oregano.

Working in layers, add the tomatoes, onion, egg, celery, olives and tuna. Season with salt and pepper. Sprinkle the basil on top, dress with a little more oil and vinegar and serve. A more modern approach is to cut the toast into small pieces and toss it through the ingredients.

SERVES 4

Insalata alle noci

Walnut salad

2 witlof (Belgian endives), trimmed
1 celery heart, thinly sliced
2 hard-boiled eggs, peeled and quartered
4 anchovy fillets, roughly chopped

15 walnuts, toasted and roughly chopped
30 ml (1 fl oz) olive oil
juice of ½ lemon
sea salt and freshly ground black pepper

Remove the outer leaves of the witlof, slice lengthwise and cut into julienne.

Combine the celery, witlof, eggs, anchovies and walnuts in a salad bowl.

In another bowl, whisk the olive oil, lemon juice and salt and pepper until emulsified. Pour over the salad, mix gently and serve. **SERVES 4**

Insalata di farro

Warm spelt salad

Farro is an ancient variety of wheat that was much loved by the Romans. It is sometimes called spelt in English and looks more like barley than wheat. *Insalata di farro*, a specialty of the mountain people in Liguria, is a classic example of peasant cooking: the base is water and a *soffritto* of oil, garlic and leeks, and enough is prepared for at least two meals. It is a simple and rustic dish that is rich in the quality of the ingredients.

1 kg (2 lb) farro
5 bay leaves
60 ml (2 fl) olive oil, plus extra
200 g (6½ oz) piece pancetta, diced

3 leeks, cleaned and thinly sliced
2 garlic cloves, finely chopped
45 g (1½ oz) freshly grated parmesan cheese
sea salt

Cook the farro and bay leaves in plenty of boiling salted water following the instructions on the packet. (Some farro comes pre-cooked and need less boiling time.) Drain but leave moist.

Heat the oil in a heavy-based saucepan over a low heat. Add the pancetta and sauté, stirring with a wooden spoon, until the pancetta starts to change colour. Add the leeks and garlic, season with salt (not too much as the pancetta is already salty). Stir, and cook for 5 minutes, or until the pancetta is crispy and the leeks are soft. At this point (when your kitchen is full of an amazing aroma), add the farro, and stir well so the grains absorb all the flavours, and cook for 5 minutes. The grains should be puffed up and moist. Place the farro in a serving dish, sprinkle with olive oil and parmesan and take it to the table. **SERVES 4**

Carciofi all'inferno

Hell's artichokes

Artichokes, tough on the outside but tender at the heart, arrived in Liguria from the Middle East in the fourteenth century (their Italian name supposedly comes from the Arabic *kharshuf*), but two centuries went by before they were fully appreciated. Now they are grown all over the region and prepared in many different ways—as an antipasto, as a side dish or as a complement to other preparations.

This particular dish is called *all'inferno* (Hell style) because the artichokes are crammed into a baking dish and cooked in a hot oven so they look like the damned souls in the Underworld.

12 globe artichokes
1 lemon, cut in half
100 ml (3½ fl oz) olive oil
2 garlic cloves, finely chopped
2 tbsp finely chopped flat-leaf
  parsley

4 sprigs marjoram, leaves
  picked and chopped
sea salt and freshly ground
  black pepper

Preheat the oven to 180°C (350°F/gas 4). To clean the artichokes pull off and discard all the tough outer leaves, leaving only the heart. Cut off the stem to make a flat base. Keep about 2 cm (¾ inch) of the top part of the stems, peel them and put to one side as these will be added to the stuffing. Rub the cut portion of the artichoke with the lemon to stop discolouring. Cut off the top 3 cm (1¼ inches) of the artichoke to expose the centre. Scrape out the hairy choke, being careful not to touch any of the tender heart, and rub the inside with some more lemon. Bang the artichoke gently on the bench, top side down, to widen the cavity and make it easier to stuff.

Finely chop the artichoke stems and combine them with the garlic, parsley and marjoram in a bowl. Stir about 20 ml (¾ fl oz) of olive oil through the mixture and season with salt and pepper.

Place the artichokes in a line on an oiled oven dish and spoon the garlic and parsley mixture into the cavity of each. Pour a generous amount of olive oil on top, sprinkle with salt and bake in the oven for 40 minutes. Serve immediately. **SERVES 4**

Carciofi e patate a funghetto
Pan-fried artichokes and potatoes

The phrase *a funghetto* in Italian title means 'done mushroom style', and refers to the way the artichokes and potatoes are thinly sliced.

1 litre (32 fl oz) water
juice of ½ lemon
10 globe artichokes
150 ml (5 fl oz) olive oil
2 garlic cloves, finely chopped
5 potatoes, peeled and
  thinly sliced

250 ml (8 fl oz) vegetable stock
1 tsp chopped flat-leaf parsley
1 tsp chopped thyme leaves
1 tsp oregano leaves
sea salt and freshly ground
  black pepper

To prepare the artichokes, first make the acidulated water. Combine the water and lemon juice in a large bowl and set aside. Pull off all the tough outer leaves of the artichokes, leaving only the yellowy green heart. Trim the stem to about 2 cm (¾ inch). Peel the remaining stem with a knife and shape it. With a sharp knife remove the points and the hairy choke in the middle. Thinly slice the artichokes lengthwise and immerse in the acidulated water.

Heat the oil in a heavy-based frying pan or terracotta pot over a low heat. Add the garlic and fry, stirring with a wooden spoon, until the garlic starts to change colour, about 1 minute. Add the drained artichokes and the potatoes and cook for 5 minutes, or until the potatoes take on a golden colour. Add the stock, mix gently, cover, and cook for 35 minutes. Remove the lid, sprinkle on the herbs, season with salt and pepper, and stir gently but thoroughly. Allow to cook for another 5 minutes and serve immediately. **SERVES 4**

Carciofi e piselli in umido
Stewed artichokes and peas

6 globe artichokes
100 ml (3½ fl oz) olive oil
1 onion, thinly sliced
250 ml (8 fl oz) dry white wine
500 g (1 lb) fresh peas, shelled

250 ml (8 fl oz) vegetable
  stock or water
sea salt and freshly ground
  black pepper

To prepare the artichokes see the recipe above.

Heat the oil in a heavy-based saucepan, preferably terracotta, over a low heat. Add the onion and fry for 3 minutes. Add the drained artichokes, mix well with a wooden spoon, and cook for 10 minutes. Add the wine and cook for 10 minutes. Add the peas and stock or water, season with salt and pepper, mix thoroughly, and cook gently for 10–15 minutes, or until the artichokes are tender. Serve hot. **SERVES 4**

Imbrogliata di carciofi
Sautéed artichoke hearts with eggs

An *imbrogliata* is a trick. We guess this dish got its name because it tricks people who expect a combination of eggs and vegetables to be a frittata, which this isn't.

12 globe artichokes
100 ml (3½ fl oz) olive oil
sea salt
1 tsp chopped flat-leaf
  parsley

6 eggs
100 g (3½ oz) freshly grated
  parmesan cheese
2 garlic cloves, chopped

To prepare the artichokes see the recipe opposite.

Heat the oil in a heavy-based frying pan over a low heat. Add the garlic and cook gently for 2 minutes. Add the drained artichokes, season with salt, and mix well with a wooden spoon. Cover and cook gently for 20 minutes, adding water if it seems to be drying out and shaking the pan from time to time. Uncover the pan, add the parsley, mix well, and cook for 5 minutes.

Beat the eggs, parmesan and a pinch of salt in a bowl and pour onto the artichokes. Mix gently and cook over a medium heat for 5 minutes, until the eggs are just set. Serve hot.

If you prefer to serve the *imbrogliata* individually, when the artichokes are tender, place in individual dishes or ramekins, pour the egg mixture on top and bake in a preheated 190°C (375°F/ gas 5) oven for 3 minutes, then serve. **SERVES 4**

Asparagi al burro di acciughe

Asparagus in anchovy butter

3 bunches asparagus
sea salt and freshly ground
  black pepper
60 g (2 oz) butter
4 anchovy fillets
45 g (1½ oz) parmesan
  cheese, grated

Wash the asparagus and tie into bunches with string. Chop off the tough ends on each stalk. Fill a saucepan with water and bring to the boil. Add a little salt, then immerse the asparagus, tips up, and simmer for 3 minutes, checking that the bubbling water does not damage or break the asparagus tips. Carefully remove and untie the bundles.

In the meantime, combine the butter and anchovies in a small pan over a low heat and cook, stirring, until the butter is bubbling and the anchovies are melted.

Arrange the asparagus on a serving dish with the tips facing towards the centre. Pour the melted anchovy butter over the asparagus, mainly on the tips. Scatter on the parmesan, add a little salt and a good grind of pepper and serve. **SERVES 4**

Fagioli e bietole

Beans sautéed with silverbeet

250 g (8 oz) dried
  cannellini beans
2 bunches silverbeet
2 garlic cloves, lightly crushed
  with the blade of a knife

100 ml (3½ fl oz) olive oil
sea salt and freshly ground
  black pepper

Soak the beans overnight. Drain and cook in plenty of boiling salted water for 30 minutes. Drain well.

In the meantime, wash the silverbeet and cut out the tough white stalks. Cook the leaves in boiling water for 8 minutes. Drain and squeeze dry. Place on a chopping board and chop roughly.

Heat the oil in a heavy-based frying pan over a medium heat. Add the garlic, stir with a wooden spoon, and sauté for 2 minutes, or until the garlic changes colour. Remove and discard. Add the silverbeet and the cannellini beans, season with salt and pepper, mix thoroughly, and cook for a few more minutes. Serve hot, adding a little oil if necessary. Excellent to accompany meat.
SERVES 4

Rattatuia

Riviera ratatouille

This dish shows what a small distance lies between the coastline of southern France and the coastline of northern Italy, and how meaningless national boundaries are. Rather than get into a silly argument about which country invented *rattatuia*, or which country does the best version, we'll just say its origin is lost in the mists of time. We do know, however, that it must have been after the sixteenth century, when the tomato and the capsicum (bell pepper) arrived in Europe from the Americas as the result of the explorations of that fine Ligurian sailor Cristoforo Colombo.

400 g (13 oz) fresh borlotti
  beans, shelled
300 g (10 oz) green beans,
  trimmed and chopped into
  short lengths
100 ml (3½ fl oz) olive oil
1 white onion, finely chopped
1 garlic clove, finely chopped
2 carrots, diced
1 small celery stalk, diced
2 small eggplants
  (aubergines), diced

1 red capsicum
  (bell pepper), diced
1 yellow capsicum
  (bell pepper), diced
500 g (1 lb) ripe tomatoes,
  peeled, seeded and diced
sea salt and freshly ground
  black pepper
5 zucchini (courgettes),
  diced
1 handful basil leaves

Cook the borlotti beans in salted boiling water until soft but still a little *al dente*, about 30 minutes, then drain and set aside.

Blanch the green beans in boiling water for 2 minutes. Drain and refresh in iced water. Set aside.

Heat the oil in a large heavy-based frying pan over a low heat. Add the onion and garlic and fry, stirring regularly to prevent sticking, for 3 minutes, or until the onions are softened and the garlic is changing colour a little. Add the borlotti beans, green beans, carrots, celery, eggplants, capsicums and tomatoes. Season with salt and pepper and cook for 30 minutes, gently stirring frequently. Add the zucchini and basil, mix well and continue to cook for 30 minutes.

Serve hot, but this dish is also excellent cold, the next day. Resting will help the fusion of the flavours. **SERVES 4**

Fagiolini all' aglio e acciughe
Green beans with garlic and anchovies

600 g (1 lb 3½ oz) green
  beans, topped and tailed
4 salted anchovies
60 ml (2 fl oz) olive oil
45 g (1½ oz) butter

1 garlic clove, finely chopped
1 handful flat-leaf parsley leaves,
  finely chopped
sea salt and freshly grated
  black pepper

Finely slice the green beans. Place in a saucepan of boiling water and cook for 3 minutes. Drain and set aside.

Wash and fillet the anchovies under running water, pat dry and set aside.

Heat the oil and the butter in a heavy-based frying pan and make a *soffritto* by adding the garlic and parsley and sautéing for 2 minutes. Add the anchovies and stir until dissolved. Add the green beans, season with salt and pepper, stir well, but gently, and sauté for 3 minutes. Serve hot.

SERVES 4

Pomodori in tegame
Pan-cooked tomatoes

8 ripe tomatoes
200 ml (7 fl oz) olive oil
4 garlic cloves, finely chopped
2 tbsp chopped oregano leaves
3 tbsp chopped flat-leaf parsley
120 g (4 oz) freshly grated
  parmesan cheese
sea salt

Preheat the oven to 180°C (350°F/gas 4).

Wash and dry the tomatoes, cut in half, and remove the seeds with a teaspoon. Place in a colander to drain off excess liquid.

Heat half of the oil in a large roasting tin over a medium heat. Add half the garlic and oregano, and one-third of the parsley. Sprinkle with some salt, stir well, and fry for 5 minutes. Remove from the heat, arrange the tomatoes, cut-side up, on top and sprinkle with salt. Scatter the remaining garlic, oregano and parsley over the tomatoes and sprinkle the parmesan on top. Cover with foil and roast in the oven for 30 minutes. Serve hot. **MAKES 16**

Cavolfiore all' acciugata
Cauliflower with anchovies

600 g (1 lb 3½ oz) cauliflower
6 salted anchovies
125 ml (4 fl oz) olive oil
30 ml (1 fl oz) good red wine
  vinegar

1 garlic clove, chopped
sea salt and freshly ground
  black pepper

In abundant boiling salted water cook the cauliflower for 20 minutes. Drain and cut into florets and place in a large bowl.

In the meantime, wash and fillet the anchovies under running water, pat dry with paper towel and break into small pieces. Place on top of the cauliflower.

Make a sauce by whisking the olive oil, vinegar, garlic and salt and pepper in a bowl. Pour over the cauliflower and anchovies, mix carefully and rest for 5–10 minutes before serving as a side dish or as an appetiser. **SERVES 4**

Cipolle e zucchine in fricassea
Fricasseed onion and zucchini

100 ml (3½ fl oz) olive oil
5 white onions, thinly sliced
6 zucchini (courgettes),
  thinly sliced
sea salt and freshly ground
  black pepper
4 eggs

Heat the oil in a heavy-based frying pan over a medium heat. Add the onions and sauté, stirring well with a wooden spoon, for 5 minutes or until softened and translucent. Add the zucchini, season with salt and pepper and cook for 15 minutes. Beat the eggs and a pinch of salt in a bowl and add to the pan. Stir quickly until the eggs set slightly, and serve immediately. **SERVES 4**

Spinaci alla genovese

Spinach with pine nuts and sultanas

This spinach is excellent served as *crostini* on top of slices of Italian bread which have been fried in a little olive oil.

45 g (1½ oz) sultanas (seedless
  white raisins)
1.5 kg (3 lb) English spinach
60 ml (2 fl oz) olive oil
45 g (1½ oz) pine nuts
pinch of freshly grated nutmeg
pinch of sea salt

Soak the sultanas in warm water for 5 minutes to revive them, and dry well with paper towel.

Wash the spinach leaves thoroughly, then cook the wet leaves in a saucepan over a medium heat for 2 minutes, or until wilted. Gently squeeze out the excess water.

Heat the oil in a heavy-based frying pan over a low heat, add the spinach, sultanas and pine nuts and season with nutmeg and salt. Mix well with a wooden spoon and cook for 10 minutes, stirring occasionally. Serve hot. **SERVES 4**

Fiori di zucchine ripieni al forno

Baked stuffed zucchini flowers

20 zucchini (courgette) flowers
2 potatoes, scrubbed
120 g (4 oz) green beans,
   topped and tailed
3 zucchini (courgettes),
   trimmed
2 eggs
60 g (2 oz) freshly grated
   parmesan cheese

1 garlic clove, finely chopped
3 sprigs marjoram leaves
8 basil leaves, finely chopped
30 g (1 oz) butter, melted
60 ml (2 fl oz) olive oil, plus
   extra
sea salt and freshly ground
   black pepper

Preheat the oven to 240°C (475°F/gas 8).

Remove and discard the pistils from inside the zucchini flowers. Set the flowers aside.

Cook the potatoes in abundant boiling salted water for 15 minutes. Drain and when cool enough to handle, peel and place in a bowl. Cook the beans in boiling water for 10 minutes, or until tender. Drain and combine with the potatoes.

Cook the zucchini in boiling salted water until tender. Drain and add to the beans and potatoes. Pass through a sieve into another bowl. Add the eggs, parmesan, garlic, marjoram, basil, butter and olive oil. Season with salt and pepper and mix well.

Separate the petals on the zucchini flowers and spoon in the stuffing. Seal the petals around the stuffing and place the flowers in a row on an oiled roasting tin.

Pour a little oil on top and place in the oven for 10 minutes.

VARIATION

You can fill the flowers with fish if you like. Just replace the potatoes and the green beans with 300 g (10 oz) of soft fish fillets (snapper, bream, whiting or red mullet). Cook the fish in salted boiling water with half an onion, a celery stalk and a carrot until it is really soft. Discard the onion, celery and carrot and puree the fish. Proceed as for the recipe above. I would add a chopped small red chilli to the mixture with the fish, before stuffing the zucchini flowers. **SERVES 4**

Radicchio in padella

Pan-fried radicchio

There are two types of radicchio—one is round and is called *radicchio di Chioggia* (a town just south of Venice); the other is long and oval shaped and comes from the town of Treviso (north-west of Venice). The Treviso version is more bitter than the Chioggia version, but sweetens when cooked—which is why we're using it in this recipe.

3 radicchio, base trimmed and outer leaves discarded
125 ml (4 fl oz) olive oil
3 garlic cloves, finely chopped
1 small bunch rosemary, leaves picked and chopped
sea salt and freshly ground black pepper
45 ml (1½ fl oz) red wine vinegar

Roughly chop the radicchio lengthwise. Wash and blanch in boiling salted water for 2 minutes. Drain and dry well.

Heat the oil in a heavy-based frying pan over a medium heat. Add the garlic and fry for 1 minute or until the garlic starts to change colour. Add the radicchio, sprinkle with rosemary, season with salt and pepper and pour in the vinegar. Stir well and cook for 2 minutes.

Remove from the heat, place in a bowl, allow to cool and serve. **SERVES 4**

Funghi a funghetto
Fried mushrooms 'mushroom style'

The Italian name is a joke that means mushrooms in a mushroom style, referring to the way they are cooked. These mushrooms are excellent served on *crostini*.

1 kg (2 lb) mixed mushrooms (not too big), such as button, shiitake, brown and enoki
2 garlic cloves, peeled

1 handful flat-leaf parsley leaves
100 ml (3½ fl oz) olive oil
sea salt
oregano

Wipe the mushrooms with a damp cloth and thinly slice. Finely chop the garlic and parsley with a mezzaluna, if you have one.

Heat the oil in a heavy-based frying pan over a low heat. Add the garlic and parsley mixture and sauté for 2 minutes, or until the garlic is just starting to change colour. Increase the heat to medium-high, add the mushrooms, stir and season with salt. Stir in the oregano and cook for 15–20 minutes, or until the liquid has evaporated. Serve hot. **SERVES 4**

Funghi e patate
Mushrooms and potatoes

1 kg (2 lb) large mixed mushrooms, such as brown or shiitake
4 garlic cloves
1 handful chopped flat-leaf parsley leaves
90 ml (3 fl oz) olive oil

60 ml (2 fl oz) dry white wine
6 large potatoes, peeled and cut into 5-mm (¼-inch) slices
sea salt and freshly ground black pepper
1 tsp oregano leaves

Preheat the oven to 180°C (350°F/gas 4).

Wipe the mushrooms with a damp cloth. Detach the stems, put to one aside, and thinly slice the remainder lengthwise.

Chop the garlic and parsley very finely to make a trito (literally, a mince). Chop the reserved mushroom stems and add to the garlic and parsley mixture. Whisk 20 ml (¾ fl oz) of oil and 45 ml (112 fl oz) of white wine and pour into an ovenproof dish. Arrange a layer of the potatoes in the dish. Sprinkle on salt and pepper and a little of the garlic and parsley trito. Place a layer of mushrooms on top, season with more salt and pepper and add another sprinkle of the trito. Cover with another layer of potatoes, salt, pepper and trito.

Pour the remaining oil on top, cover the dish (if you don't have a lid use foil), and bake in the oven for 30 minutes. Remove the cover, sprinkle the oregano leaves on top and return to the oven to brown for 15 minutes. Cool a little and serve. **SERVES 4**

Polpettine di patate

Potato croquettes

We'd better explain the difference between *polpettine* and *polpettone* (the next recipe). Both words come from *polpette*, which means meatball. A *polpettone* is a large meatball—a meat loaf (or, by extension, anything in a loaf shape). *Polpettine* are small balls of minced ingredients, sometimes meat, but in this case, potatoes. Are you more confused now?

500 g (1 lb) potatoes, peeled
  and chopped
sea salt and freshly ground
  black pepper
pinch of freshly grated nutmeg
45 g (1½ oz) butter
100 g (3½ oz) freshly grated
  parmesan cheese

2 egg yolks
2 eggs
60 g (2 oz) plain (all purpose)
  flour
150 g (5 oz) breadcrumbs
olive oil, for frying

Place the potatoes in a large saucepan, cover with cold water, add a pinch of salt and boil until soft. Drain, mash and place in a bowl. Season with salt and pepper and nutmeg. Add the butter, parmesan and egg yolks and mix well to amalgamate. Shape into small croquettes about 5 cm (2 inches) long.

In the meantime, place the eggs in a shallow bowl and lightly whisk. Place the flour and the breadcrumbs on separate plates.

Roll each croquette in the flour, then dip in the egg and then roll in the breadcrumbs, shaking off the excess coating each time.

Pour enough oil into a large heavy-based frying pan to cover the base and come about 8 mm (⅜ inch) up the sides. Heat the oil over a high heat. Add the croquettes, as many as you can fit without overcrowding, and cook, turning occasionally, until a golden crust has formed on all sides. Remove from the pan with a slotted spoon and place on paper towel to drain, and keep them warm in an oven heated to 120°C (230°F/gas ½). Repeat with the remaining croquettes. Serve hot.

SERVES 4

Polpettone di zucchine

Zucchini and potato cake

3 medium potatoes, scrubbed
125 ml (4 fl oz) olive oil
½ white onion, finely chopped
1 garlic clove, finely chopped
800 g (1 lb 10 oz) zucchini
  (courgettes), thinly sliced
sea salt and freshly ground
  black pepper
1 handful flat-leaf parsley leaves,
  finely chopped

4 eggs
60 g (2 oz) freshly grated
  parmesan cheese
pinch of freshly grated nutmeg
4 sprigs marjoram,
  roughly chopped
4 tbsp breadcrumbs

Preheat the oven to 190°C (375°F/gas 5).

Cook the potatoes in plenty of boiling salted water.

Heat the oil in a heavy-based frying pan over a low heat. Add the onion and garlic and sauté for 2–3 minutes. Add the zucchini, mix with a wooden spoon, season with salt, mix again and cook for 15 minutes. Sprinkle the parsley on top, mix well, remove from the heat and place in a bowl.

By this time the potatoes should be ready, drain and when cool enough to handle, peel and puree using a mouli. Combine with the zucchini. Add the eggs, parmesan, nutmeg and marjoram. Mix well to amalgamate and season with salt and pepper if necessary.

Oil the base of an ovenproof dish. Pour in the zucchini and potato mixture, smooth the surface and sprinkle with the breadcrumbs. Drizzle over a bit more olive oil and bake in the oven for 40 minutes, or until golden brown.

This *polpettone* can be enjoyed either warm or cold, as a light lunch accompanied by a salad of radicchio and tomato. **SERVES 4**

Insalata di patate
Potato salad

3 waxy potatoes, such as
  large Pontiacs
1 tbsp capers
4–6 anchovy fillets, broken
  into small pieces
1 garlic clove, finely chopped
1 tbsp oregano leaves
sea salt
60 ml (2 fl oz) olive oil
1 handful basil leaves

Peel and cook the potatoes in plenty of boiling water for 15 minutes, or until soft. Drain and when cool enough to handle, cut into thick slices. Arrange the potatoes in a serving bowl, add the capers, anchovies, garlic, oregano and a little salt. Pour the olive oil on top, mix gently and rest for 15 minutes. Tear the basil leaves and scatter over the potatoes, give another gentle mix and serve immediately while the basil is still aromatic. **SERVES 4**

Patate arrosto alle erbe Liguri
Roasted new potatoes with mixed herbs

1 kg (2 lb) new potatoes, washed
60 ml (2 fl oz) olive oil
45 g (1½ oz) butter, chopped
30 g (1 oz) chopped mixed
  herbs, such as rosemary,
  marjoram, thyme and sage
6 garlic cloves, peeled
sea salt

Preheat the oven to 180°C (350°F/gas 4).

Parboil the potatoes for 3 minutes in abundant salted water. Drain well.

Lightly oil an ovenproof dish and add the potatoes. Scatter the butter over the potatoes, and sprinkle the herb mixture on top. Add the garlic cloves at random. Season with salt and pour on the rest of the olive oil. Toss well and bake in the oven for 30 minutes, or until golden brown. **SERVES 4**

Scorzanera alla salsa appetitosa
Salsify with spicy sauce

Salsify is an earthy winter vegetable that's a bit like celeriac or parsnip (which would also benefit from the sauce in this recipe).

1 kg (2 lb) salsify

FOR THE SAUCE
2 salted anchovies
½ garlic clove
1 tsp chopped flat-leaf parsley
 leaves
30 g (1 oz) pine nuts

15 g (½ oz) capers
30 g (1 oz) soft inside of Italian
 bread, soaked in a little of the
 vinegar
60 ml (2 fl oz) good white
 wine vinegar
75 ml (2½ fl oz) olive oil
sea salt

Scrape clean and wash the salsify then cook in abundant salted water for 5 minutes. Drain and cut lengthwise into julienne. Place in a bowl and dress with the sauce.

To make the sauce, wash and fillet the anchovies under running water and pat dry with paper towel.

Combine the garlic, parsley, pine nuts, capers, anchovies and bread soaked in vinegar in a mortar and pound with a pestle until creamy. Pass through a sieve into a bowl. Add the remaining vinegar and the olive oil, season with salt, and pour over the salsify. **SERVES 4**

Marinata di melanzane
Marinated eggplant

5 long thin eggplants
 (aubergines)
150 ml (5 fl oz) olive oil
30 ml (1 fl oz) white wine
 vinegar
2 garlic cloves, finely chopped
thyme

oregano
1 small handful flat-leaf
 parsley leaves, chopped
sea salt and freshly ground
 black pepper

Wash the eggplants and boil in plenty of water for 4 minutes. Drain and pat dry, trim the ends, and slice the eggplants into thin discs.

Whisk the olive oil, vinegar, garlic, thyme, oregano, parsley and a pinch of salt and pepper in a bowl. Arrange a layer of eggplants on the bottom of a large dish, pour some of the herb dressing on top and continue layering in this manner until all the ingredients are used.

Set aside in a cool place for 5 hours, checking after 1 hour that it is not becoming too dry. If it is, add some oil and vinegar. **SERVES 4**

Melanzane fritte
Pan-fried eggplant

2 large round eggplants
  (aubergines), thickly sliced
sea salt
3 eggs
15 ml (½ fl oz) milk
100 g (3½ oz) plain (all
  purpose) flour
100 g (3½ oz) breadcrumbs
olive oil

4 ripe tomatoes, peeled,
  seeded and chopped
sea salt and freshly ground
  black pepper
1 handful basil leaves, roughly
  chopped
200 g (6½ oz) parmesan cheese

FOR SAUCE
20 ml (¾ oz) olive oil
4 garlic cloves, peeled

Sprinkle the eggplant with salt and place in a colander for about 15 minutes to purge the bitter juices. Pat dry with paper towel.

In the meantime, beat the eggs, milk and a pinch of salt in a shallow bowl. Place the flour and the breadcrumbs on separate plates. Dip the eggplant slices first in the flour, then in the egg mixture and finally in the breadcrumbs, pressing firmly.

Heat the olive oil to a depth of about 1 cm (½ inch) over a high heat in a heavy-based frying pan. Add the eggplant and fry until golden. Drain on paper towel to remove excess oil, sprinkle with salt and serve hot.

VARIATION

At this point, instead of serving the eggplant immediately you can add a tomato and parmesan cheese sauce.

Preheat the oven to 180°C (350°F/gas 4). Heat the olive oil in a pan add the garlic and sauté until aromatic and lightly golden. Discard the garlic and add the tomatoes. Season with salt and pepper, mix well and cook for 5 minutes. Place in a bowl and set aside.

Spread some tomato sauce in the base of an ovenproof dish, place a layer of eggplant on top, not overlapping. Now on top of that layer of eggplant put some more tomato sauce, some basil leaves and a sprinkle of parmesan. On top of that add another layer of eggplant, tomato sauce, basil and parmesan and continue until all the ingredients are used. Finish with some pepper and a sprinkle of olive oil on the top layer. Bake in the oven for 5 minutes, or until the parmesan has formed a crust.

Allow to rest and serve at room temperature. **SERVES 4**

Piccoli peperoni ripieni di inzimono

Stuffed Bellarossa capsicums

8 small round deep red Bellarossa
  capsicums (bell peppers)
olive oil
sea salt
⅓ quantity of spinach and pine
  nuts mixture (see page 283)
2 tbsp breadcrumbs

Preheat the oven to 220°C (425°F/gas 7).

Coat the capsicums with oil and salt and roast them in the oven for 15–20 minutes, or until the skin blisters.

Allow to cool, and peel. Cut away the stem, and scoop out the seeds with a spoon, making sure not to break the flesh. Fill each cavity with the spinach and pine nut mixture and place on a greased roasting tin. Sprinkle with breadcrumbs and a little olive oil and bake at 180°C (350°F/gas 4) for 10 minutes. Serve warm.

VARIATION

The roasted capsicums can be preserved in garlic- and oregano-scented olive oil with an anchovy and a caper inside each cavity. **SERVES 4**

Dolci

Desserts

Desserts

302 PESCHE RIPIENE ALL'AMARETTO ~ Stuffed peaches with amaretti biscuits

304 SACRIPANTINA ~ Coffee and chocolate sponge

305 PANDOLCE GENOVESE ~ Genoa cake

306 PACIUGO ~ Ice cream sundae

307 CROSTATA DI RICOTTA E RABARBARO ~ Rhubarb and ricotta tart

309 BUDINO DI CASTAGNE ~ Chestnut mousse with basil sauce

310 TORTA DI FICHI E MASCARPONE ~ Fig and mascarpone tart

313 TORTA DI RICOTTA E NOCCIOLE ~ Flourless hazelnut and ricotta cake

314 AMARETTI ~ Almond biscuits

316 BISCOTTINI ~ Almond and chocolate biscuits

317 ANICINI ~ Aniseed biscuits

317 BACI DI DAMA ~ Lady's kisses

318 PINOLATE ~ Pine nut cookies

318 FOCACCIA DOLCE ALLO SCIACCHETRÀ ~ Focaccia cake with dessert wine

320 CASTAGNACCIO ~ Chestnut flour cake

322 SEMIFREDDO ALLA MENTA ~ Mint ice cream cake with chocolate fudge

325 SEMIFREDDO DI NOCI ~ Walnut semifreddo

Desserts are not exactly a standard part of the daily diet of Ligurians. Most of the time they end their meals with unadorned pieces of fruit, which grow abundantly in Liguria's mild climate.

Elaborate *dolci* are too frivolous for hardworking sailors and farmers, who might nibble on an almond biscuit with their coffee, but can only give themselves permission to fully relax with a sweet treat when it's an official feast day or occasion for celebration.

Fortunately, there are many official feast days along the Riviera and thus there are many opportunities to put cavities in a sweet tooth with a purchase from the pastry shop. The *pandolce*, for example, which is the antecedent of the more familiar *panettone*, comes out at Christmas, while the *sacripantina* is a wedding cake.

In Liguria, the desserts developed in relation to the natural produce of the land and its aromas. Aniseed and fennel seeds feature in an array of biscuits across the province, with almost every village proud of its own recipe.

Some biscuits are eaten for breakfast dipped in caffe latte, which is usually served in huge cups like a soup bowl. And what a wonderful moment of the day that is, with the strong tastes of the seeds and the aroma of the coffee in the air. Other biscuits are made with nuts—almond *amaretti* and the irresistible soft *pinolate*, pine nut biscuits.

A few desserts are made with chestnuts or its flour. Chestnuts were part of the life of the people of the inland villages away from tourist traps. For those people, their cooking was a matter of survival. For us it has led to some great dishes. Chestnut flour is used in dishes ranging from simple pancakes to an elegant and delicate chestnut mousse.

A few desserts are influenced by the Middle East, such as the little pastries filled with nuts and covered in honey that you find in cake shop windows all along the Riviera, as well as many other tempting and provocative *pasticcini*.

We're offering a mixture of the classic traditional—such as the almond biscotti—and the adventurous modern—such as the chestnut parfait with basil sauce—and quite a few points in between. Some are challenging, but we've left the most difficult to last. We begin with a not-so-unadorned piece of Liguria's finest fruit.

Pesche ripiene all' amaretto

Stuffed peaches with amaretti biscuits

5 yellow peaches
150 g (5 oz) candied fruit
150 g (5 oz) amaretti, chopped
caster (superfine) sugar, for
 sprinkling
splash of white wine or Marsala

Preheat the oven to 180°C (350°F/gas 4).

Cut the peaches in half and remove the stones. Using a spoon, scrape out a little of the flesh from each cavity. Place this peach flesh, the candied fruit and amaretti in a bowl and mix well.

Arrange the peaches cut-side up on a baking tray. Divide the filling between the 10 peach halves, sprinkle with a little of the wine or marsala and top with a sprinkling of sugar. Bake for 20 minutes, or until golden on top. Serve with mascarpone or ice cream. **SERVES 4**

Sacripantina

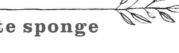

Coffee and chocolate sponge

4 sweet biscuits
3 amaretti biscuits
180 g (6 oz) icing
  (confectioners') sugar
200 g (6½ oz) butter, softened
  to room temperature
30 ml (1 fl oz) rum
30 ml (1 fl oz) strong espresso
  coffee

30 g (1 oz) bitter cocoa powder
500 g (1 lb) plain sponge cake
  (bought at your local cake
  shop)
1 small bottle Marsala

Crush the biscuits to a fine powder and mix with 30 g (1 oz) of the sugar. Set aside.

Cream the butter and the remaining sugar until soft and fluffy. Add the rum, then divide into two portions. Slowly add the coffee to one portion and add the cocoa to the other.

Slice the sponge crossways into 6 discs to fit the cake tin. You can cut the sponge into pieces to fit the size if necessary.

Line a springform cake tin with plastic wrap, allowing enough overhang to cover the top of the cake. The idea is to have layers of sponge alternating with layers of the coffee cream and the cocoa cream.

Set aside enough of the cocoa cream to cover the cake at the end. Layer the bottom of the tin with sponge. Brush with marsala and put a layer of cocoa cream on top, add another layer of sponge brushed with marsala, then place a layer of coffee cream on top. Finish with a layer of sponge. Cover with the overhanging plastic wrap, place a plate the same size as the cake on top and place a weight on top of that. Refrigerate for at least 3–4 hours.

Unmould the cake onto a serving plate and spread the remaining cocoa cream over the surface. Sprinkle on the reserved biscuit and sugar powder, to decorate as you like. **SERVES 4**

Pandolce Genovese

Genoa cake

This is a classic Christmas cake from mediaeval times, but now it is consumed all year round. On Christmas Day, it was presented to the family with a little bunch of bay leaves or olive leaves sticking out of it. The youngest person would cut it, the oldest would pass it round and each portion was kissed by all the people at the table. Health concerns make this a less popular ritual nowadays.

Again, the recipe varies along the Riviera. In La Spezia, where I come from, it is made with fewer candied fruits and with the addition of fennel seeds.

½ tsp active dry yeast
125 ml (4 fl oz) warm milk
150 g (5 oz) butter, softened
180 g (6 oz) caster
  (superfine) sugar
20 g (¾ oz) fennel seeds
1 tsp ground coriander
1 egg, lightly beaten
10 ml (13 fl oz) vanilla extract

20 ml (34 fl oz) orange
  blossom water
500 g (1 lb) plain
  (all purpose) flour
45 g (1½ oz) currants
45 g (1½ oz) finely
  chopped candied zest
45 g (1½ oz) pine nuts

Combine the yeast and milk in a small bowl and stir to dissolve the yeast. Set aside for 10 minutes, or until foaming.

Cream the butter and sugar until light and fluffy. Add the fennel seeds and coriander, and mix well, then add the egg, vanilla and orange blossom water and mix thoroughly. Slowly stir in the yeast and milk mixture. Gradually sift in the flour and mix until smooth and moist. Add the currants, zest and pine nuts. Mix well to evenly distribute all the ingredients, and knead until you have a smooth and pliable consistency, adding some water if necessary. Cover with a tea towel and rest in a warm place for 4–5 hours.

Preheat the oven to 200°C (400°F/gas 6).

Transfer the dough to a greased baking tray and shape the cake into a mound about 15 cm (6 inches) in diameter. You will have to moisten your hands with water as the dough will be a little sticky. With a sharp knife cut a cross into the top of the cake. Place in the oven and bake for 45 minutes to 1 hour, lowering the temperature if the cake browns too quickly. The finished cake should be a deep golden brown. Allow to cool completely before serving. **SERVES 4**

Paciugo
Ice cream sundae

Let's go back to childhood. This specialty of Portofino, where the rich go to play like children, is a fruit and ice cream sundae that you build to your taste. We have not put any quantities in this recipe because you know what you like. The main thing is to display a variety of colours in the layers. It should be served in a large cocktail glass or a tall sundae glass.

whipped cream
chocolate ice cream
strawberry or raspberry ice
  cream
fresh fruit, peeled and chopped,
  such as peaches, apples and
  pears, depending on the season

mixed berries, such as
  strawberries, blueberries
  and raspberries

Assemble this dessert by placing a little cream in the bottom of the glass, then layer in the ice creams and the fruit and top with a little more whipped cream.

Crostata di ricotta e rabarbaro

Rhubarb and ricotta tart

FOR THE PASTRY
500 g (1 lb) plain
  (all purpose) flour
75 g (2½ oz) almond meal
75 g (2½ oz) caster
  (superfine) sugar
15 g (½ oz) salt
375 g (12 oz) unsalted
  butter, diced
3 eggs

FOR THE FILLING
20 rhubarb stalks

100 g (3½ oz) caster
  (superfine) sugar
1 nip of grappa

FOR THE TOPPING
250 g (8 oz) ricotta
  cheese
2 eggs
100 g (3½ oz) caster
  (superfine) sugar
½ cup mascarpone

To make the pastry, combine the flour, almond meal, sugar, salt and butter in a bowl and rub together quickly until all the butter is incorporated into the dry ingredients and the mixture resembles breadcrumbs. Add the eggs and mix gently by hand to form a ball. Wrap the pastry in plastic wrap and refrigerate for 30 minutes.

Preheat the oven to 180°C (350°F/gas 4).

Place the pastry on a lightly floured surface and roll out to a round shape until 5 mm (¼ inch) thick. Ease the pastry into a fluted 28-cm (11¼-inch) tart tin and refrigerate for 20 minutes. Blind bake (see the Fig and mascarpone tart recipe on page 310) for 15 minutes, or until pale golden.

To make the filling, wash the rhubarb and cut into 3-cm (1¼-inch) lengths. Place in a stainless steel saucepan, add the sugar and grappa and cook over a low heat until the rhubarb is tender but still holds its shape. Remove from the heat and allow to cool.

To make the topping, place the ricotta, eggs, sugar and mascarpone in a blender and puree until smooth. Spread the rhubarb in the pastry shell and pour the ricotta mixture on top. Refrigerate until ready to serve. **SERVES 4**

Budino di castagne
Chestnut mousse with basil sauce

The notion of putting a basil sauce with a dessert would have surprised my parents. They'd have thought of basil as best suited to boosting pasta. But when we tried this experiment, we found the combination of the two classic Ligurian ingredients curiously addictive. After all, chestnut isn't sure if it's sweet or savoury, just as basil has something in common with such invigorating herbs as peppermint.

FOR THE CHESTNUT MOUSSE
550 ml (17½ fl oz) single cream, divided into two batches: 300 ml (10 fl oz) and 250 ml (8 fl oz)
120 g (4 oz) caster (superfine) sugar
1 vanilla bean, split lengthwise and seeds scraped
300 ml (10 fl oz) milk
120 g (4 oz) chestnut flour
3 gelatine leaves, titanium strength
45 g (1½ oz) toasted chestnuts, finely chopped (optional)

FOR THE BASIL SAUCE
½ bunch young basil, leaves picked
iced water
125 ml (4 fl oz) milk
1 egg
1 egg yolk
45 g (1½ oz) sugar
125 ml (4 fl oz) single cream

To make the chestnut mousse, heat 300 ml (10 fl oz) of the cream, the sugar, vanilla bean and seeds and 150 ml (5 fl oz) of the milk in a heavy-based saucepan over a low heat. Bring to a simmer. In a bowl, mix the remaining milk with the chestnut flour to make a paste. Add to the mixture in the saucepan, remove from the heat and stir constantly for at least 5 minutes—the mixture should be thick and smooth. Soak the gelatine in cold water for 3 minutes. Stir into the mixture, until completely dissolved. Allow to cool (but not set) in the fridge. When the mousse is a semi-jelly-like consistency, whip the remaining 250 ml (8 fl oz) cream to soft peaks. Fold into the mousse and add the chestnuts. Pour into four individual moulds and chill.

To make the basil sauce, blanch the basil leaves in boiling water for 10 seconds. Remove and refresh in iced water. Squeeze out excess water and place in a blender. Add the milk and puree until frothy and green.

Whisk the egg, egg yolk and sugar until pale and thick. Heat the cream and basil milk in a saucepan until just below a simmer. One spoonful at a time, add the hot basil cream to the egg and sugar mixture, stirring constantly until all the cream has been added.

Return the basil sauce to a very low heat and stir until it starts to thicken. Do not let it boil. Remove from the heat and continue stirring until cool. Chill and pour around the mousse when serving. **SERVES 4**

Torta di fichi e mascarpone

Fig and mascarpone tart

FOR THE SWEET PASTRY
250 g (8 oz) plain
  (all purpose) flour
150 g (5 oz) butter
150 g (5 oz) icing
  (confectioners') sugar
2 eggs
1 egg yolk
1 egg, lightly beaten,
  for brushing the pastry

FOR THE FILLING
500 g (1 lb) mascarpone
75 g (2½ oz) caster
  (superfine) sugar
1 egg

1 egg yolk
zest of 1 orange
zest of 1 lemon
1 vanilla bean, split
  lengthwise and seeds
  scraped
1 nip of Cointreau or
  orange-flavoured liqueur

FOR THE SYRUP
250 ml (8 fl oz) water
250 g (8 oz) caster
  (superfine) sugar

6 ripe figs, sliced into discs

First make the pastry. Combine the flour, butter and sugar in a food processor and process until the mixture resembles breadcrumbs. Place in a bowl. Add the whole eggs and egg yolk and work the dough with your hands for 2 minutes. Cover in plastic wrap and place in the fridge for 1 hour. Makes two 24-cm (9½-inch) tart shells.

Preheat the oven to 180°C (360°F/gas 4). Grease and flour a 24-cm (9½-inch) tin.

Roll out half of the pastry until very thin and line the prepared tin. Trim excess pastry around the edge. Rest it in the fridge for 30 minutes. Line the pastry with a sheet of baking paper and fill with a light weight such as rice or dried beans.

Bake the pastry in the oven for 25 minutes. Remove the weights and paper and lightly brush the pastry with the beaten egg to seal the surface. Set aside to cool.

To make the mascarpone filling, combine the mascarpone, sugar, egg, egg yolk, zests, vanilla seeds and liqueur in a bowl and set aside.

Reduce the oven temperature to 110°C (225°F/gas ½).

When the pastry is cool, fill the tart case with the mascarpone mixture three-quarters full. Bake in the oven for 1 hour and 10 minutes, or until the top looks set after a gentle shake.

To make the sugar syrup, heat the water and sugar over a medium-high heat, stir and bring to the boil for 4 minutes. Allow to cool.

Arrange the fig discs on the filling, glaze with sugar syrup and serve. **SERVES 4**

VARIATION

An equally delicious tart can be made by replacing the sliced figs with an assortment of fresh berries—particularly raspberries and strawberries. For a great visual effect arrange one line of strawberries around the outside of the pie. Line the inside of that with raspberries, and continue in concentric circles alternating the berries until you reach the centre where you can place one large strawberry. Brush with sugar syrup and serve.

Torta di ricotta e nocciole

Flourless hazelnut and ricotta cake

FOR THE CAKE
1 egg
75 g (2½ oz) caster (superfine)
  sugar
1 vanilla bean, split lengthwise
  and seeds scraped
500 g (1 lb) ricotta cheese
finely grated zest of 1 lemon
finely grated zest of 1 orange
30 ml (1 fl oz) Frangelico
75 g (2½ oz) toasted hazelnuts

FOR THE MASCARPONE CREAM
1 egg
45 g (1½ oz) caster (superfine)
  sugar
400 g (13 oz) mascarpone
60 g (2 oz) dark chocolate
  shavings

Preheat the oven to 110°C (225°F/gas ½). Grease a 25-cm (10-inch) springform cake tin.

To make the cake, place the egg, sugar and vanilla seeds in the bowl of a food processor and process for 5 minutes or until light and creamy. Add the ricotta, zests and Frangelico and mix well. Remove from the food processor and fold in the hazelnuts. Pour into the prepared tin. Place in the oven and bake for 50 minutes, or until the sides can be pulled away with the fingers and will not stick. Set aside to cool for 20 minutes.

To make the mascarpone cream, cream the egg and sugar until light and fluffy. Add the mascarpone and mix until smooth. When the cake is cool, cover with the mascarpone cream and sprinkle some chocolate shavings on top. **SERVES 4**

Amaretti
Almond biscuits

75 g (2½ oz) hazelnuts
500 g (1 lb) caster
  (superfine) sugar
500 g (1 lb) almond meal
5 egg whites

2 tbsp plain (all purpose) flour
75 g (2½ oz) icing
  (confectioners') sugar

Preheat the oven to 180°C (350°F/gas 4). Roast the hazelnuts on a baking tray for 10 minutes stirring occasionally. Remove and cool and rub off the papery skin using a tea towel. Place in a mortar, add the sugar and pound until the mixture resembles breadcrumbs. Add the almond meal and mix well.

In a very clean stainless steel bowl, beat the egg whites until soft peaks form and, using a wooden spoon, slowly incorporate the almond meal mixture. Add the flour to create a soft and pliable paste.

Lightly flour a baking tray and drop on spoonfuls of the biscuit mixture, allowing space for spreading. Use the back of a teaspoon to make an impression in the centre of each biscuit, sprinkle with the icing sugar and rest for 1 hour.

Preheat the oven to 180°C (350°F/gas 4) and place the baking tray on the top shelf. As soon as they start to brown, remove the tray from the oven and set aside to cool. Serve straight away, or store in an airtight container. Many people believe that the amaretti improve with a few weeks' ageing. **MAKES ABOUT 30 BISCUITS**

Biscottini

Almond and chocolate biscuits

150 g (5 oz) dark chocolate,
  roughly chopped
200 g (6½ oz) brown sugar
250 g (8 oz) plain
  (all purpose) flour
30 g (1 oz) cocoa powder
1 tsp baking soda

pinch of salt
3 large eggs
5 ml (⅛ fl oz) vanilla extract
60 ml (2 fl oz) very strong
  espresso coffee
150 g (5 oz) toasted
  almonds, chopped

Preheat the oven to 150°C (300°F/gas 2).

Line a large baking tray with baking paper.

Combine the chocolate and brown sugar in the bowl of a food processor and process until the chocolate is very fine. Set aside.

Sift the flour, cocoa, baking soda and salt into a bowl.

Whisk the eggs and vanilla in another bowl and add the coffee. Slowly add the dry ingredients and the almonds and mix until a stiff dough forms. Divide the dough in half. Place one half on a floured work surface and, using your hands, form into a log about 30 cm (12 inches) long, rolling backwards and forwards and flouring your hands if the mixture gets sticky. Repeat with the other half.

Place the logs well apart on the prepared baking tray (they will spread during the baking process) and bake for 35–40 minutes, or until almost firm to the touch. Transfer to a wire rack to cool for about 10 minutes.

Cut the logs on the diagonal into *biscottini* about 2 cm (¾ inch) thick using a serrated knife. Place the biscottini, cut side facing down, back on the baking tray and return to the oven for 10–15 minutes on each side, or until dry and crisp.

When completely cool they will keep in an airtight container for a few weeks.

MAKES ABOUT 30

Anicini
Aniseed biscuits

500 g (1 lb) caster
  (superfine) sugar
10 eggs, separated
1 tbsp aniseeds

45 ml (1½ fl oz) orange
  blossom water
400 g (13 oz) plain
  (all purpose) flour

Cream the sugar and egg yolks until light and fluffy. Add the aniseeds and the orange blossom water and mix to incorporate.

Place the egg whites in a very clean stainless steel bowl and beat until stiff peaks form. Gently fold into the creamed mixture, then fold in the flour. Knead gently and rest for 10 minutes.

Preheat the oven to 160°C (315°F/gas 2–3). Line a baking tray with baking paper and shape the dough into a 10-cm (4-inch) wide log, flatten slightly and place in the oven for 20 minutes.

It will still be soft and chewy at this stage. When cool enough to handle, cut the dough into 2-cm (¾-inch) thick biscuits.

Lay them on their sides on the baking tray and bake for 10 minutes to dry out completely.

MAKES ABOUT 30 BISCUITS

Baci di dama
Lady's kisses

¾ cup almonds, toasted
1 cup caster (superfine) sugar
250 g (8 oz) unsalted butter,
  softened
finely grated zest of ½ lemon

pinch of salt
1 cup plain (all purpose) flour
75 g (2½ oz) good-quality dark
  chocolate, chopped

Preheat the oven to 180°C (350°F/gas 4) and line a large baking tray with baking paper.

Process the almonds and sugar in a food processor until powdery (be careful not to process to a paste).

Cream the butter, zest, salt and the nut mixture in a large bowl, add the flour and stir until just incorporated (do not overwork).

Roll level ½ teaspoons of dough into tiny balls the size of marbles and place 2.5 cm (1 inch) apart on the prepared baking tray. Bake in batches until very pale golden, 12–14 minutes, then slide onto a wire rack to cool completely.

Melt the chocolate, stirring occasionally, in a metal bowl set over a saucepan of barely simmering water. Working with two at a time, spoon a little of the just-melted chocolate onto the flat side of one biscuit and immediately press on another to form the 'kiss'.

If you like, make the biscuits ahead of time and store in an airtight container. Assemble the kisses just before you are ready to serve them. **MAKES ABOUT 50 BISCUITS OR 25 KISSES**

Pinolate
Pine nut cookies

100 g (3½ oz) bitter
  almonds, peeled
100 g (3½ oz) sweet
  almonds, peeled
500 g (1 lb) caster
  (superfine) sugar

4 egg whites
pinch of active dry yeast
60 g (2 oz) pine nuts

Preheat the oven to 200°C (400°F/gas 6). Line a baking tray with baking paper.

Combine the almonds and some of the sugar in a food processor and process to a dry fine powder. Beat the egg whites in a clean bowl until stiff peaks form. Fold in the almond mixture, the yeast and the rest of the sugar and mix well. Roll into walnut-sized balls and coat with the pine nuts. Place on the prepared baking tray and bake for 10–20 minutes, or until golden.

Serve warm from the oven, or set aside to cool and sprinkle with icing sugar. **MAKES 30**

Focaccia dolce allo Sciacchetrà
Focaccia cake with dessert wine

Sciacchetrà is the great, rare and very expensive dessert wine of the Cinque Terre, made from grapes left to dry in the sun to concentrate their sugars. We thought it appropriate to pay tribute by including it in a dessert, even though connoisseurs would consider it a criminal waste to mix it with dough and bake it. Feel free to use any sweet wine in the mixture, then pour a glass of Sciacchetrà to drink with it.

2 firm apples, peeled, cored
  and sliced
1 tbsp sultanas (seedless white
  raisins), soaked in water
1 tbsp pine nuts
45 ml (1½ fl oz) Sciacchetrà
  or any dessert wine

4 eggs
250 g (8 oz) caster
  (superfine) sugar
200 g (6½ oz) butter
450 g (14 oz) plain
  (all purpose) flour
2 tsp baking powder

Place the apples, sultanas and pine nuts in a bowl. Pour over the wine and set aside for 30 minutes.

Preheat the oven to 200°C (400°F/gas 6).

Beat the eggs and sugar in another bowl, add the butter and flour and mix well. Add the apple mixture and stir to combine. Add the baking powder and mix well.

Lightly oil a 30-cm (12-inch) baking dish. Add the dough and flatten, evenly pushing it into place with your fingers. Bake in the oven for about 50 minutes, until golden brown. **SERVES 4**

Castagnaccio
Chestnut flour cake

Peasants and shepherds have for centuries exploited the chestnut in various ways. The chestnut tree represented a safe and economic food source. The flour was used to make bread—because wheat was rare in the Ligurian hills—fresh pasta, thick pancakes and a type of polenta which was pan-fried.

The nuts were eaten fresh, roasted, or peeled and cooked in milk and rice. Another method was to boil them in their skins with pig trotters. Then stale bread rubbed with garlic (a primitive *bruschetta*) was dipped in the broth.

This chestnut cake has many small variations from the north of Tuscany and across the whole of Liguria. Some use water, others use milk, some have just pine nuts, others have hazelnuts, apples and raisins as well. Near the Tuscan border, it is made with rosemary. Towards Genoa, fennel seeds are used. But all have extra virgin olive oil in common.

We offer a classic local recipe, from the province of La Spezia, topped with pine nuts and sprigs of rosemary which are removed before eating, leaving only the wonderful flavour.

1 kg (2 lb) chestnut flour
3 litres (96 fl oz) tepid water
1 tsp fennel seeds
sea salt
125 ml (4 fl oz) olive oil
120 g (4 oz) raisins

75 g (2½ oz) pine nuts
75 g (2½ oz) roughly
  chopped hazelnuts
2 apples, peeled and diced
finely grated zest of 1 orange
3 sprigs rosemary

Sift the chestnut flour into the water and mix well to remove lumps. Add the fennel seeds and a pinch of salt, and set aside to rest for half a day.

Preheat the oven to 180°C (360°F/gas 4).

Into a bowl, add the olive oil, raisins, pine nuts, hazelnuts, apples and orange zest. Mix well and pour into a well-oiled cake tin that is 25 cm (10 inches). Decorate the top of the mixture with rosemary sprigs. Cook in a hot oven for about 1 hour. The *castagnaccio* is ready when the crust is cracked like the land in a drought.

Enjoy with a little glass of *passito* (sweet wine made with late-picked Muscat grapes).

SERVES 4

Semifreddo alla menta

Mint ice cream cake with chocolate fudge

Now we've reached the complicated part of the chapter. This and the following recipe require an electric beater and a sugar (candy) thermometer. Including freezing time, this recipe takes about 13 hours, but the results are spectacular.

FOR THE FUDGE CAKE
120 g (4 oz) unsalted butter
120 g (4 oz) dark chocolate
3 eggs, separated
1 egg yolk extra
150 g (5 oz) caster
  (superfine) sugar
60 g (2 oz) plain
  (all purpose), sifted flour

FOR THE MINT SEMIFREDDO
2 bunches mint, leaves picked
375 ml (12 fl oz) single cream
1 nip of crème de menthe
⅓ cup caster (superfine) sugar
30 ml (1 fl oz) dark corn syrup
60 ml (2 fl oz) honey
4 egg whites, at room
  temperature
pinch of salt

To make the fudge cake, preheat the oven to 160°C (315°F/gas 2–3). Grease a 25-cm (10-inch) springform cake tin with butter and sugar. Cover the entire outer surface of the cake tin with foil to make it completely waterproof.

Melt the butter and the chocolate in a heatproof bowl over a saucepan of simmering water. Remove and allow it to cool.

In a medium bowl, whisk the egg yolks and half the sugar until pale and thick.

In a separate bowl, whisk the egg whites with the remaining sugar until soft peaks form.

Add the yolk mixture to the chocolate, fold in the flour, then fold in the egg white mixture. Pour into the prepared cake tin and cover with baking paper. Transfer the cake tin to a baking dish. Half-fill with hot water so that the cake tin sits in the dish without floating and cooks at a constant temperature. Bake in the oven in the water bath for 25 minutes or until the centre is set.

Remove from the oven and set aside to cool wile you make the *semifreddo*.

To make the mint *semifreddo*, blanch the mint in boiling water for 10 seconds and refresh in iced water. Drain, squeeze dry and chop finely.

Combine 60 ml (2 fl oz) of the cream, the mint and the crème de menthe in a blender and puree until amalgamated.

Whip the remaining cream until soft peaks form. Cover and refrigerate.

Place the sugar, corn syrup and honey, in a small saucepan, clip a sugar (candy) thermometer to the side of the pan and place over a medium heat.

Place the egg whites and salt in the bowl of an electric mixer and whisk until soft peaks form.

Cook the sugar syrup to soft-ball stage—112–115°C (234–240°F) on the thermometer. Keep a close eye on the pan as this will happen quickly. While whisking the egg whites on low speed, slowly and carefully drizzle the hot syrup down the side of the bowl. Increase the mixer speed to medium-high and beat until the meringue is cool to the touch. Add the mint puree and fold in the whipped cream.

Line the bottom and sides your mould of choice with plastic wrap and spoon in the meringue. Smooth the top and cover with chocolate fudge cake (which you can cut into slabs that will fit together over the *semifreddo* in the mould). Wrap and freeze for 12 hours.

When you're ready to serve, unwrap the mould, turn out the *semifreddo* onto a plate, and carry it triumphantly to the table with a big knife. Serve as slices. **SERVES 4**

Semifreddo di Noce
Walnut semifreddo

This recipe requires an electric mixer and sugar thermometer, so it's challenging. It uses the sweet walnut liqueur called Nocello, which originated in Modena (not in Liguria, we admit, but good enough to make a contribution). If you can't find it, you could substitute Frangelico.

250 g (8 oz) chopped walnuts
600 ml (20 fl oz) single cream
75 g (2½ oz) caster
  (superfine) sugar
45 ml (1½ fl oz) corn syrup

125 ml (4 fl oz) honey
6 egg whites
pinch of salt
30 ml (1 fl oz) Nocello
  (walnut liqueur)

Preheat the oven to 180°C (350°F/gas 4) and toast the walnuts on a baking tray for 10 minutes.

Whip the cream until soft peaks form, cover and refrigerate.

Place the sugar, corn syrup and honey in a small saucepan, clip a sugar (candy) thermometer to the side of the pan and place over a medium heat.

Place the egg whites and salt in the bowl of an electric mixer and whisk until soft peaks form.

Cook the sugar syrup to soft-ball stage—112–115°C (234–240°F) on the thermometer. While whisking the egg whites on low speed, slowly and carefully drizzle the hot syrup down the side of the bowl. Increase the mixer speed to medium-high and beat until all the syrup is incorporated and the meringue is cool to the touch. Add the Nocello liqueur and slowly fold the meringue into the whipped cream.

Fold in the walnuts and pour into eight small bowls. Cover and freeze for 12 hours before serving. **SERVES 4**

THE AUTHORS' BURDEN

Poor us. To research this book we had to travel up and down the coastline of north-west Italy—eating, drinking, talking and occasionally swimming. When we got back to Australia, we had to prepare, photograph and eat close to 200 examples of modern Ligurian cooking, some of them several times. Just as well it's one of the healthiest cuisines in the world.

We had one big advantage in our research—Lucio grew up on the Italian Riviera, and was already an expert on ravioli and on the many permutations of pesto, Liguria's best-known contributions to the world. But even he was surprised at the diversity and sophistication of the eating places along what Italians call La Riviera di Levante (the coast of the rising sun).

A new generation of chefs has been busily adapting tradition to the needs of the future. The Ligurians' habit of conserving and recycling every resource, born out of poverty and isolation, serves them well in a new century when we all must walk softly on the landscape and leave a small carbon footprint.

We decided this book had to be written while we were researching our earlier book, *Soffritto: A delicious Ligurian memoir.* The three of us (David Dale, Lucio Galletto and Paul Green) were in Lunigiana, an area which stretches from the mountains to the sea on the border of Liguria and Tuscany (the eastern end of the sunrise coast). We realised that the coastline to the west of Lunigiana—so near geographically and yet so far gastronomically—needed a cookbook of its own. So we convinced our publisher that we had to go back to try the food and interview the farmers, fishermen, winemakers, waiters and cooks.

One of Lucio's inspirations was a recurring memory from his childhood. One night he looked out to sea from the front of the family restaurant in the village of Bocca di Magra and saw a row of little lights bobbing up and down on the ocean. His parents explained that they were the anchovy fishermen from further up the coast. By the light of kerosene lamps they were trying to net the tiny silver fishes before they got snapped up by passing tuna.

The fishermen would put their catch into flat baskets, which were neatly aligned along the dockside in the morning to be collected by the wives. Each woman would load a basket onto the front of her bicycle and pedal off to sell the anchovies in the villages further inland. When the baskets were empty, the women would fill them with wild herbs they'd picked on the steep hillsides. Then they'd pedal back to the coast to stuff the herbs into their ravioli.

The fishing methods of the Riviera are more systematic these days, and the wild herbs are harder to find, but Ligurians retain their dedication to sourcing their food supplies close to home. That's the story we wanted to tell.

We must thank many people for their help in constructing *Lucio's Ligurian Kitchen*: Logan Campbell, the head chef at Lucio's restaurant, contributed essential advice and applied his intelligence and imagination to ensuring the dishes looked their best for the camera of the genius Paul Green. Sally Galletto applied her disciplined mind to interpreting Lucio's recipe notes.

Mario and Wendy Guelfi gave us valuable ideas and warm hospitality at the eastern end of the sunrise coast. Barbara Raffellini brilliantly organised our stay in the Cinque Terre and access to its scholars and cooks. Salvatore Marchese, *enogastronomo* (wine and food expert) provided deep historical and cultural background.

Sue Hines of Allen & Unwin believed in the idea and put up with our idiosyncratic working methods, which were finally reined in by editor Alexandra Nahlous and designer Hamish Freeman.

Books that provided stimulating background for us included *The Food of Italy* by Waverley Root (Vintage Books, 1977); *Recipes from Paradise* by Fred Plotkin (Little Brown and Company, 1997); *Enchanted Liguria* by David Downie (Rizzoli, 1997); *La Cucina Ligure di Levante* by Salvatore Marchese (Franco Muzzio Editore 1990); *Il Grande Libro della Cucina Ligure* by Franco Accame, Silvio Torre and Virgilio Pronzati's (De Ferrari 1994); and *La Cuciniera Genovese* by G.B. and Giovanni Ratto (Fratelli Frilli Editori, first published 1863).

Lucio also wants to thank his friend Neil Wood of Traveltoo for organising his trips to Italy, and wants to dedicate this book to his children, Matteo and Michela, who will carry on the Ligurian tradition in Australia.

David Dale,
2008

INDEX